TABLE OF CONTENTS

Chapter 1: Property Ownership and Land Use Controls and Regulations   6

    1.1   Land vs. Real Estate vs. Real Property   6
    1.2   Classes of Property   6
    1.3   Land Characteristics and Descriptions   10
    1.4   Appurtenant Rights   15
    1.5   Encumbrances   17
    1.6   Restrictions on Use of Property   19
    1.7   Ownership   25
    1.8   Liens   28
    1.9   Homesteads   29

    Study Smart Guide   31

    Chapter 1: Quiz and Answers   34

Chapter 2: Acquisition, Transfer, Escrow and Taxation of Property   36

    2.1   Acquisition of Property   36
    2.2   Transfer of Property   39
    2.3   Deeds   41
    2.4   Title Insurance   44
    2.5   Sale Escrows and Settlements   47
    2.6   Taxation   52

    Chapter 2: Study Smart Guide   57

    Chapter 2: Quiz and Answers   59

Chapter 3: Laws of Agency and Fiduciary Duties   61

    3.1   Agency and Fiduciary Duties   61
    3.2   Creation of Agency and Agency Agreements   63
    3.3   Responsibilities of Agent to Seller/Buyer as Principal   64
    3.4   Types and Disclosure of Agency   65
    3.5   Termination of Agency   68
    3.6   Agency Contracts   69

    Chapter 3: Study Smart Guide   71

    Chapter 3: Quiz and Answers   73

Chapter 4: Contracts   75

    4.1   General Contract Law Overview   75
    4.2   Statute of Frauds   80
    4.3   Interpretation, Performance & Discharge of Contracts   82
    4.4   Real Estate Contracts Overview   85
    4.5   Listing Agreements   86
    4.6   Exclusive Authorization & Right to Sell (MLS Agreement)   88
    4.7   Real Estate Purchase Agreements & Receipt for Deposit   92
    4.8   Option Contracts   99
    4.9   Negotiating Contracts   101
    4.10   Disclosures   102

    Chapter 4: Study Smart Guide   109

    Chapter 4: Quiz and Answers   111

Chapter 5: Practice of Real Estate   113

    5.1   Responsibilities of Principal Broker to Salespeople   113
    5.2   Licensing & Continuing Education Requirements   115

5.3	Permitted Activities of Unlicensed Sales Assistants	121
5.4	Compensation and Related Regulations	123
5.5	Consumer Protections	124
5.6	Servicing Diverse Populations	125
5.7	CalBRE Jurisdiction and Disciplinary Actions	131
5.8	Trust Account Management (Broker's Escrow)	133
5.9	Accounting Records	138
	Chapter 5: Study Smart Guide	141
	Chapter 5: Quiz and Answers	143

Chapter 6: Leases, Landlord/Tenant Law and Specialty Areas — **145**

6.1	Leases	145
6.2	Lease Terminations	154
6.3	Disclosures Required by Owner/Rental Agent to Tenant	159
6.4	Specialty Areas	161
6.5	Development	164
6.6	Sale and Leasing of Businesses (Business Opportunity)	167
	Chapter 6: Study Smart Guide	170
	Chapter 6: Quiz and Answers	172

Chapter 7: Property Valuation and Appraisals — **174**

7.1	Values	174
7.2	Principals of Valuation	176
7.3	The Appraisal Process	179
7.4	Sales Comparison Approach	181
7.5	Cost Approach	182
7.6	Income Approach	187
7.7	Appraisal Licensing and Regulation	189

Chapter 7: Study Smart Guide 193

Chapter 7: Quiz and Answers 196

Chapter 8: Financing Concepts and Regulations **198**

    8.1   General Financing Concepts   198

    8.2   Lenders, Mortgage Brokers & Mortgage Originators   203

    8.3   Conventional and Alternative Financing   205

    8.4   Primary Financing Documents and Instruments   207

    8.5   Types and Purposes of Secured Loans   211

    8.6   Foreclosures   213

    8.7   Real Estate Finance Regulations   221

Chapter 8: Study Smart Guide 225

Chapter 8: Quiz and Answers 227

Chapter 9: The Mortgage Process **229**

    9.1   The Path to Homeownership   229

    9.2   Preliminary Documentation   230

    9.3   The Mortgage Application   232

    9.4   Loan Processing   234

    9.5   Loan Underwriting Analysis   236

    9.6   Loan Approval, Document Signing and Settlement   237

Chapter 9: Study Smart Guide 238

Chapter 9: Quiz and Answers 239

Study Smart Aids   **241**

    Real Estate Math   241

    Real Estate Glossary   274

Practice Exams   **298**

    Real Estate Sales **Exam I**   298

    Real Estate Sales **Exam I Answers**   324

    Real Estate Sales **Exam II**   330

    Real Estate Sales **Exam II Answers**   356

    Real Estate Sales **Exam III**   362

    Real Estate Sales **Exam III Answers**   388

    Real Estate Sales **Exam IV**   394

    Real Estate Sales **Exam IV Answers**   420

*Money Back Guarantee

We have full confidence this book will prepare you to pass the exam. However, if after going through the whole book, and taking and passing the practice exams, you do not pass the actual exam you may return it for the full purchase price, excluding taxes and shipping & handling. Simply return this book with your original sales receipt to 100 Cummings Ctr. 426C, Beverly, MA 01915.

All refund claims must be made within 180 days of purchase.

One offer per person and address. U.S. residents only. Refunds will be issued within 1 month of receipt.

Chapter 1

Chapter 1: Property Ownership and Land Use Controls and Regulation

1.1   Land vs. Real Estate vs. Real Property

Land is the physical property and any natural objects on it—like trees and bodies of water, often referred to as a "lot", "site" or "parcel".

Real estate generally refers to land with permanent manmade improvements.

Real Property refers not only to the land and its improvements, but also the bundle of rights, powers, and privileges ("bundle of rights") that are legally connected to ownership of that land.

1.2   Classes of Property

There are two main types of property discussed in real estate. They are *real* property and *personal* property, also referred to as "chattel."

Real Property

Collectively, the land, its improvements, and its accompanying tangible and intangible rights are the "real property." Real property refers to the land and things permanently attached to it, such as buildings, plant life and ground minerals. In addition, any fixture (plumbing, kitchen cabinetry) that is permanently affixed or causes damage were it to be removed is considered a part of real property. **Real Property is transferred by deed.**

Ownership of real property is not simply a lot and some buildings, but a bundle of rights with each stick in the bundle representing a right associated with property ownership. A property owner can take a stick from that rights bundle and sell it without necessarily affecting the other rights. For example, allowing another party access without jeopardizing the ownership of the land. The sticks in this bundle of rights can be separated into two basic categories:

- **Tangible rights** based on the physical aspects of a property, such as claims to:
    - Land

- Buildings, garages, barn/sheds or other improvements
- Forests
- Farmland, Vineyards
- Trees, plant life, floral gardens (with some minor exceptions)
- Fixtures (such as fences, plumbing, etc.)

- **Intangible rights** associated with areas above and below the land surface, access and privileges such as:
  - Air rights
  - Water rights
  - Subsurface rights (mineral rights)
  - Easements
  - Licenses
  - Profits
  - Leases
  - Mortgages

The most common categories of real property are:

- **Residential property**—single-family homes, co-ops and condominiums, apartment buildings.
- **Commercial property**—retail spaces, business offices, hotels, restaurants, gas stations, and other service businesses.
- **Industrial/Manufacturing property**—manufacturing facilities, distribution centers, and warehouse spaces.
- **Agricultural property**—including crop fields, grazing lands, orchards etc.
- **Vacant land**—land that does not contain buildings or other improvements ("unimproved land").

Another category referred to as **special purpose properties** includes:

- **Parks and recreational areas:** lands preserved for recreational, ecological, and educational purposes by either the local government or by the Department of Environmental Conservation (DEC) and the Office of Parks, Recreation, and Historic Preservation (OPRHP) and/or all three agencies.

- **Institutional properties:** universities, public schools, hospitals, prisons, libraries, and other buildings for public entities.

Personal Property

Personal property refers to property those tangible and moveable, such as furniture and swing sets. Although plant life is generally seen as real property, it can be classified as personal property if it is superficially planted and can be removed without damage to the property. Personal property does not include rights to the land and is **transferred by "Bill of Sale"**.

Personal property can become real property when it becomes a permanent fixture of the land. For instance, a house built on a secure and sturdy foundation is real property. A mobile home can be moved at any time and is a piece of personal property. Were the mobile home to be affixed to a permanent foundation, it becomes part of the real property.

Fixtures

Fixtures are items that have been permanently attached to real property. An example would be a built in bookcase. The bookcase becomes a fixture because it is nailed or fastened in a way that is considered permanent. Fixtures can be pieces of personal property that have been "**physically or constructively annexed**" to a structure. For example, a swimming pool made of concrete can't be removed and is "constructively annexed."

Fixtures must be defined in each instance so each party is clear exactly what is being transferred on sale. The exact nature of what separates personal property from fixtures may be decided on a case-by-case basis. Courts of law have established a method known as 'tests of a fixture' and include five points to test. You can memorize the five tests through the acronym M-A-R-I-A;

M - Method of attachment,
A - Adaptability,
R - Relationship of the parties,
I - Intent,
A - Agreement between the parties

M-Method of attachment

Determining how a fixture is attached often decides whether the item is personal or a fixture. For example, wood paneling on the walls is a fixture. A less obvious example would be cabinets. Cabinets that have been attached, such as kitchen cabinets are fixtures and part of real property. A moveable cabinet, such as an armoire or china cabinet is the owner's personal property, as it has not been permanently attached.

A-Adaptability of attached item

Some items become a fixture because they have been specifically adapted or modified. An example would be rugs or carpeting. Wall-to-wall carpeting has been cut and modified (adapted) and attached to the property. Yet a moveable area rug (even if the dimensions match the room size) is not a fixture, since no adaptation has taken place. In essence, if something is altered and specifically adapted for use on the property, it may be called 'constructively attached' and becomes a fixture.

R-Relationship of the parties

Sometimes the relationship of the fixture to its owner is overriding. For example, a tenant attaches a stained glass window to a window frame. A homebuyer, not realizing it doesn't belong to the owner of the property, may assume it is attached and part of the real property when in fact it is excluded from the sale as "tenant's belongings."

I-Intent

Intent relates to what the owner intended when they placed an item on the property. For example, a stained glass window hanging on a nail in front of a window clearly has a different intention than a window that has been nailed and puttied into a custom cut hole in the wall.

A-Agreement

A written agreement is the most obvious determination whether or not an item is a fixture. Having a discussion about which fixtures are "included" and "excluded" from the sale (refrigerators, clothes washer/dryers, Grandma's chandelier) and incorporating the result into the purchase agreement then creates an explicit agreement.

1.3 Land Characteristics and Descriptions

Land Characteristics

There are two main characteristics to describe land and land function; physical characteristics and economic characteristics.

Physical characteristics of land are:

- **Immobility** – Land cannot be moved in its entirety; therefore, it is considered immobile. Although pieces can be removed or replaced, the original part of the land still remains.

- **Indestructibility** – Although land can be damaged by storms or disasters, ultimately, it cannot be destroyed because it continues to change, adjust and develop over time.

- **Non-homogeneity** – Simply stated: no two pieces of land are identical. Differences in features and structures situated on a parcel affect the whole 'package.'

Economic characteristics of land:

- **Scarcity** – In some areas, land is considered a rarity, and ownership is even more unlikely. When land is scarce, prices are higher driving value as an investment over time.

- **Permanence** – Also known as "fixity," permanence refers to the lasting potential of the land.

- **Situs** – The concept that some locations are more and less valuable. It should be noted the preferences for a particular location can change over time keeping this aspect of values fluid.

- **Improvements** – Structures and landscaping add value to land.

Land Descriptions

There are many different types of property. Each type describes different characteristics of the property in question and can change the whole context in which someone views it.

Metes and bounds – A method of describing real property that uses geography and land features with direction and distances to define and describe the boundaries of the land. (See an example on the following page)

Rectangular survey system – Traditional method of surveying property and it measures factors such as the precise length of line run, natural materials (flora/fauna), and surface and land soil.

Government or US public land system – Most commonly used method to survey and spatially identify land or property parcels before designating ownership, whether for sale or transfer. (See an example following in two pages)

Townships – A survey method that refers to a square unit of land that is six miles on each side. Townships exist at the intersection of a range and a tier. Each 36-square-mile township is divided into 36 one-square mile sections that can be further subdivided for sale.

Principal meridians – Method that uses a principal meridian line for survey control in a large region, which divides townships between north/south/east/west. The meridian meets its corresponding initial point for the land survey.

Base line and meridian intersections – In California, there are three base line-meridian intersections that are used for legal descriptions. Base lines run horizontally (east to west) and meridians run vertically (north to south). Base lines and meridians mark land into tiers every six miles. The three base line-meridian intersections used in California are:

- Humboldt Base Line and Meridian (HBBM), in the northern part of the state
- Mt. Diablo Base Line and Meridian (MDBM), in the central part of the state
- San Bernardino Base Line and Meridian (SBBM), in the southern part of the state

Recorded plat – Also known as the lot and block survey system, this system is used for lots in a variety of areas (e.g. heavily populated metropolitan, suburban, and exurban areas). Especially used to plot large areas of a property into smaller lots and land areas.

Assessor's parcel number (APN) – Also known as an appraisal's account number, a number assigned to parcels of property by the area's jurisdiction for identification and record keeping. Each APN is unique within the particular jurisdiction, and may conform to certain formatting standards that hold identifying information, such as the property type or location within the plat map.

Metes and Bounds map example

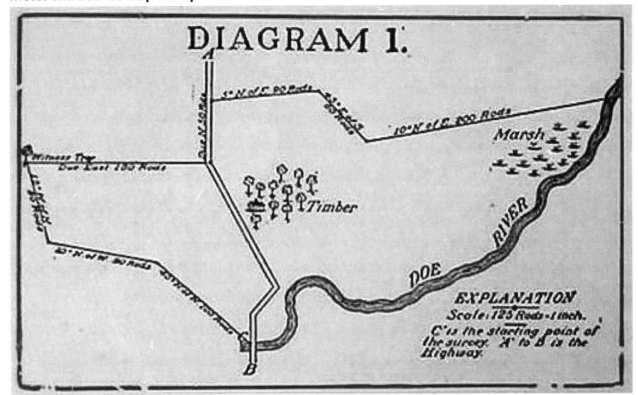

U.S. government sections and townships method

The U.S. government sections and townships method utilizes a grid of lines; the horizontal lines are township, or tier, lines. The vertical lines are called range lines, both types of lines run in six mile increments; i.e. they are spaced with a six mile distance. See the following example;

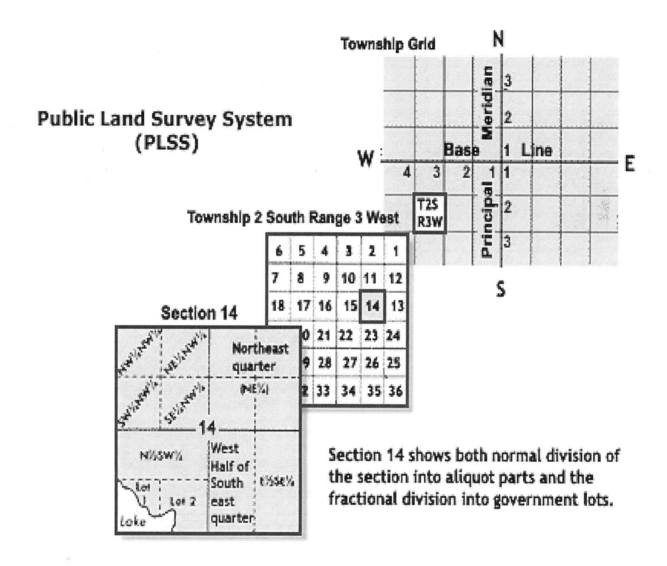

Section 14 shows both normal division of the section into aliquot parts and the fractional division into government lots.

THE LOT AND BLOCK OR PLAT MAP SYSTEM

```
                    GORDON STREET
         ┌─────────┬─────────┬─────────┬─────────┐
         │   75    │   75    │   75    │   75    │
C        │         │         │         │         │  O
A        │75  7  75│75  8  75│75  9  75│75 10  75│  G
N        │         │         │         │         │  L
D        │   75    │   75    │   75    │   75    │  E
L        ├─────────┼─────────┼─────────┼─────────┤  T
E        │         │         │         │         │  H
R        │75 11  75│75 12  75│75 13  75│75 14  75│  O
         │         │         │         │         │  R
S        │   75    │   75    │   75    │   75    │  P
T        └─────────┴─────────┴─────────┴─────────┘  E
R
E                   BULLOCH STREET                  D
E                                                   R
T                                                   I
                                                    V
                                                    E
```

Plat of survey for CHESTNUT RIDGE DEVELOPMENT

PLAT VOLUME 2, PAGE 412, LIBERTY COUNTY, GEORGIA

1.4 Appurtenant Rights

Appurtenances are additional beneficial rights, interests and items associated with land ownership beyond just the physical soil. Major appurtenant rights are: water, air and mineral rights.

Water Rights

Individual states issue water permits for the purpose of allotting scarce water resources, this is especially necessary in states in the west. Although water rights vary by state, there are two basic types that are common nationwide: riparian rights and littoral rights.

> **Riparian rights** – Refers to a land owner's right to "reasonable use" of water flowing through or abutting the property. When dealing with **a navigable body of water**, the property owner's boundary will extend to the water's accretion line (edge). With a **non-navigable body** of water, the property owner's boundary will extends to the water's center point.
>
> **Littoral rights** – Refers to a land owner's right to "reasonable use" of the water abutting the property as in lakes and oceans.

Some terms to keep in mind with regarding water rights:

- Accession – **Attaining land** due to the soil deposited by **natural elements** such as accretion or alluvial deposit
- Erosion – **Natural elements** cause a **steady decrease** in land
- Accretion – Deposit of soil **by water** that results in the **steady increase** in land
- Alluvial – Water shifts alluvium soil resulting in **gradual increase** of land
- Avulsion – **Water** abruptly changes its course resulting **rapid decrease** in land
- Reliction – Retreat of **water** causes a **steady increase** in land

Other nationally recognized water rights:

- **Natural flow doctrine** – Riparian owner's use cannot cause the water to diminish in the amount, quality or pace. All riparian owners have the right to have access to the water in its natural state.
- **Doctrine of reasonable use** – Each riparian owner is entitled to "reasonable use of the water".
- **Doctrine of prior appropriation** - Refers to the water rights that not linked to land ownership. These can be sold and mortgaged as real property.

- **Doctrine of beneficial use** – States that the first users of the water have priority, but must use the water in a beneficial manner and within a reasonable time frame.
- **Doctrine of correlative rights** – Imposes a limit on landowners regarding their share of the water. Generally, this limit "correlates to the amount of land owned by each.

Mineral Rights

Mineral rights are the rights to minerals, such as oil, gas, coal etc., found beneath property. Mineral rights belong to the owner and can be sold separately from the land. A mineral lease may be created to allow non-owners access to specific minerals on a piece of real property.

Liquid Minerals, as in oil and gas are subject to **the law of capture** which grants the surface owner only the right to legally drill and remove as much oil and gas as possible. Ownership of the actual mineral liquids cannot be claimed until they are brought to the surface and become personal property which can then be conveyed by a "Bill of Sale".

Solid Minerals, as in coal and other metals, grants similar rights and restrictions, except that ownership of solids automatically passes with sale.

Air Rights

A property owner is entitled to exclusive use of a "reasonable amount" of airspace above the land which can be conveyed separately. With the advent of air travel, the definition of "reasonable amount" can only be defined as a result of lawsuits between parties.

1.5 Encumbrances

An encumbrance is a claim or lien on a parcel of real property. Specific types of include:

Easement – A right granted for a specific use of the land of another, most often related to rights of way or utility (i.e., gas and water) easements for properties that don't abut a public way. The land granting the easement is considered **encumbered** and referred to as the **servient tenement**, "serving" the easement. The land benefiting from the easement is considered to have an **easement appurtenant** and is referred to as the **dominant tenement**. Further, an easement appurtenant "runs with the land", meaning it automatically transfers when property is conveyed and cannot be sold separately.

Easement in Gross – This easement doesn't benefit a specific property, but rather a person or business entity, as in to construct and maintain power lines running through several pieces of property. In California, this easement can be assigned unless specifically prohibited by the original grant.

Easements are granted in several ways, specifically:

- **express grant** - a property owner expressly grants a specific right to use servient land to another.

- **express reservation** - Rather than granting the right to use, the property owner reserves a specific right to use servient land after they sell the property.

- **easement by implication** - an implied easement is created when a buyer can only reach their property by crossing land owned by the person from whom they purchased.

- **easement by necessity** - granted by court order when a buyer discovers later they can only reach their property by crossing land owned by the person from whom they purchased.

- **easement by prescription** - granted when land is used "openly and notoriously" for a period of time. While this is similar to adverse possession, it only grants "use" and not ownership or exclusivity.

Easements are terminated when:

- The dominant tenement acquires the encumbered land

- The land of both the dominant and servient tenements is combined as one property.

- Easement by Prescription is terminated by lack of use.

Encroachment – A situation in which a structure or fixture is built on another person's property or land, and "encroaches" on their property, often due to poor surveying or incorrectly marked boundary lines. Generally corrected by destruction of the encroaching structure or by obtaining/granting an easement.

Liens – The official definition is "a form of security granted over an item of property to secure the payment of a debt or obligation."

1.6 Restrictions on Use of Property

Restrictions on use of property falls into two main categories: governmental restrictions and private restrictions.

Governmental Restrictions

Governmental Restrictions are the local, state or federal authority's right to limit uses of real property to protect the general public safety, i.e. building codes and environmental protections.

Eminent domain – The government's power to take private property for public use by a federal, state, municipality, or private person or corporation; some common examples are property for government buildings and facilities, highways or railroads, or for public safety reasons. The legal term for this action is referred to as condemnation proceedings.

Three basic requirements must be upheld in order for a government to exercise eminent domain:

1. The property must be taken for public good;

2. The property needs to be used for the public purpose it is being taken for;

3. The property owner must be given just compensation. Note: A court or local government usually decides the definition and amount of just compensation which should reflect 'fair market value'.

- **Condemnation** – The process of exercising powers of eminent domain

- **Severance damage** – Payment to a property owner for an inconvenience that is caused once a portion or all of the land is purchased and used under eminent domain.

- **Inverse condemnation** – A situation where the government seizes the property, but fails to pay the compensation required by the Fifth Amendment of the Constitution.

Police power – Government entities typically "control" the rights to the property by creating laws or guidelines that must be followed when owning a parcel of property. Some common examples include development and zoning laws which designate or restrict what structures or improvements can be made on the property.

Zoning

Zoning laws are adopted by federal authority all the way down to neighborhood and homeowner association authority. They range from restrictions on size, height and use of land or structures to population density and income levels. There are four main categories for land use:

- Residential,
- Commercial,
- Industrial,
- Rural,

and further broken down into seemingly endless subcategories such as: R-1 Single family residential housing; R-2 Two unit residential housing and so on.

Zoning Exemptions

Landowners can apply for exceptions to the existing zoning codes in their area under these main categories:

- **Non-conforming use** - generally applies to areas that have been re-zoned and pre-existing structures and uses no longer conform to the new zoning laws. When new laws are passed, granting of this exception is usually automatic and often referred to as "grandfathering". While it permits continued non-conforming use, major changes or abandoning that use would revoke the exception and then require modifications to meet current standards.
- **Conditional use** - generally applies to hospitals or churches located in residential neighborhoods.
- **Variance** - generally requested by local builders or individual homeowners for **minor exceptions** such as parking, deck size or in the case of builders, the number of residential units allowed in a neighborhood or particular piece of land.

State & Local Permitting & Codes

All buildings in California must comply with the Uniform Building Code. Building codes are the minimum construction standards for construction and framing, wiring, plumbing and other components of buildings. Local authorities each have additional codes outlining restrictions on zoning and other aspects of construction such as local building or fire codes. When a new building or remodeling is proposed, the local authorities issue a building permit for the specified work. When construction is complete, a certificate of occupancy is issued after all building code requirements are satisfied and passed inspection.

Environmental Hazards and Regulations – Laws, guidelines, and regulations the government puts in place to help monitor and regulate different aspects of the country, including physical property, plant life, animals and surrounding environments.

Federal

- The Clean Air Act – Signed into law in 1970 and aimed at controlling air pollutants produced by industrial companies. Since 1970, more than 40 amendments have been added to the original law.

- The Clean Water Act – Passed in 1972 and aimed at controlling water pollution; addresses a popular problem of contaminant dumping by companies and individuals.

- National Environmental Policy Act – Created after the 1969 Santa Barbara oil spill, it made the entity of the property, commercial or private, responsible for ensuring the safety of the environment, including pollution or any chance of accidents.

- Comprehensive Environmental Response, Compensation, and Liability Act (CERCLA) – Created in 1980, it was designed to be a "superfund" that supplies resources to deal with hazardous waste sites, such as oil spills or spilled contaminants. Through CERCLA, entities responsible for the spill are also responsible for the cleanup.

- The Endangered Species Act – Created in 1973 and designed to provide protection for wildlife and flora that are at risk of becoming extinct; among many provisions, it states that animals considered endangered cannot be hunted or harmed and that state government can seize any land that is needed to preserve the species.

- The Safe Drinking Water Act – Created in 1974 to ensure the safety and quality of America's drinking water, it is designed to protect drinking water sources, such as rivers, lakes and reservoirs.

- The Toxic Substances Control Act (TSCA) – Passed in 1976 and it regulates any new or existing chemical substances and its use, and it requires companies to submit notifications and information regarding any new chemical created and added to the TSCA list.

- Residential Lead-Based Paint Hazard Reduction Act – Passed in 1992 and aimed at reducing the number of residences that have lead-based paint, as this type of paint has been associated with many health hazards.

State of California

- Alquist-Priolo Earthquake Fault Zoning Act – Applies to any California development in an earthquake fault zone. This act helps to control the construction of residential properties or other properties designed for human use within a quarter-mile of the fault.

- Seismic Hazards Mapping Act – Applies to any California property that is located in an area considered a defined seismic hazard zone.

- Coastal Zone Conservation Act – Applies to any California property that is located within a defined coastal zone.
- The California Environmental Quality Act (CEQA) – Passed in 1970, this act may require an environmental impact report (EIR) before any subdivision is approved.

Private Controls

Private Controls are **voluntary** use restrictions adopted by landowners or homeowner associations. Restrictive covenants and deed restrictions are methods that private land owners use to control the property even after they have passed ownership to another person or party. These regulations are designed to impose rules for future owners regarding new buildings or use of the land. The restrictions are plainly laid out in the deed or in an additional covenant and binding on all future owners

Forms of private controls are:

- **Conditions** – Generally refers to the status of property, such as current structures and how the property is sustained. Many restrictions are attached to the condition of the property and how it will look in the future.
- **Covenants** – Simply defined as a promise to uphold a requested action or use. Covenants are often added to deeds to restrict actions taken against the property, such as physical or structural changes.
- **Restrictions** – Strict prohibitions that generally "restrict" certain actions or behaviors. Owners identify specific prohibited actions often ranging from adding structures or modifications to restrictions on ownership and transfer of ownership.

Subdivisions

Subdivision is a form of private control. For the most part, a subdivision is a division of contiguous land for the purpose of sale, lease or financing. Subdivisions in California are essentially regulated by two basic subdivision laws: the **Subdivision Map Act** and the **Subdivided Lands Law**. Generally, the subdivider must prepare a map for approval by the local government agency. The major types of subdivisions are:

- planned developments,
- condominiums,
- community apartment projects, and
- stock cooperatives.

Subdivision Map Act

The Subdivision Map Act lays out the conditions for approval of a subdivision map and requires that local governments enact ordinances through which they can directly control the types of subdivisions and the physical improvements required. This act has two major objectives: a) to coordinate a subdivision's design (lots, street patterns, rights-of-way for drainage and sewers, etc.) with the community plan; and b) to ensure the subdivider will properly complete the public areas.

Subdivided Lands Law

The Real Estate Commissioner administers the Subdivided Lands Law as a set of consumer protections from fraud, misrepresentation and/or deceit in the sale of subdivided property. Nearly all subdivisions require the Commissioner to issue a subdivision public report laying out essential consumer information and disclosures prior to the sale offering of a subdivision. The report cannot be issued until the subdivider meets the statutory requirements, including financing to assure completion of the project and evidence that the individual lots or units being purchased can be used for the purpose intended.

Subdivision Types and Definitions

Standard - A standard subdivision has no common areas.

Common Interest - Purchasers in a common interest subdivision own or lease a separate lot, unit, or interest, as well as an undivided interest or membership interest in a portion of the common area of the entire project. There are four types:

- **Condominium** - a common undivided interest in a portion of real property together with a separate interest in a unit, the boundaries of which are described on a recorded final map, parcel map, or condominium plan. The undivided interest portion may be all of the real property or may include a particular portion thereof as described on a recorded final map, parcel map, or condominium plan. Typically, an owner of a condominium owns an undivided interest in common in certain other defined portions of the whole property involved. An association and its elected governing board perform the management functions.

- **Planned development** - consists of lots or parcels owned separately and lots or areas owned in common, reserved for the use of some or all of the individual lot owners. Generally, an owner's association provides management, maintenance and control of the common areas and has the power to levy assessments and enforce obligations which attach to the individual lots.

- **Stock cooperative** - a corporation formed to hold title to improved real property, either in fee simple or for a term of years. Shareholders own stock in the corporation and receive a right of exclusive occupancy of a portion of the real property, which right can only be transferred with the transfer of the stock ownership. Most stock cooperatives are operated by a board of directors.

- **Community apartment project** - an undivided interest in the land coupled with the right of exclusive occupancy of an apartment located thereon. The owners elect a governing board which operates and maintains the project.

Undivided Interest

A partial/fractional interest in an entire parcel of land is called an undivided interest. The land itself has not been divided, but its ownership has been divided. Creating five or more undivided interests in land for the purpose of sale, lease or financing constitutes a subdivision and requires a public report be issued prior to offering. There are exemptions, including the purchase by people related by blood or marriage or by ten or fewer persons who: are informed concerning the risks of ownership; are not purchasing the property for resale; and waive the protections offered by the Subdivided Lands Law.

Time Share Interest - there are two forms of timeshare ownership:

- **time share estate** - ownership interest in real property along with an exclusive right to occupy for specific time periods.

- **time share use** - ownership of the exclusive right to occupy, but not ownership of the real property. Time share use is generally only transferable through a license or membership.

Homeowner's Associations - A homeowners' association (HOA) is a corporation or private party formed by a real estate developer to manage (and sometimes market and sell) a subdivision. Many HOAs are managed by the residents often through "board members" who govern any final rulings or decisions.

1.7 Ownership

Ownership Rights and Restrictions

When someone acquires real property, not only the rights of ownership are considered. There are several degrees of ownership, often relating to duration and transferability. The two major categories of estates are **"freehold"** and **"non-freehold"** and divided into several sub-categories, each with specific rights and limitations.

Freehold Estates

Freehold estates grant the exclusive right to lawfully own, use and transfer for an indefinite period of time. This type of ownership is inheritable. Examples of freehold estates are:

Fee simple absolute – The most common type of freehold estate. Rights include:

- live in, rent or mortgage the property
- sell, demolish or convey ownership of the property
- build and construct on the property
- test for and mine minerals, gas and oil
- deny the use of the property to others

Fee simple defeasible - Same rights as "absolute", but contains one or more conditions that, if violated, would cause the property to revert to the prior owner, such as partitioning the land and selling separate parcels. It should be noted that the conditions must be lawful.

Life estates –The owner of the life estate is granted all the rights of ownership for their entire lifespan and can sell or lease their interest. However, upon death all interests are terminated.

- **Pur autre vie** – "for another's life" similar to 'life estate'. Just as the translation from the French says, this ownership is based on the lifespan of another person.
- **Life estate in reversion** – A life estate ownership that reverts to the original owner or grantor.
- **Remainder man** – An individual who inherits a life estate, typically upon death or by transfer from the original owner.

Non-freehold Estates

A non-freehold estate is a lease or contract generally granting only possession and use for a period of time. Generally the holder of a non-freehold estate is referred to as the "lessee/tenant" and the owner, "lessor/landlord". There are four types of non-freehold estates in California:

- **Estate at Will** – Also known as a tenancy at will. Either party can terminate the contract at any time. Note: California law requires a 30-day notice of termination.

- **Estate for Years** – Includes fixed start and end dates. The contract period can be as short as hours or days, or as long as 100 years or more.

- **Estate from Period to Period** – Also known as a periodic tenancy or periodic estate. Similar to an Estate for Years, but automatically renews from period to period unless one of the parties gives notice of termination.

- **Estate at Sufferance** – Use and/or occupancy against the owner's wishes, i.e., a tenant who does not vacate at the end of the lease.

- **Fee upon condition** – The tenant's costs of holding the property can vary and are based on external fluctuations like changes in market rental or leasing rates, increases in property taxes, etc.

Legal Designations of Ownership

There are multiple ways in California to hold title to real property. If you're single, you can take title as sole owner; married owners often take title as Joint Tenants and so on. Title can also be held jointly with someone other than your spouse. Each form of ownership contains different rights, restrictions and tax or liability consequences.

The two major designations of Ownership are:

Estate/Ownership in severalty – Ownership by a single person only.

Co-Ownership - Ownership by two or more owners. California recognizes the following five types of co-ownership:

1. **Joint Tenancy** – A form of ownership in which two or more parties own an undivided interest in the property. With joint tenancy, the right of survivorship is applicable. This means that a co-owner cannot transfer his ownership interest when he dies. Instead, the surviving co-owner will automatically take over the decedent's interest. These are the "unities" inherent in joint tenancy:

   a. **Unity of time** – Interest acquired by both tenants at the same time.

   b. **Unity of title** – Interests held by co-owners from the same property.

   c. **Unity of interest** – All tenants have the same interest in the same property.

   d. **Unity of possession** – All tenants have the same right to possess the property.

2. **Tenancy in common** – A form of ownership in which two or more parties possess the property simultaneously. This form of ownership does NOT include a "right of survivorship."

3. **Community property** – A form of ownership commonly defined as property owned by spouses or **registered** domestic partners. All real and personal property acquired during the marriage is considered community property, as is any separate property that is commingled with community property. Exceptions exist for property owned prior to marriage or acquired through gift or inheritance.

   Both spouses have the legal right to manage community property. Community property can only be attached by a creditor of **both** the parties. As of 2001, California adopted a law allowing for **Community Property with a right of survivorship** (as in Joint Tenancy above).

4. **Tenancy in Partnership** – A form of ownership in which two or more people combine assets and property for business purposes, each sharing in profits and losses. A joint venture is similar to a partnership, though typically for a specific "project" and a limited amount of time. Two classes of Partnership are:

   a. **General partnership** – An association of people or an unincorporated company that create an agreement formed by two or more people where all parties are personally responsible for action, debts and liability of the partnership.

   b. **Limited partnership** – A partnership in which at least one person is required to be a general partner assuming the responsibilities of the role. All limited partners have no liability beyond their own investment in the partnership.

1.8 Liens

Liens are an encumbrance against real property, generally to guarantee a debt. Some are voluntary as when a homeowner obtains a second mortgage. Others are involuntary as when the government obtains a lien to secure payment of real estate or income taxes. Common types of liens and terms associated with them are:

Judgment liens – A type of **general lien** that is meant to secure payment or property that was awarded as a result of a legal judgment or settlement. Judgment liens are valid for 10 years, can be renewed and remain valid even if a property is transferred.

Attachment liens - A type of lien created by one of the actions below:

- **Writ of attachment** – A court order to seize a portion of an asset in an amount to satisfy a lien.

- **Writ of execution** – A court order to enforce a judgment, usually to seize and sell an asset to satisfy a judgment.

Mechanic's lien – A lien initiated by licensed contractors who have supplied labor and/or materials to improve real property (carpenters, landscapers). This is a type of **specific lien** in that it applies to a specific piece of improved property.

Materialman's lien – Similar to a mechanic's lien, but applies to the person or company who supplies the materials used to improve the property.

Design Professional's Lien - Also similar to a mechanic's lien. In California, effective in 1991, a "design professional" is defined as a certificated architect, a registered professional engineer, or a licensed land surveyor who furnishes services under a written contract with a property owner for the design, engineering, or planning of improvement work.

Tax liens – Types of liens imposed by the government's taxing authority used for collection of unpaid taxes.

- **Property tax lien** – a **specific lien** against a piece of real property to collect unpaid property taxes.

- **Federal tax lien** – a **general lien** to secure unpaid federal taxes.

- **State tax lien** – a **general lien** to secure unpaid taxes.

Lis Pendens - A "notice of pending litigation" attached to a piece of real property. This is generally done by a creditor as warning to prospective purchasers or lenders of a pending lawsuit that could result in a negative judgment affecting the value or salability of real property.

1.9 Homesteads

Homestead Protection

First - do not confuse this with the Homestead Act of 1862 which is no longer legal. Homestead protection laws allow individuals to declare a portion of their property as "homestead", offering limited protection in the event of a lien or lawsuit. This declaration exempts a portion of their equity from seizure.

Homestead Exemption Amounts

The amount of the homestead exemption varies depending on the factors below:

1. $75,000 for an individual;

2. $100,000 for a head of household (others who live in the home have only a community property interest in the property);

3. $175,000, if the judgment debtor or spouse who resides in the homestead is at that time of the attempted sale of the homestead any one of the following:

    I. A person 65 years of age or older

    II. A person physically or mentally disabled and because of that disability is unable to engage in substantial gainful employment.

    III. A person 55 years of age or older; for singles with a gross annual income of not more than $25,000, or married with a combined annual income not more than $35,000 and in both instances the sale is involuntary.

Homestead Filing Services

Non-attorney "Homestead Filing Services" can provide homeowners with assistance. Due to predatory practices, California developed the following regulations for all non-attorney providers who charge for their services:

- A provider must properly prepare a homestead declaration;
- A provider must have the declaration notarized and pay the notary's fee;
- A provider must have the declaration recorded at the county recording office within 10 days of being notarized and pay the recording fee;

- A provider must give the homeowner a written disclosure statement before requiring payment; and
- A provider may not charge more than $25 for his or her services (including notary and recording fees).

Study Smart Guide

Real property - land and things permanently attached to it. Transferred by deed

Personal property - property that is tangible and moveable. Does not include rights to the land and transferred by bill of sale

Fixtures - items that have been permanently attached to real property. Can be personal property that has been "**physically or constructively annexed**" to a structure.

Appurtenant Rights - additional beneficial rights, interests associated with land ownership beyond just physical soil. Major appurtenant rights are: water, air and mineral rights.

Encumbrance - a claim or lien on a parcel of real property.

Easements – right granted for a specific use of the land of another created by: express grant, express reservation, easement by implication, easement by necessity and easement by prescription

Encroachment – a structure or fixture is built on another person's property or land, and "encroaches" on their property

Eminent domain – The government's power to take private property for public use executed by a condemnation proceeding.

Police power – Government entities typically "control" the rights to the property by creating laws or guidelines

Private Controls - **voluntary** use restrictions adopted by landowners or homeowner associations.

Standard Subdivision - has no common areas.

Common Interest Subdivision - ownership or lease of a lot, unit, or interest, with an undivided interest or membership interest in the common area.

Condominium - a common undivided interest in a portion of real property together with a separate interest in a unit.

Planned development - lots or parcels owned separately and lots or areas owned in common, reserved for the use of some or all of the individual lot owners.

Stock cooperative - a corporation formed to hold title to improved real property. Shareholders own stock in the corporation and receive a right of exclusive occupancy. Can only be transferred with the transfer of the stock ownership.

Freehold estates - grant the exclusive right to own, use and transfer for an indefinite period of time; inheritable.

Fee simple absolute - most common type of freehold estate.

Fee simple defeasible - Same rights as "absolute", but contains conditions that would cause the property to revert to the prior owner.

Life estates - all the rights of ownership for a person's entire lifespan. May be sold or leased, but is terminated upon their death.

Non-freehold Estates - lease or contract for possession only and for a defined period of time. Holder is "lessee" or "tenant" and owner is "lessor" or "landlord".

Estate at Will – tenancy at will. Can terminate at any time. California law requires a 30-day notice of termination.

Estate for Years – Lease that includes fixed start and end dates. Can be as short as hours or days, or as long as 100 years or more.

Estate from Period to Period – periodic tenancy or periodic estate. Similar to an Estate for Years, but automatically renews unless one of the parties gives notice of termination.

Estate at Sufferance – Use and/or occupancy against the owner's wishes, i.e., a tenant who does not vacate at the end of the lease.

Estate/Ownership in severalty – Ownership by a single person only.

Co-Ownership - Ownership by two or more owners.

Joint Tenancy – two or more parties own an undivided interest with the right of survivorship must include **unity of time, unity of title, unity of interest** and **unity of possession.**

Tenancy in common – two or more parties possess the property simultaneously; does NOT include a "right of survivorship."

Community property – property owned by spouses or **registered** domestic partners; with a right of survivorship.

Tenancy in Partnership – two or more people combine assets and property for business purposes

Judgment liens – A type of **general lien** to secure payment or property that was awarded as a result of a legal judgment or settlement. Valid for 10 years, can be renewed and remain valid even if a property is transferred.

Liens – security granted over an item of property to secure the payment of a debt or obligation. Types are: **mechanic's lien, materialman's lien, design professional's lien** and **tax liens.**

Lis Pendens - "notice of pending litigation" attached to a piece of real property as warning of ongoing lawsuit.

Homestead Protection - limited protection that exempts a portion of equity from seizure.

Chapter 1
Quiz & Answers

1) Fixtures are:
    a) personal property
    b) real property
    c) permanently attached
    d) all of the above

2) Personal property is transferred:
    a) along with a deed
    b) as part of a sale
    c) only if the buyer pays for it
    d) by bill of sale

3) An Assessor's Parcel Number is:
    a) used for local identification
    b) used for federal taxes
    c) used for directions
    d) used for national mapping

4) Appurtenant rights include:
    a) the right to use a common driveway
    b) the right to use common areas in a subdivision
    c) the rights to air, land and minerals
    d) all of the above

5) The steady increase of land deposited by water is:
    a) Alluvium
    b) Accretion
    c) Erosion
    d) Reliction

34

6) An easement is:
   a) an appurtenant right
   b) transferrable
   c) the right to use the land of another
   d) all of the above

7) Tenancy in common is:
   a) common areas owned by a subdivision
   b) enforced police power
   c) a lease held by more than one person
   d) none of the above

8) An older building that does not meet current building codes:
   a) is illegal and must be renovated
   b) is legal and considered non-conforming
   c) is illegal and must be demolished
   d) a and c

9) An attachment is:
   a) a fixture that is attached
   b) a type of lien
   c) a right of ownership
   d) personal property

10) A life estate is:
    a) a lease for life
    b) a non-freehold estate
    c) an ownership for life
    d) all of the above

ANSWERS:

1. d
2. d
3. a
4. c
5. b
6. d
7. d
8. b
9. b
10. c

Chapter 2

Chapter 2: Acquisition, Transfer, Escrow and Taxation of Property

The regulations governing how property is transferred are many and do not differentiate between real and personal property.

2.1 Acquisition of Property

In California, the ways to acquire property are: will, succession, accession, occupancy, and by transfer as follows:

- By will
- By succession of separate property or community property.
- By accession: through accretion (alluvion or reliction); through avulsion; through addition of fixtures and through improvements made in error.
- By occupancy: Abandonment, prescription and adverse possession.
- By transfer: Private or public grant; Gift (to private person or by public dedication).
- Alienation by court-ordered partition or foreclosure.
- By marriage.
- By escheat.
- By eminent domain.
- By equitable estoppel.

Wills

Property accumulated during a lifetime may be transferred at death to designated beneficiaries. The instrument directing this transfer is called a will. The defining difference between wills and other instruments of transfer, such as deeds and contracts, is that will only become effective upon death. The types of wills are:

- **witnessed will** - formal written instrument signed by the maker and declared made by free will in front of at least 2 people who then also sign the document as witnesses.

- **holographic will** - written, dated and signed in the maker's own handwriting, requiring no declaration or witnesses.
- **statutory will and statutory will with trust** - usually a pre-printed form written according to a format authorized by law. Upon death, title passes temporarily to an executor/executrix before passing to the beneficiaries or heirs. Title is not immediately marketable or insurable until released from the control of a probate court who settles any creditor claims and establishes the identity of the heirs

Probate

Probate begins with a *petition for probate* of a will or for letters of administration if there is no will. A hearing is held and a representative is appointed to handle the estate. This person is referred to as an executor or executrix if there is a will, or an administrator or administratrix if there is no will or no executor was name in the will.

Notice to creditors is published, giving all creditors four months to file claims. An inventory and appraisal of the estate listing all the assets is filed with the county clerk. During administration of the estate, the representative may only sell estate property by permission of the probate court.

After the time for filing and "creditors" claims have expired, the representative files an accounting for court review and approval. Lastly, the representative petitions the court to approve distribution of the remaining assets to the proper heirs and devisees. Small estates may be exempt from probate administration.

Succession

If a person dies without leaving a will, the law provides for disposition of their property, called *intestate succession.* There can be many special rules depending on the nature of the property and the relationship of the next of kin. In the simplest cases, *separate property* is divided equally between a surviving spouse and one child, or split one-third to the surviving spouse and one-third to each of two children, etc. One-half of the *community property* belongs to the surviving spouse and the other half is dispersed by the will. If there is no will, the decedent's half of the community property remaining after payment of his or her liabilities goes to the surviving spouse.

Accession

By accession, an owner's title to improvements or additions to his or her property may be extended as a result of either man-made or natural causes, such as accretion or reliction or annexation.

Abandonment. Abandonment is the voluntary surrender of a lease and/or possession of real property. This is a willful termination of possession and/or interest, without assigning the interest to another. If the holder of a leasehold interest (i.e., the lessee) abandons the property, the landlord re-acquires possession and full control of the premises. Non-use is not abandonment.

Adverse possession. The actual physical possession of property plays heavily when weighing rights and obligations. Upon occupancy, the adverse possessor acquires a title to the property good against all except the state and the true owner. The occupancy can become *legal* title by adverse possession if the possession is:

- by actual occupation;
- open and notorious;
- hostile to the true owner's title;
- under claim of right or color of title;
- continuous and uninterrupted for a period of five years; and
- accompanied by payment of all real property taxes for a period of five years.

Since title by adverse possession cannot be traced through the county registrar, it is neither marketable nor insurable until declared by a court decree. Title by adverse possession usually cannot be acquired against a public body.

Prescription. An easement created by prescription is similar to adverse possession. However, an easement grants only the right to use someone else's land, rather than gaining an ownership interest.

2.2 Transfer of Property

Property is transferred when the lawful owner conveys title from one person to another.

Private Grant - By deed from one private party to another. Most property is transferred in this manner.

Gift - transfer of property through a gift deed. The owner (or grantor) cannot receive compensation for the property.

Public dedication - property given to a public body for use by the public. Examples include land for a park, a street, or public access to a body of water or beach. To be valid, the public body must formally accept the public dedication.

Public Grant - the government grants land at little or no cost, but with stipulations. Often granted to private individuals or institutions such universities or railroads. Originally began with the Homestead Act of 1862 which has now been abandoned in all states.

Alienation by court action - Below are the most common situations in which courts establish legal title regardless of the desires of the record owners.

- **Quiet Title** - the usual way of clearing tax titles, titles based upon adverse possession, and the title of a seller under a forfeited recorded contract of sale.

- **Partition** - A co-owner of property may sue the other co-owners, requesting a separation ("partition") of the respective interests. If the property cannot be divided physically, the court may order a sale and divide the proceeds among the former owners.

- **Foreclosure** - A person holding a lien based on a delinquent contract may ask the court to order sale of the property and the proceeds applied to the unpaid balance due under the contract.

- **Declaratory Relief** - In the case of controversy or dispute, a person may ask the court to determine their rights and obligations under any contract.

- **Execution sale** - A plaintiff obtaining a money judgment against a defendant can get a *writ of execution.* This court order directs the sheriff to satisfy the court's judgment by seizing and selling real property at public auction.

- **Forfeiture.** An owner may impose a *condition subsequent* in a deed. If the condition is breached, the grantor (or successor) has the power to terminate ownership and reacquire title. Similarly, the owner may impose a *special limitation* in a deed. If the referenced event occurs, ownership automatically terminates and the grantor (or successor) reacquires title. In both cases, property is acquired by forfeiture with no need for consideration.

Marriage - Under California law, marriage does not effect a transfer of title. However, *subsequent* earnings and acquisitions of either spouse during marriage are *community property.* Each spouse has a present, existing and equal interest in that property.

Escheat - transfer of property from someone who died without heirs or without a will (intestate). Property is usually transferred to the state to ensure it is not left unattended.

Eminent domain - a governmental entity acquires private property for public use, paying compensation based on fair market value.

Equitable estoppel - a former owner is legally barred ("estopped') from denying the title of the innocent claimant. For example, if an owner permits a friend to appear to the world as the owner of certain property, and an innocent third party buys the land from that apparent owner; the true owner is barred under equitable estoppel from claiming ownership.

Bankruptcy - transfer through legal bankruptcy (insolvency) proceedings. When a person or business declares bankruptcy, the courts transfer the property ownership to a trustee, who sells the property and disperses the proceeds to satisfy creditors under court supervision.

2.3 Deeds

The deed is the legal document transferring the ownership interest in real property from one party (grantor) to another (grantee). Deeds do not have to be recorded to be valid, but when recorded, it gives legal notice of the transfer of ownership.

Validation of Deeds

There are several key elements that must be included in the deed in order for it to be valid. These are:

- Must be in writing;

- Properly identify all parties involved; Grantor must be legally competent and Grantee must be legally capable;

- "Granting clause"- specific language (i.e., I "grant," or I "transfer," etc.);

- Consideration - declares money or other value being exchanged;

- Details of the rights or interest being transferred;

- Legal property description;

- Properly executed - signed by Grantors using the same names as when property was acquired;

- Delivered to Grantee - can be voided if not actually delivered (by recording or otherwise). It should be noted that recording after death is considered "undelivered";

- Accepted by Grantee - either by action (use by Grantee or recording);

- Grantor must sign and declare that the transfer is his "free act and deed" in the presence of a Notary Public if the deed is to be recorded.

Types of Deeds

The main types of deeds are:

1. **Grant deed** - conveys interest in property with 2 implied warranties: a) Grantor has not transferred interest to another party and b) Property is free of encumbrances assumed by Grantor other than disclosed. This is the most common deed in California.

2. **Trust deed** - conveys strict legal title only. Used as a security instrument for mortgages. The borrower ("trustor") is granted "use and possession" of the property; the lender ("beneficiary") receives payments on the note; and the "trustee" holds title as security for the note, with no rights to use or possession until the terms of the note are satisfied and the lien discharged.

Additionally, this deed grants the trustee the power to sell the property if the trustor defaults or otherwise breaches the terms of the note.

3. **Reconveyance deed** - reconveys full title from the trustee to the borrower under a trust deed once the promissory note is paid in full.

4. **Quitclaim deed** - conveys interest in property but makes no warranties regarding previous title or encumbrances.

5. **Sheriff's deed** - given at the foreclosure and conveys only the former owner's title, with no warranties whatsoever.

6. **Special warranty deed - conveys** interest in property with warranties that the property is free and clear of all encumbrances, along with the Grantor's responsibility to defend the title against all future claims. This deed is rarely use due to the legal liabilities.

7. **Gift deed** - conveys title for which no consideration is given in exchange. This deed can be voided if it is deemed to have been conveyed for fraudulent reasons.

Title

When transferring ownership, the grantor must disclose and usually discharge any encumbrances or outstanding interests depending on the type of deed granted. This is referred to as providing "clear and marketable" title. If the seller does not properly clear encumbrances to the title, the buyer may not receive the full rights and benefits of ownership.

Possession

Possession of the property or interest therein, is important in establishing who owns the title to a particular piece of real estate as well as the right to grant the property to another party. To back the claim of possession, ownership is recorded in the appropriate office of the county in which the property is located, generally a Registry of Deeds, or in the case of court ordered transfer, sometimes a Land Court. These offices are where actual deeds and other instruments affecting title are recorded establishing a **chain of title**, ideally traced back to the property's original conveyance from the government. The offices maintain these records in two ways:

- **Grantee index** – An alphabetical list of purchasers of the property.

- **Grantor index** – An alphabetical list of sellers of the property.

A record of the "chain of title" is not always complete or properly maintained due to missing or erroneous records. Prior to any deed being recorded, a process known as a **Title Search** is performed to determine true ownership and any others who may have a claim or encumber the property, i.e., a bank holding a mortgage.

Abstract of Title

An abstract of title is a statement summarizing the history of conveyances appearing in the public record. Since most individual buyers and lenders are not equipped to make the necessary investigation, a title specialist is retained to study the records and prepare summaries or abstracts of title of all pertinent documents discovered in the search.

Cloud on the title

A "cloud on the title" is any outstanding claim or encumbrance that would, when validated, affect or impair the owner's rights to a particular property/estate. While the cloud remains, the owner is prevented from selling, transferring or conveying marketable title. The ability to further encumber the property (for instance, get a mortgage) may also be impaired.

Examples are:

- a mortgage is paid off but without official recording of a discharge or reconveyancing deed;
- an apparent interest in the property remains because an heir fails to sign a deed ;
- or a notice of action (lis pendens) which remains on the public record even after the plaintiff and defendant have agreed to dismissal of the court action.

2.4 Title Insurance

Since public records can be erroneous or incomplete, lenders require new owners to obtain Title insurance to protect their interest against future claims of ownership or debt. Title insurance covers most risks that are a matter of public record and can be extended to protect non-recorded risks. The general practice in California for buyers, sellers, lenders, attorneys, and real estate brokers is to rely on title insurance companies for title information, title reports, and policies of title insurance.

Preliminary report

The title insurance industry typically issues a preliminary report rather than a "search" or "abstract". The Insurance Code defines "preliminary report" as a "commitment" or "binder" furnished in connection with an application for title insurance. These reports are **offers to issue a title policy** and not abstracts or searches.

Title Insurance Polices

Policies of title insurance are now almost universally used in California, largely in the standardized forms prepared by the California Land Title Association (CLTA) for standard coverage and American Land Title Association (ALTA) for extended coverage.

Standard coverage - In addition to risks of record, the standard policy protects against:

- off-record hazards such as forgery, impersonation, or lack of competency of a party to any transaction involving title to the land (e.g., a deed from grantor considered incompetent, or an agent whose authority has terminated);

- the possibility that a deed of record was not in fact delivered with intent to convey title typically excluding a fraudulent conveyance);

- the loss which might arise from the lien of federal estate taxes, which is effective without notice upon death; and

- The expense, including attorneys' fees, incurred in defending the title, whether the plaintiff prevails or not.

The standard policy of title insurance does *not* protect the policyholder against defects known to exist at the date of the policy and not previously disclosed to the insurance company. Additionally, the standard policy does not protect against:

- easements and liens which are not shown by the public records;
- rights or claims of persons in physical possession of the land/property not shown by the public records;

- rights or claims not shown in public records which could be ascertained by physical inspection of the land/property or inquiry of persons on the land/property;
- by a correct survey;
- zoning ordinances;
- mining claims;
- reservations in patents; and
- water rights.

Extended Coverage - In California, many loans secured by real property have been made by out-of-state financial institutions/licensed lenders that were not in a position to make a personal inspection of the property. For them and other non-resident lenders, the special ALTA (American Land Title Association) Policy was developed. This policy expands the risks normally insured to include:

- rights of parties in physical possession, including tenants and buyers under unrecorded instruments;
- reservations in patents; and
- unmarketable title.

The ALTA Loan Policy also covers **recorded** notices of enforcement of excluded matters (like zoning), as well as **recorded** notices of defects (liens or encumbrances) affecting title that result from a violation of matters excluded from policy coverage.

Rules and Regulations for Title Insurance Companies

Every title insurer must make available to the public a schedule of fees and charges for title policies.

Rebate Law

Title insurance companies are legally required to charge for preliminary reports and prohibited from accepting direct or indirect payments from principals in a transaction as consideration for additional business. Further, they are prohibited from paying any commission, rebate or other consideration as either an inducement or compensation to escrow or other title businesses in connection with a policy.

Domestic Title Insurance Companies in California

Section 12359 of the Insurance Code of California requires that a title insurance company organized under the laws of this State have:

- At least $500,000 paid-in capital represented by shares of stock.

- That the insurer deposit with the Insurance Commissioner a "guarantee fund" of $100,000 in cash or approved securities to secure protection for title insurance policy holders.

- Must also set apart annually, as a title insurance surplus fund, a sum equal to 10 percent of its premiums collected during the year until this fund equals the lesser of 25 percent of the paid-in capital of the company or $1,000,000.

- Title insurance companies can furnish "the name of the owner of record and the record description of any parcel or real property" without charge. Such information may be referred to as a "property profile" or "subject property history".

2.5 Sale Escrows and Settlements

Sale Escrows

An escrow is essentially a small and short-lived trust arrangement. It is the process by which real property transfers and other transactions such as exchanges, leases, sales of personal property, sales of securities, loans, and mobile home sales are transferred.

Legal Definition of an Escrow

California Civil Code Section 1057 provides this description of an escrow:
> "A grant may be deposited by the grantor with a third person, to be delivered on the performance of a condition, and, on delivery by the depositary, it will take effect. While in the possession of the third person, and subject to condition, it is called an escrow."

Section 17003 of the Financial Code provides this description of an escrow:
> "Escrow means any transaction wherein one person, for the purpose of effecting the sale, transfer, encumbering or leasing of real or personal property to another person, delivers any written instrument, money, evidence of title to real or personal property, or other thing of value to a third person to be held by such third person until the happening of a specified event or the performance of a prescribed condition, when it is then to be delivered by such third person to a grantee, grantor, promisee, promisor, obligee, obligor, bailee, bailor, or any agent or employee of any of the latter."

Escrows are used for the transfer of funds between buyer and seller. In California, escrow instructions vary by regions of the state. In Northern California, most real estate transactions involve what are known as **unilateral escrow instructions**. Buyer and seller each prepare their own separate documents, which are given to the escrow agent shortly before closing. In Southern California, most real estate transactions involve what are known as **bilateral escrow instructions**. A single set of instructions is signed by both buyer and seller and given to the escrow agent at the time the escrow is opened.

Essential Elements of an Escrow

The essential elements for a valid sale escrow are:
- a binding contract/agreement between buyer and seller outlining the conditions to be met prior to transfer; and
- the delivery to the neutral party (escrow holder) something of value (the deed) and any accompanying documentation for transfer, all of which may only be returned by consent of both parties.

Escrow Holder

The escrow holder (escrow agent) is defined a neutral third party lawfully engaged in the business of receiving escrows (money, documents, things of value) for deposit on behalf of and/or for delivery to the designated principal(s). The escrow holder is a fiduciary in performing duties and must, at all times, demonstrate reasonable care, loyalty, and good faith towards the principals of the escrow. While the escrow holder can be held liable for violating written instructions, they are only a neutral stakeholder and cannot resolve conflicts among the principals. In the event of a conflict the escrow holder must ask a court for resolution and direction on how to proceed.

Who May Act as Escrow Holder/Agent

Escrow holders/agents who conduct public escrows must be licensed. However, under certain circumstances, banks, title insurance companies, underwritten title companies, trust companies, attorneys and real estate brokers have exemptions from the licensing requirements and can act as Escrow agents.

The buyer in the real estate sales transaction generally makes the selection of the escrow holder/agent and the title insurance company intending to issue the title insurance coverage.

Escrow Companies Must Be Incorporated

An individual cannot be licensed as an escrow holder/agent. Instead, a corporation conducting an escrow business must hold the license. Applicants for escrow licenses must meet the follow standards:

- financially solvent and furnish a surety bond in the amount of $25,000 or more, based upon yearly average trust fund obligations.
- all officers, directors, trustees, and employees having access to money or negotiable instruments must furnish a bond of indemnification against loss.
- all money deposited in escrow must be placed in a trust account that is exempt from execution or attachment.

Real Estate Brokers as Escrow Holder

A licensed real estate broker is exempt from holding an escrow license when acting in the normal course of a real estate transaction. The exemption further requires that the real estate broker must either be an agent or a party to the real estate transaction *and* performing an act for which a real estate license is required. For example, if a real estate broker is acting as an agent of a buyer or seller, the broker may lawfully perform the escrow. In contrast, if the real estate broker is acting solely as a party (i.e., they are the buyer or seller) and not acting as a real estate agent for another party, the broker is not authorized to perform the escrow.

Responsibilities of the Escrow Holder

The escrow holder ensures that all parties to the transaction comply with the terms and conditions of the sale agreement and escrow instructions. They generally coordinate the activities the lender(s), the title company (if different), the title insurance company, and the obligations of the buyer, seller and real estate broker. The escrow holder is responsible for:

- holding money
- written instruments and documents
- personal property and other things of value such as securities etc.

The escrow holder maintains control of these items until the performance of specified events and contract conditions.

Audit
An escrow holder/agent licensed under the Escrow Law is required to keep accurate accounts and records. These records are subject to examination and the must submit an independent audit prepared by a Certified Public Accountant annually.

Real estate brokers conducting sale escrows are subject to the audit of their trust funds and the examination of their accounts and records by the Real Estate Commissioner.

Definition of Principals to the Escrow
In a real estate sale escrow, the principals include the buyer and the seller and, if applicable, the lender(s) making the "purchase money" loan. While principals are parties to the escrow, not all parties involved are principals.

Escrow Instructions
Escrow instructions govern the conditional delivery of a deed or encumbrance, money, or other things of value accompanied by instructions to the escrow holder authorizing the delivery of the instruments, funds and related documents after certain events and performance of stipulated conditions. In California, there are two forms of escrow instructions:

- bilateral instructions - signed by both and binding on each buyer and seller

- unilateral instructions - separate sets of instructions, each executed by the buyer and seller and binding for both.

The escrow instructions implement and may supplement the original contract agreement; thus both are interpreted together as part of one complete agreement. However if the escrow instructions contain a conflict with the original contract/agreement, the instructions (being the later contract/agreement) will usually control.

When the buyer and seller have each fully performed under an agreement (all conditions of escrow have been satisfied or waived), the escrow holder becomes the agent of the seller relative to the purchase money and the agent of the buyer relative to the deed. As such, the escrow holder delivers the money to the seller and the deed to the buyer.

Prohibited Actions

An escrow holder/agent may not pay fees to real estate brokers or others for referral of business.

An escrow holder/agent cannot disburse a real estate broker's commission from the escrow proceeds prior to closing of the escrow.

Escrow holders/agents may not solicit or accept escrow instructions, or amended or supplemental instructions containing any blank to be filled in after signing or initialing. Further, they may not permit any person to add, delete or alter an escrow instruction, unless it is signed or initialed by all parties who previously signed or initialed the instructions.

At the time of execution, escrow holders/agents are charged by law with delivering a copy of any escrow instruction, or amended or supplemental instruction, to all parties executing the instructions. However, escrow instructions, being privileged and confidential, may not be disclosed to non-principals.

Real estate brokers, when conducting escrows, must follow similar standards of conduct and may not nominate an escrow holder/agent as a condition to a transaction, but may suggest an escrow holder/agent, if requested by the principals to the transaction.

Developer-controlled Escrow Prohibition

No real estate developer (defined as any person or entity having an ownership interest in real property which is improved by them and offered for sale to the public) may require, as a condition to the sale, that escrow services be provided by an escrow entity in which the developer has a "financial interest." A developer who violates this statute is liable for damages of $250 or three times the charge for escrow services, whichever is greater, plus attorney's fees and costs.

Closing or Terminating Escrow

Completed Escrow
Properly drawn and executed escrow instructions become an enforceable contract/agreement. An escrow is termed "completed" or "perfected" when each of the terms has been met, performed, satisfied or waived.

Termination of Escrow
Escrows are voluntarily completed by full performance/execution and closing, or the escrow may be terminated by mutual consent. The termination of the sale escrow is accomplished by cancellation of the escrow, and by rescission or cancellation of the original residential purchase agreement.

"Time is of the Essence"
Compliance with the escrow instructions must be completed within the timeframe outlined in the instructions unless mutually extended by the principals. The escrow holder has no authority to enforce or accept performance after the time limit expires.

When the time limit has expired and either party to the escrow has not performed, the principals may elect to mutually cancel the sale escrow and each entitled to the return of their respective property, funds, instruments and related documents. The escrow holder does not have authority to determine that a principal has not performed, and must follow clear and precise instructions from the principals.

Cancellation of Escrow - Cancellation or Rescission of Purchase Agreement/ Contract
Cancellation of escrow may not also cancel or rescind the original purchase agreement/contract. The distinction between cancelling and rescinding the purchase agreement/contract is:

- **cancellation** - the principals stop the transaction in place (subject to whatever limited fees, costs, and expenses imposed by third parties and/or to the payment of liquidated damages pursuant to the agreement of the principals), or
- **rescission** - the principals are returned to their respective status prior to the transaction.

2.6 Taxation

Taxes are a levy imposed by various, and often multiple, governmental authorities impacting the ownership, transfer and value of real property.

Types of Taxes

There are many tax consequences of owning or investing in real estate, transferring real estate and even inheriting or receiving real property as a gift. The most common categories of taxation are:

- **Real Property Tax** - Annual tax imposed by local government based on value (ad valorem)

- **California Transfer Tax** - Local authorities impose a transfer fee on real property based on value

- **Estate/Inheritance Tax** - California does not tax estates, however the Federal government may

- **Gift Tax** - California does not tax gifts of real property, however the Federal government may when the value of the gift exceeds a certain amount, which can change from year to year

- **Income Tax** - Owning or transferring real property can have significant tax ramifications for both Federal and State tax.

Real Property Taxes

Property taxes are required on all land and improvements and paid to the local government. The tax is imposed by the government in which the property is located. The owner of property in San Francisco pays tax to the local authority in San Francisco, regardless if their principal residence is in Los Angeles. Multiple areas or jurisdictions can tax the same property at the same time if it straddles more than one jurisdiction or claims more than one address.

For property tax purposes, the government performs an appraisal of the size and value of each property, including land and any improvements. Tax is assessed in proportion to that value at a rate equal to 1% of the taxable value.

Ad valorem taxes are created specifically based on the monetary value of the property as a whole. This is the most common type of property tax and is usually created at the time of the purchase of the property, although it also can be done on an annual basis. California law specifies how often real property may be assessed or reassessed. Property owners who disagree with the assessment of their property may appeal to the Board of Equalization by presenting an independent appraisal. Ad valorem property taxes account for nearly 90 percent of the revenue collected from property tax bills in California.

Property Tax in California

Figure 1
Sample Annual Property Tax Bill

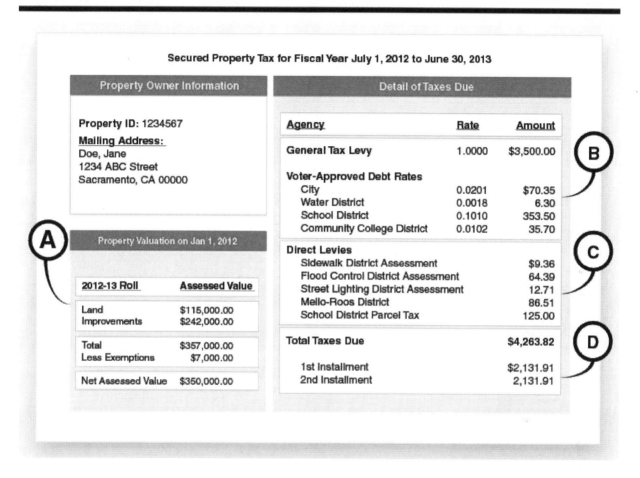

- "Box A" -identifies the taxable value of the property

- "Box B" -shows the property's tax levies that are calculated based on this value.

- "Box C"- special assessments. These are additional charges based on factors such as the benefit to the property owner from improvements in the surrounding district or county.

- "Box D"-total amount due divided into two equal payments, payable on November 1 and April 1 and delinquent as of December 10 and April 10 respectively.

Charges Based on Property Value

The 1 Percent Rate. The largest component of most property owners' annual property tax bill is the 1 percent rate—often called the 1 percent general tax levy or countywide rate. The State Constitution limits this rate to 1 percent of assessed value. As shown on our sample property tax bill, the owner of a property assessed at $350,000 owes $3,500 under the 1 percent rate. The 1 percent rate is a general tax, meaning that local governments may use its revenue for any public purpose.

Calculating Property Value for Ad Valorem Taxes

One of the first items listed on a property tax bill is the assessed value of the land and improvements. Assessed value is the taxable value of the property, which includes the land and any improvements such as buildings, landscaping, or other improvements. The assessed value of land and improvements is important because the 1 percent rate and voter–approved debt rates are levied as a percentage of this value, meaning that properties with higher assessed values owe higher property taxes.

Acquisition value

The county assessor assigns an assessed value that is equal to a property's most recent purchase price. This process was established by Proposition 13. Local real property is assessed at acquisition value and adjusted upward each year. When property is sold, the county assessor again assigns it an assessed value equal to its most recent purchase price/market value.

Important Tax Amendments

- **Proposition 13** - established the maximum of 1% rate and a maximum increase of 2 percent or the rate of inflation, whichever is lower. This applies only to ad valorem taxes and does not limit special assessments.

- **Proposition 8** - requires assessing authority to use the lower of Proposition 13 value or current market value. In times of declining values, this can lower ad valorem taxes.

Tax Exemptions

Exemptions (reductions) from property taxes are available for certain classes of property and classes of people. Generally, only one exemption can be claimed. For example:

- **Homeowner Exemption** - Homeowners occupying as a primary residence as of Jan 1 of that year can file for a $7000 reduction in the following year's assessed value.

- **Veteran's Exemption** - Some veterans may qualify for a $4000 reduction from the assessed value based on their time and type of military service.

- **Disabled Veteran's Exemption** - Some disable veterans or their surviving spouses may qualify for an exemption depending on their income and type of disability.

- **Government Property** - All government property in California is exempt from tax.

- **Other Exemptions** - Civic organizations such as schools, churches, libraries etc may be entitled to exemptions.

Relief for Older Homeowners

Homeowners age 62 and older may qualify for property tax relief under the Property Tax Postponement Law. This law allows low-income homeowners 62 and older to postpone property tax payment until their principal residence is either sold or no longer occupied. These homeowners may also qualify for a property tax rebate through the Homeowner Assistance Program.

Supplemental Tax Assessments

On the sale of a property or the completion newly constructed property, the local assessor establishes the current market (taxable) value. The prior assessed value is then subtracted from the current value to establish a net value for the supplemental tax. This is then used as the taxable value from the date of sale or completion of construction through remaining tax (fiscal) year ending on June 30.

Owners of property of 4 residential units or less are required to provide a disclosure notice to prospective buyers regarding Supplemental Tax Assessments.

California Transfer Tax

California charges a transfer tax when real property is sold. When sale documents are recorded, the local authority collects a fee. The local rate for counties is $0.55/$500 across the state. Individual cities can also impose an additional transfer tax. This rate varies from city to city and set by the city authorities. Transfer taxes are paid by the seller and collected in advance by the escrow holder as part of the closing/settlement of the Escrow.

Income Taxes

Both State and Federal authority are empowered to tax income. Income taxes are quite complicated and the tax codes elaborate. Below are some very simplified explanations of some of the terms relating to the income tax consequences of owning and transferring real property:

Benefits

- Mortgage interest paid for both a principal residence and one second home are deductible from personal income.

- Property taxes are also deductible from personal income

Investment Property Tax

- **Depreciation** - Tax Depreciation is a method of accounting that calculates the lessening value of an asset due to wear and tear from use. A depreciation deduction is allowed annually, except on a primary residence. Land is also exempted, meaning the calculation for real property subtracts out land value before the deduction is taken.

- **Capital Gain** - Gains (profit) on the sale of a capital asset is taxed at a different rate than regular income and known as the "capital gain rate". The idea of a capital asset can be very fluid depending on the expertise of your attorney or account. *Very* simply, capital assets are things owned by businesses (excluding inventory) and people for personal or investment purposes, including houses, furniture, stocks etc.

- **1031 Exchange** - A vehicle to defer the tax on a large capital gain from the sale of investment property. There are many restrictions, but simply put, an investor can simultaneously sell and buy another "like kind" property that will be held for business or investment. This allows for deferment of the capital gain tax until the sale of the new property. "Like kind" refers to one income-producing or investment property for another; therefore, primary residences, vacations homes etc. do not qualify. These are sometimes referred to as "tax-free" exchanges, but tax is merely deferred, not forgiven.

Study Smart Guide

Ways to acquire property are: will, succession, accession, occupancy, and by transfer through private or public grant, gift, alienation by court-ordered partition or foreclosure, marriage, escheat, eminent domain or equitable estoppel.

Ways to transfer property are: private grant, gift, public dedication, public grant, alienation by court action, marriage, escheat, eminent domain, equitable estoppel and bankruptcy.

Deed - The deed is the legal document transferring the ownership interest in real property from one party (grantor) to another (grantee).

Types of Deeds are: Grant deeds, Trust deed, Reconveyance deed, Quitclaim deed, Special Warranty deed, Sheriff's deed and Gift Deed.

Title - When transferring ownership, the grantor must disclose and discharge encumbrances, referred to as providing "clear and marketable" title.

Grantee index – An alphabetical list of purchasers of the property.

Grantor index – An alphabetical list of sellers of the property.

Abstract of Title - a statement summarizing the history of conveyances appearing in the public record.

Cloud on the title - any outstanding claim or encumbrance that would prevent the owner from selling, transferring or conveying marketable title.

Title Insurance - required insurance on title that covers most risks that are a matter of public record.

Preliminary report - an offer to issue a title policy.

Title Insurance Polices - largely standardized forms prepared by the California Land Title Association (CLTA) for standard coverage and American Land Title Association (ALTA) for extended coverage.

Sale Escrows - a trust arrangement by which real property transfers and other transactions such as exchanges, leases, sales of personal property, sales of securities, loans, and mobile home sales are transferred.

Essential Elements of an Escrow - a binding contract/agreement between buyer and seller outlining the conditions to be met prior to transfer; and the delivery to the neutral party (escrow holder) something of value (the deed) and any accompanying documentation for transfer, all of which may only be returned by consent of both parties.

Escrow Holder - a neutral third party lawfully engaged in the business of receiving escrows.

Escrow Instructions - instructions governing the delivery of a deed or encumbrance, money, or other things of value.

Bilateral instructions - signed by both parties and binding on each buyer and seller

Unilateral instructions - separate sets of instructions, each executed by the buyer and seller and binding for both.

Taxes - a levy imposed by governmental authorities.

Types of Taxes - Real Property Tax, California Transfer Tax, Estate/Inheritance Tax, Gift Tax and Income Tax

Real Property Tax - required on all land and improvements and paid to the local government.

Ad Valorem Taxes - the most common type of property tax, specifically based on the monetary value of the property as a whole; meaning that properties with higher assessed values pay higher property taxes.

The 1 Percent Rate - a general levy limited to 1% of assessed value, the largest component of property tax bills

Acquisition value - assessed value for tax purposes must be equal to a property's most recent purchase price and adjust upward annually until the next sale or evaluation.

Proposition 13 - established the maximum ad valorem tax rate of 1% rate and a maximum increase of 2 percent or the rate of inflation, whichever is lower. Does not limit special assessments.

Proposition 8 - requires assessing authority to use the lower of Proposition 13 value or current market value.

California Transfer Tax - a state-wide county tax of $.55/$500 levied when property is sold. Cities assess and levy an additional tax. Transfer taxes are paid by the seller and collected at the close of escrow.

Depreciation - a method of accounting that calculates the lessening value of an asset due to wear and tear from use.

Capital Gain - a tax on gains (profit) on the sale of a capital asset.

1031 Exchange - a vehicle to defer the tax on a large capital gain.

Chapter 2
Quiz & Answers

1) Property is acquired by:
    a) will
    b) alienation
    c) eminent domain
    d) all of the above

2) A holigraphic will is:
    a) a digital copy of a will
    b) not witnessed
    c) handwritten
    d) b and c

3) Property transferred by private grant is:
    a) by one private party to another
    b) a private inheritance transferred by will
    c) includes private money for upkeep
    d) by a private person for public use

4) A reconveyance deed is used to:
    a) discharge a mortgage
    b) transfer title under a will
    c) transfer title when a Deed of Trust is terminated
    d) none of the above

5) The Grantor Index is:
    a) a national registry homeowners
    b) an alphabetical list of people granting deeds
    c) an index of property recently sold
    d) an index of property granted to the government

6) A "cloud on title" is created by:
   a) an undischarged lien
   b) a lien that was discharged, but not documented
   c) an unpaid tax bill
   d) all of the above

7) An escrow holder must be:
   a) incorporated
   b) a licensed attorney
   c) an accountant
   d) a neutral party

8) Escrow instructions:
   a) can be amended at any time
   b) are private and confidential
   c) can never expire
   d) b and c

9) Which of the following is true of property taxes:
   a) they can be paid to any state authority
   b) they are based on the property value
   c) they are paid once a year
   d) they are paid every month

10) An assessment is:
    a) an appraisal of the property
    b) a charge for public improvements
    c) a value on which taxes are calculated
    d) all of the above

ANSWERS:

1. d	3. a	5. b	7. d	9. b
2. d	4. c	6. d	8. b	10. c

Chapter 3

Chapter 3: Laws of Agency and Fiduciary Duties

3.1 Agency and Fiduciary Duties

The leading category for claims and lawsuits against real estate companies is made for breaching the fiduciary duty of license holders. More specifically, negligence and misrepresentations are the leading causes for a principal (buyer or seller) seeking compensation.

Agency Relationships

An agency relationship creates a fiduciary duty owed by the agent to the principal.

- **Agent** - An agent is represents another, called the principal, in dealings with third persons. The act of representation is called agency. In an agency relationship, the principal delegates to the agent the right to act on his or her behalf **continuously, without additional authority from transaction to transaction.**

- **Special Agent** - The agency relationship between a real estate broker and principal resulting in a **special agency,** typically limited to soliciting/negotiating related to a **single transaction** involving real property or secured by real property. Generally, real estate brokers are not empowered to act in the place of or to bind their principals to an agreement. They must have new authority for each transaction.

- **Real Estate Broker** - A special agent who is authorized by the principal to carry out certain defined acts within the course and scope of the agency established by the principal.

- **Real Estate Salesperson** - An agent of the real estate broker, regardless of employee or independent contractor status.

The broker is responsible for his or her salesperson acting as an agent of the broker. A salesperson or broker associate owes a duty to the buyer, the seller, or any principal or party in a transaction equivalent to the duty owed by the real estate broker.

Even where a broker or salesperson is acting for his or her own account, as a principal to the transaction, they are obligated to act honestly and fairly, in good faith, and without fraud or deceit. These duties and obligations are expected of all parties to agreements.

Fiduciary Duty

The fiduciary duty owed by real estate brokers to their principals has been compared by the courts to the duty owed to the beneficiaries by a trustee under a trust. The CalBRE Reference Book cites Black's Law Dictionary for its description of a fiduciary relationship as "*one founded on trust or confidence reposed by one person in the integrity and fidelity of another. A fiduciary has a duty to act for the principal's benefit and not for the fiduciary's own personal interest.*"

Specific Fiduciary Duties
- confidentiality (to all parties in a transaction)
- full and complete disclosure of material facts (to all parties in a transaction)
- acting fairly and honestly without fraud or deceit (to all parties in a transaction)
- loyalty (to principal)
- accounting of funds (to all parties in a transaction)
- duty to "explain" and "counsel" about disclosures and real estate concepts permitting the principal to make an informed decision (to all parties in a transaction)
- utmost care (to all parties in a transaction)

Some common breaches of fiduciary duty are:

- **Non- Disclosure** - concealing defects in the property. The real estate broker, as a fiduciary and the seller both have a duty to disclose facts materially affecting the value, desirability, or intended use of property.

- **Misrepresentation**- An untrue representation (whether mistaken or intentional) which becomes part of the purchase contract may cause for voiding and/or damages by the buyer or seller.

- **False Promise**- Usually a promise about future events. Example: Saying, "Property values will go up by 20 percent in this neighborhood by next year." when in fact, the agent has no control over values and should make no representations about future market performance.

- **Commingling funds** - mixing (depositing) of principal's funds into the same account with the broker's funds. Monies given by principals (down payments, fees, etc.) must be kept in separate dedicated accounts for each transaction and principal.

- **Secret Profit** - an agent acquiring an undisclosed interest in a property for personal profit or falsely representing the true value to an owner with the intention of purchase for personal gain.

3.2 Creation of Agency and Agency Agreements

For the purposes of Agency, it is necessary to understand the distinctions in the following relationships.

- **Real Estate Broker** is duly licensed as such by the State of California to represent another in the transfer of an interest in real property for compensation or an expectation of compensation.

- **Real Estate Salesman** (Salesperson) is duly licensed as such by the State of California and **must be employed by a duly licensed Real Estate Broker** to represent another in the transfer of an interest in real property for compensation or the expectation of compensation.

- **Associated Broker** (or Broker Associate) is a duly licensed Real Estate Broker that chooses to be employed by another duly licensed Real Estate Broker to represent another in the transfer of an interest in real property for compensation or the expectation of compensation.

There are two distinct categories of Agency relationships in the normal course of a real estate career:

- Between the Principal Broker (binding upon their Salespeople/associated Brokers) and the principal parties in a transaction (Buyers, Sellers, etc) and

- Between the Principal Broker (Broker designated to be legally responsible for your office) and their Salespeople (or associated Brokers). Sales people/associated Brokers are **agents** of the Principal Real Estate Broker.

The principal and agent relationship is created by agreement between the parties, known as *actual agency*. Real estate brokers and salespeople act as a "special agent" of a principal by "**express agreement**" (a contract), at which point all fiduciary obligations are owed.

Contracts for Agency

An agency agreement must be in writing for the agent to be able to enforce a commission claim. Due to the real estate broker's knowledge and expertise, it is generally the broker's duty to see that the Agency contract is constructed fairly and correctly formatted.

3.3 Responsibilities of Agent to Seller/Buyer as Principal

A real estate company can be set up so that *all* agents in the company have the same relationship with the principal (client) OR *only* the agent listed on the disclosure form represents the client.

According to the California Mandatory Licensee-Consumer Relationship Disclosure Form, there are several relationship options between the agent and the potential client (Buyer, Seller, Landlord). These are:

- **Seller's agent** – Represents the seller in all aspects of the transaction and owes all fiduciary duties to the seller, known as single agency

- **Buyer's agent** – Represents the buyer in all aspects of the transaction and owes all fiduciary duties to the buyer, known as single agency

- **Facilitator** – Brings the buyer and seller together but does not act on behalf of either party as agent. Does not owe fiduciary duties to either party other than confidentiality, honesty, fairness and disclosure.

- **Dual agent** – Represents both the buyer and seller. Since all fiduciary duties (such as loyalty) cannot be given to both parties, the agent must maintain impartiality to each client. Since the nature of the fiduciary duties is changed, it is unlawful to have an undisclosed dual agency. Both Buyer and Seller must agree to this relationship in writing.

- **Designated seller's or buyer's agent** – Represents either the buyer or seller and owes all fiduciary duties to client. If the client agrees, the agent can be "designated" as the client's only agent.

    Generally this comes up when a Buyer client of a Seller Agent wants to purchase the property. In this situation, the Principal Broker for the office "designates" which client the agent will represent and assigns another agent to represent the now unrepresented client. The initial agent continues to owe confidentiality to their former client for any information previously obtained.

3.4 Types and Disclosure of Agency

Under California law, all real estate agents must disclose in writing the exact nature of their relationship to each party in the transaction. A paper document must be created; and when signed by all parties, constitutes a consent form. The same applies to all types of agency (agent of seller, agent of buyer etc.).

Single and Dual Agency

There are two types of agencies:

Single agency-agent works on behalf of either the buyer, seller or other principal

Dual agency- agent works on behalf of both the buyer and the seller.

Dual Agency Defined

Dual agency occurs when a broker represents both parties. The practical effect limits the ability of a real estate broker, acting as a dual agent, to engage in the negotiation of price and terms in a sale transaction. The broker should present the buyer the listed price and terms requested by the seller and ask the buyer to make whatever offer the buyer deems appropriate. Equally, the broker should present the seller the price and terms set forth on the buyer's written offer to purchase. The seller should be asked to accept the offer or counter the price and terms as the seller deems appropriate.

Should either principal require professional assistance to ascertain the price and terms to request or offer (or counter-offer), the dual agent real estate broker is not in the position of offering that assistance. They must recommend the principals seek independent advice from qualified professionals in determining what price and terms are appropriate. The limitation placed upon the real estate broker as a dual agent does not preclude the broker from providing both principals with the same comparative market data upon which the principals may independently rely.

The disclosure consent form must be signed by a seller before signing the listing contract. A separate disclosure consent form must be signed by a potential buyer (and their agent, if applicable) and delivered to seller or seller's agent "as soon as is practical" and before the purchase contract is put in place. The disclosure process is broken down as a three step process:

> **Disclosure** –the document is presented and read by the parties;
>
> **Election**- the timeframe where the receivers of the disclosure statement decide to accept or not;
>
> **Confirmation**-signatures.

Agency Relationship Disclosures Example

To provide an explanation of agency relationships and duties, the law requires that a real estate broker disclose in writing the duties and responsibilities under certain agency relationships. Additionally, the broker's status as agent of the seller, agent of the buyer, or agent of both the seller and buyer (dual agent) must be disclosed to the principals, who must then consent to the agency relationship(s) disclosed. This requirement applies to the sale, exchange, or lease (for more than one year) of real property improved with 1 to 4 dwelling units.

The required agency disclosure form includes the following specific language:

DISCLOSURE REGARDING REAL ESTATE AGENCY RELATIONSHIP   (As required by the Civil Code)

When you enter into a discussion with a real estate agent regarding a real estate transaction, you should from the outset understand what type of agency relationship and representation you wish to have with the agent in the transaction.

SELLER'S AGENT

A Seller's agent under a listing agreement with the Seller acts as the agent for the Seller only. A Seller's agent or a subagent of that agent has the following affirmative obligations:

To the Seller:

(a) A fiduciary duty of utmost care, integrity, honesty, and loyalty in dealings with the Seller.

To the Buyer and the Seller:

(a) Diligent exercise of reasonable skill and care in performance of the agent's duties.

(b) A duty of honest and fair dealing and good faith.

(c) A duty to disclose all facts known to the agent materially affecting the value or desirability of the property that are not known to, or within the diligent attention and observation of, the parties.

An agent is not obligated to reveal to either party any confidential information obtained from the other party which does not involve the affirmative duties set forth above.

BUYER'S AGENT

A selling agent can, with a Buyer's consent, agree to act as agent for the Buyer only. In these situations, the agent is not the Seller's agent, even if by agreement the agent may receive compensation for services rendered, either in full or in part from the Seller. An agent acting only for a Buyer has the following affirmative obligations:

To the Buyer:

(a) A fiduciary duty of utmost care, integrity, honesty, and loyalty in dealings with the Buyer.

To the Buyer and the Seller:

(a) Diligent exercise of reasonable skill and care in performance of the agent's duties.

(b) A duty of honest and fair dealing and good faith.

(c) A duty to disclose all facts known to the agent materially affecting the value or desirability of the property that are not known to, or within the diligent attention and observation of, the parties. An agent is not obligated to reveal to either party any confidential information obtained from the other party which does not involve the affirmative duties set forth above.

AGENT REPRESENTING BOTH SELLER AND BUYER

A real estate agent, either acting directly or through one or more associate licensees, can legally be the agent of both the Seller and the Buyer in a transaction, but only with the knowledge and consent of both the Seller and the Buyer.

In a dual agency situation, the agent has the following affirmative obligations to both the Seller and the Buyer:

(a) A fiduciary duty of utmost care, integrity, honesty and loyalty in the dealings with either the Seller or the Buyer.

(b) Other duties to the Seller and the Buyer as stated above in their respective sections.

In representing both Seller and Buyer, the agent may not, without the express permission of the respective party, disclose to the other party that the Seller will accept a price less than the listing price or that the Buyer will pay a price greater than the price offered.

The above duties of the agent in a real estate transaction do not relieve a Seller or Buyer from the responsibility to protect their own interests. You should carefully read all agreements to assure that they adequately express your understanding of the transaction. A real estate agent is a person qualified to advise about real estate. If legal or tax advice is desired, consult a competent professional.

Disclosure of Acting as Principal or Other Interest

Brokers or salespersons have added responsibilities when acting as principals for their own purposes. Duties of disclosure of facts to the principal extend to the point that a principal must be informed by the agent if the buyer is related to the agent or has any other relationship which includes both a marital or business relationship.

3.5 Termination of Agency

Agency contracts can be terminated by:

- completion of the objective
- time limit expiration
- rescission
- revocation
- death of the principal or broker
- property destruction
- bankruptcy of either party

Because the relationship between a principal and agent is a personal one founded on trust and confidence, the principal has an absolute power under the law to revoke the agency at any time. As a rule, unless a real estate broker's authority is coupled with an interest in the property, the broker's authorization may be revoked at any time.

Nevertheless, while the principal generally has the power to revoke the agency relationship, it does not necessarily revoke the contract (as in a listing contract). The principal may be liable for breach of contract by revoking the agency without good cause.

Warranty of Authority

The principal to the contract authorizes the agent to do what is necessary to complete the objective; however, they are also is liable for the actions of their agent. When an agent acts without authority or in excess of the agent's authority, the agent may be held liable for resulting damages for having breached the agent's implied warranty of authority.

3.6 Agency Contracts

The agent is also personally liable for the performance of the contract if the agent fails to reveal the name of the principal, or the fact that the agent is acting in an agency capacity.

If the fact of agency is disclosed in the contract, but the name of the principal is not, the rule in California can be that the agent is personally liable for the performance of the contract.

To avoid the possibility of personal liability of the agent, the name of the principal for whom the agent is acting must appear on the face of the contract.

Torts

Torts are private wrongs committed upon the person or property of another and arising from a breach of duty created by law rather than by contract.

Where a person misrepresents his or her authority to act as agent for another, such person may be liable in tort to the third party who relies on the representation to the third party's detriment.

Material representations which are false or misleading may result in liability of the real estate broker. The same may be said of failure of the broker to disclose material facts about the property to the prospective buyer.

Fraud v. Negligence

Misrepresentation may be either fraudulent (intentionally misleading) or negligent (intentionally or unintentionally obtaining and conveying pertinent facts).

In either case the agent may be liable for damages incurred by the injured party, subject to disciplinary action by the real estate board and legal action. The dividing line between fraud and negligence is a grey area. Unfortunately for the agent there can be a significant difference in the punitive damages placed on the agent depending on whether the misrepresentation is found to be negligent or fraudulent.

Certain misrepresentations, even though made by an agent with no ill intent, can be defined by law as actual fraud if they are positive assertions of that which is not true.

Constructive fraud- California Civil Code defines constructive fraud as, "any breach of duty which, without an actually fraudulent intent, gains an advantage to the person in fault, or anyone claiming under him or her, by misleading another to his or her prejudice, or to the prejudice of anyone claiming under him or her."

Nondisclosures and Constructive Fraud

Duty of disclosure usually involves the failure to disclose known defects in the property. Legal cases have held that the real estate broker acting as an agent of the seller and the seller both have a duty to disclose facts materially affecting the value, desirability, or intended use of property.

If the broker knows that the buyer is unaware of certain facts, and they are not found during the buyer's inspection of the property or diligent attention, then the broker must disclose those facts.

"Puffing"

Statements by a real estate broker that embellish or exaggerate. Advertising or portraying a property as the "best available", or that the buyer "will receive a good return on the investment", were once considered expressions and not to be taken literally.

Today the courts are more likely to treat such statements as representations of fact. A statement by a real estate broker, salesperson or broker associate that a house was "in perfect shape," while obviously not literally true, has been described as a representation of a material fact by an appellate court considering the question.

Gratuitous Agent

In addition to negotiating the "meeting of the minds" of seller and buyer in a real estate transaction, brokers do a multitude of other things in order to consummate sales. For example, they order preliminary reports, complete forms, arrange for pest inspections, and assist in the preparation of escrow instructions. If the real estate broker aids the buyer or seller in the many details of completing a transaction and does not charge for the additional service (which is an expected standard of service), the broker is a gratuitous agent of the buyer or seller for those purposes. A broker's failure to use reasonable care while acting in these "gratuitous" capacities can result in the liability of the broker, if the party sustains an injury as a result of negligence.

STUDY SMART GUIDE

Agent - represents another, called the principal, in dealings with third persons, **continuously, without additional authority from transaction to transaction.**

Special Agent - typically limited to soliciting/negotiating related to a **single transaction** involving real property or secured by real property and **requires new authority for each transaction.**

Real Estate Broker - A special agent authorized to carry out certain defined acts established by the principal.

Real Estate Salesperson - An agent of the real estate broker.

Fiduciary - a relationship between a principal and agent based on trust and confidence in the integrity and fidelity of another.

Fiduciary duty - the duty to act for the principal's benefit and not for the fiduciary's own personal interest."

Specific Fiduciary Duties of Real Estate Agents
- confidentiality (to all parties in a transaction)
- full and complete disclosure of material facts (to all parties in a transaction)
- acting fairly and honestly without fraud or deceit (to all parties in a transaction)
- loyalty (to principal)
- accounting of funds (to all parties in a transaction)
- duty to "explain" and "counsel" about disclosures and real estate concepts permitting the principal to make an informed decision (to all parties in a transaction)
- utmost care (to all parties in a transaction)

Common breaches are: Non- Disclosure, Misrepresentation, False Promise, Commingling funds and Secret Profit.

Types of Agency - Seller's agent, Buyer's agent, Facilitator, Dual agent, Designated seller's or buyer's agent.

Single agency-agent works on behalf of either the buyer, seller or other principal

Dual agency- agent works on behalf of both the buyer and the seller

Agency is terminated by: completion of the objective; time limit expiration; rescission; revocation; death of the principal or broker; property destruction and bankruptcy of either party

Torts - private wrongs arising from a breach of duty created by law rather than by contract.

Fraud v. Negligence - Misrepresentation may be either fraudulent (intentionally misleading) or negligent (intentionally or unintentionally obtaining and conveying pertinent facts).

Constructive fraud - breach of duty, without fraudulent intent that gains an advantage.

Disclosure - the real estate broker acting as an agent of the seller and the seller both have a duty to disclose facts materially affecting the value, desirability, or intended use of property

Puffing - Statements by a real estate broker that embellish or exaggerate.

Gratuitous Agent - If the real estate broker aids the buyer or seller in the many details of completing a transaction and does not charge for the additional service (which is an expected standard of service), the broker is a gratuitous agent of the buyer or seller for those purposes.

Chapter 3
Quiz & Answers

1) A special agent:
   a) represents another continuously
   b) represents only one person
   c) both a and b
   d) none of the above

2) A real estate salesperson is:
   a) a special agent
   b) an employee
   c) an agent of the broker
   d) b and c

3) The duty to be honest and fair is:
   a) a fiduciary duty
   b) ethical, but not required
   c) a duty to your client only
   d) something your mother told you

4) Agency contracts are:
   a) between a seller and real estate broker
   b) between a buyer and real estate broker
   c) both a and b
   d) none of the above

5) Which of the following is true:
   a) fraud must be intentional
   b) misrepresentation is considered fraud
   c) a mistake isn't considered fraud
   d) you're not responsible if you don't know something

6) Buyer Agency is:
   a) a single agency
   b) a contract between an agent and a buyer
   c) requires loyalty to the buyer only
   d) all of the above

7) Commingling happens when:
   a) you give advice to another person's client
   b) you share a listing with another agent
   c) you have two client for the same property
   d) you deposit personal money into an escrow account

8) Dual Agency is:
   a) illegal
   b) must be disclosed and agreed to
   c) releases you from confidentiality
   d) a and c

9) Which of the following is false:
   a) a salesperson must be licensed
   b) a salesperson must deposit escrows
   c) a salesperson must work for a broker
   d) a salesperson must sign contracts

10) Which of the following is true:
    a) Agency disclosures can be given verbally
    b) Agency disclosures are between agents only
    c) Agency must be disclosed in writing
    d) all of the above

ANSWERS:

1. d	3. a	5. b	7. d	9. b
2. d	4. c	6. d	8. b	10. c

Chapter 4

Chapter 4: Contracts

4.1 General Contract Law Overview

In California, a contract is described as "...an agreement to do or not do a certain thing."

Classification of Contracts

There are four major elements used when classifying contracts. They are:

1. **Manner of Creation** - examines the method by which the contract was created

    - **Express** - parties "express" their intention in words, orally or in writing

    - **Implied** - parties "imply" a contract by their actions; need not be in words. For instance: you hail a taxi on the street. Once you give the driver an address and he drives away, you have an implied contract for him to drive and you to pay him for driving, even though this agreement is **unexpressed**, it is "implied" by your respective actions.

2. **Content of the Agreement** - examines what actions are required to complete the contract

    - **Bilateral contract** - Both *parties* have made a promise to each other. For instance: You and your neighbor agree that you'll pay them $50 *and* they will to take out your trash. Each has promised an action to benefit the other.

    - **Unilateral contract** - *One party* offers an incentive to cause another to act. For instance: You offer your neighbor $50 *if* they take out your trash. The difference being, if they don't take out the trash, no money is due; therefore one party must perform an action for the contract to be in effect.

3. **Extent of the Performance** - examines the stage of fulfillment of the contract

    - **Executed** - the obligations under a contract have been completely fulfilled. (Do not confuse this with "fully executed" in the context of all parties to a contract having signed the document.)

    - **Executory** - the obligations under a contract have not been completely fulfilled.

4. **Legal Effectiveness** - examines the legal viability of the contract

- **Valid** - contract is legally binding and enforceable by law. It has all the essential elements required by law.

- **Void**- agreement is not a legal contract and cannot be enforced (e.g., an agreement to commit a crime).

- **Voidable**- contract is valid and enforceable, but can be terminated by one (or both) parties (e.g., a contract induced by undue influence or some other fraud may be voided by the victim).

- **Unenforceable**-contract is valid, but cannot be enforced by law (e.g., because too much time has passed under the statute of limitations).

Essential Requirements of a Valid Contract

Below are the four essentials for a valid and enforceable contract:

- Legal Capacity
- Mutual consent
- A lawful object
- Sufficient consideration

It should be noted that some contracts, and more importantly, nearly **all** real estate contracts also require that they be properly written and constructed.

Legal Capacity

All parties must be legally capable of forming a contract. Generally everyone is fully capable except:

- non-emancipated minors - An emancipated minor is a person under 18 who has entered into a valid marriage (even if now divorced), is on active duty with any of the US armed forces, or has received a court ordered declaration of emancipation. This special class of minor is considered as being over the age of majority for certain purposes and has certain powers to deal with real property.

- persons of unsound mind

- aliens (non-citizens) - In California legal non-citizens have the same rights as citizen relating to real property, however, federal law does contain some restrictions.

- persons deprived of civil rights (e.g., some convicts have limited legal capacity).

Mutual consent

Parties who have capacity must mutually consent to be bound and properly communicate the contract's intention. Requirements for consent are twofold:

- both an offer and an acceptance of terms, and
- clearly defined terms and contractual intention that have been offered and accepted.

Consent must be genuine and freely given. If it is clouded by fraud or mistake, the contract may be voidable.

Fraud

Fraud may be either actual or constructive. Normally, fraud relates to a person misrepresenting a material fact they know to be untrue or with careless indifference to what may be true. A person must misrepresent with the intent to induce the other to enter the contract, and the other must rely on the representation in entering the contract. "Material fact" is defined as an important fact which significantly affects the party's decision to enter into the contract.

> **Actual Fraud.** Civil Code Section 1572 lists the following five acts as actual fraud when done with intent to induce another to enter a contract, or to deceive the other party:
>
>> 1. The suggestion, as a fact, of that which is not true, by one who does not believe it to be true;
>>
>> 2. The positive assertion, in a manner not warranted by the information of the person making it, of that which is not true, though the person believes it to be true;
>>
>> 3. The suppression of that which is true, by one having knowledge or belief of the fact;
>>
>> 4. A promise made without any intention of performing it; or,
>>
>> 5. Any other act intended to deceive.

Ordinarily, misrepresentation of law does not amount to actionable fraud, because everyone is presumed to know the law. Nevertheless, it may be considered fraudulent when one party uses superior knowledge to gain an advantage over another, or where the parties rely on a confidential relationship (i.e., real estate agent).

> **Constructive fraud.** Constructive fraud may:
>
>> a) consist of any **unintentional** breach of duty which gains an advantage for the person in fault over another; and
>>
>> b) consist of any act or omission the law specifically declares to be fraudulent.

> **Negligent misrepresentation** has been held to be a type of fraud.

> **Mistakes may also negate consent**. When both parties are mistaken about the subject matter of the contract, there can be no contract. When, unknown to the parties, circumstances surrounding the purpose of the agreement make performance impossible, there is no contract.

> Mistakes are classified in two ways: mistakes of fact or of law.
>
>> **A mistake of fact** is one ignorance or forgetfulness of a material fact or by a mistaken belief in a material fact surrounding the contract. However, the mistake cannot be caused by the neglect of a legal duty by the person making it.
>>
>> **A mistake of law** arises from a misunderstanding of the law, with all parties involved making substantially the same mistake believing they knew and understood the law.

Duress, menace, undue influence. A contract may be voidable when entered into under duress, menace, or undue influence. All three thwart the victim's ability to exercise free will, permitting that person to void the contract.

Duress - involves coercion or confinement.

Menace - is a threat to commit duress, including threatening unlawful and violent injury to a person or the person's character.

Undue influence - is an unfair advantage taken by someone who has the confidence of another, or who holds authority over another. Undue influence is most frequently between people in a confidential relationship (trustees/beneficiaries, brokers/principals, attorneys/clients, etc.)

Lawful Object

The object refers to what the contract requires the parties to do or not to do. If the contract has a single objective that is unlawful or performance is impossible, the contract is void. If there are several distinct objects, the contract is normally valid relative to the lawful objects only.

Common violations. The objects and consideration must be legal and cannot violate the law. Those commonly occurring in a real estate transaction are:

- Contracts of unlicensed "brokers" or "general contractors." These persons are not permitted to enforce their contracts.

- Forfeiture clauses in deposit receipts, contracts of sale and leases. This clause calls for a fixed amount of damages in the event of a breach ("liquidated damages") and are valid unless it can be proven they were unreasonable. Special rules apply to these provisions in the purchase of residential property.

- Contracts restraining one party from engaging in business (typically called a "non-compete clause").

- Responsibility for fraud cannot be erased by writing a clause into a contract holding a party harmless from fraudulent acts.

- A contract calling for interest payments in excess of the California Constitution's current limits may be usurious depending on the lending entity and the purpose of the loan. If such a contract is usurious, that portion of the contract relating to the payment of interest is void.

- Real estate brokers must comply with numerous additional measures incorporated in Real Estate Law. Specific violations may prevent enforcement of a listing contract (getting paid) and may be subject to criminal punishment.

Sufficient Consideration

In general, every contract requires consideration. The consideration may be either a benefit granted (like money or affection) or a detriment suffered (like paying a fine or being evicted from your home). Consideration is the price bargained for and paid for a promise. If a valid consideration exists, the promise, and therefore the contract, is binding. Typically, consideration must have some value. A purely moral obligation (love and affection) may under some circumstances be consideration. The amount is generally only challenged if one party sues for breach or if in combination with other facts may prove fraud.

4.2 Statute of Frauds

Generally, it's immaterial whether a contract is oral or written, except those specifically governed by the Statute of Frauds. The Statute was created to prevent perjury, forgery and dishonesty when proving the existence and terms of certain types of contracts.

The Statute of Frauds addresses only the remedy, not the validity of the contract. If a contract fails to comply with the statute, it is not void but merely unenforceable if breached. Once a contract has been fully performed, the Statute of Frauds no longer applies and cannot be invoked for any reason.

The statute provides that certain contracts are invalid, unless the contract is in writing and signed. In California, contracts required to be in writing are:

- An agreement that is *not to be performed within a year*;
- A special promise to answer for the debt, default, or miscarriage of another;
- An agreement for *leasing for a longer period than one year* or for the sale of real property, or of an interest therein. Such agreement, if made by an agent of the party sought to be charged, is invalid, unless the authority of the agent is in writing and subscribed by the party sought to be charged;
- An agreement authorizing or employing an agent, broker, or any other person, to purchase or sell real estate, or to lease real estate for a longer period than one year, or to procure, introduce, or find a purchaser or seller of real estate or a lessee or lessor of real estate where such lease is for a longer period than one year, for compensation or a commission;
- An agreement which by its terms is not to be performed during the lifetime of the promisor;
- An agreement by a *purchaser of real property to pay an indebtedness secured by a mortgage* or deed of trust upon the property purchased, unless assumption of the indebtedness by the purchaser is specifically provided for in the conveyance of such property.
- A contract, promise, undertaking, or commitment to loan money or to grant or extend credit, in an amount greater than one hundred thousand dollars ($100,000), not primarily for personal, family, or household purposes, made by a person engaged in the business of lending or arranging for the lending of money or extending credit. For purposes of this section, a contract, promise, undertaking, or commitment to loan money secured solely by residential property consisting of one to four dwelling units shall be deemed to be for personal, family, or household purposes.

Clearly several very important sections of the Statute of Frauds apply to real estate. Practically all contracts for the sale of any interest in real property must be in writing. This includes assignment of a percentage of the proceeds of oil produced from designated lands. It embraces any and all instruments creating liens such as trust deeds, mortgages, leases for periods of longer than one year, rights to rights of way through property and any and all encumbrances incurred or suffered by the owners, or by operation of law (judgments, attachments, zoning).

The statute does not apply to a lease for a year or less.

Commissions. Under the Statute of Frauds, in order for a broker to collect a commission, the contract providing for a commission must be in writing and signed by the property owner who employs the broker to produce a buyer; or a buyer who employs the broker to find a suitable property.

4.3 Interpretation, Performance and Discharge of Contracts

The majority of all contracts are properly performed and discharged or executed without legal complications. However, when they are not, below are some of the rules on which the courts may rely in their interpretation of contracts.

Interpretation of Contracts

Contracts are generally interpreted to enforce the *mutual intention of the parties* as it existed *at the time of contracting*; to the degree the intention is ascertainable and lawful. Most contracts relating to real estate brokers must be in writing under the Statute of Frauds; but when the contract fails to express the real intention of the parties (through fraud, mistake or accident), the courts will attempt to discover the real intention and disregard the erroneous parts of the writing.

Executing a written contract supersedes all previous negotiations, including any that may not have been required to be written. When a contract is partly written and partly printed (filling in a form), the written parts control the printed part, and the parts which are purely original control those which were copied from a form. If the two contradict the latter must be disregarded.

Modification of a contract is a change in the obligation and requires mutual assent. A contract may only be altered by a new contract in writing or by an executed (completed) oral agreement, and not otherwise.

Parol evidence rule. Parol evidence refers to prior oral or written negotiations or agreements. The (deed, contract, will, etc.)

Under the "parol evidence rule," when a contract is expressed in writing, it is intended to be the complete and final expression of the rights and duties of the parties; parol evidence is not admissible as evidence. When parties agree by mistake or fraud and the contract does not accurately express their agreement, it may be revised by the court.

Performance of Contracts

It is not uncommon for someone to want to change their mind without terminating the contract. In some circumstances, this can be accomplished by assignment or by novation.

> **Assignment** - *transfers* all the interests, rights and remedies to the assignee. It also transfers any liability or responsibility the assignor has to the other party to the original contract. Even if the assignee assumes the obligation, the assignor still remains secondarily liable as a surety or guarantor, unless the other party to the original contract releases the assignor. Generally, bilateral and unilateral contracts are assignable unless it expressly says that it cannot be assigned or requires consent to assign.

Novation - *substitutes* a new obligation for an existing one, with the intent to satisfy the existing contract. The substitution may be a new obligation between the same parties, a new party, a new debtor or a new creditor. A novation requires the new contractual intention to include the discharge of the old contract and, being a new contract, requires consideration and all other essentials of a valid contract.

Time

Timelines and expiration dates are often significant in contracts. By statute, if a timeframe is not specified for performance, a reasonable time is allowed. If the act is capable of being performed instantly, it must be done immediately unless otherwise agreed.

Discharge of Contracts

Contracts are discharged in one of two ways: full performance or breach of contract. Between these extremes are a variety of methods of discharge including:

- partial performance;
- substantial performance;
- impossibility of performance;
- agreement between the parties;
- release;
- operation of law; and
- acceptance of a breach of contract.

Statute of Limitations

The Statute of Limitations relates to the time allowed to file suit in a court of law. Statutory time running out will bar any legal action for a breach of contract. Real estate-related timeframes range anywhere from 90 days to 10 years. Most commonly, it is considered that suit for a breach of an oral contract must be brought within 2 years and a written contract, 4 years.

Remedies for Breach

As a final possibility, a contract may be discharged by the acceptance of breach of contract. If one party fails to perform, the other may choose to accept the contract as ended if it would be too difficult or costly to enforce a judgment or the awarded amount too insignificant.

On the other hand, the victim of a breach has a choice of two, and sometimes three, courses of action: unilateral rescission, action for dollar damages or action for specific performance.

Rescission - rescission based on breach must specifically comply with the following statutory rules:

- rescind promptly after discovering the facts which justify rescission; and
- restore everything of value received from other parties under the contract; or offer restoration on the condition that the other party does likewise, unless they are unable or refuse.

Damages - Whenever a party to a contract is a victim of a breach, they may recover monetary compensation called damages. The victim is entitled to interest (now 10% per annum) from the day the right to recover is vested. If the contract stipulates a legal rate of interest as a penalty for breach, that rate remains in effect until superseded by a verdict or new obligation. Damages for breach of contract must be reasonable. General guidelines are:

- **For Buyers:** The harm caused by the breach to convey real property is deemed to be the price paid and the expenses incurred in examining the title and preparing the necessary papers, with interest. In cases of bad faith, added to the above is the difference between the price agreed to be paid and the value of the estate agreed to be conveyed, at the time of the breach, as well as the expenses incurred.
- **For Sellers:** The detriment caused by the breach of an agreement to purchase real property is deemed to be the excess, if any, of the amount which would have been due to the seller under the contract, over the value of the property to the seller.

Sometimes, especially in building contracts, the parties will anticipate the possibility of a breach (e.g., construction delays). The parties may specify in the contract the amount of damage to be paid in the event of a breach. These liquidated damage agreements will be enforced by the courts provided the amount specified is:

- not so excessive as to constitute a penalty, and
- provided it would be impractical or extremely difficult to fix the actual damage, and
- if the contract expressly provides that liquidated damages shall be the only remedy available in the event of breach of the contract.

Specific Performance - Generally, if money damages cannot provide an adequate remedy, it can be ordered that the defendant perform the contract; sometimes going so far as preventing them from entering into a new contract with another party. Specific performance is especially important in real estate since the law presumes every piece of property is unique and a breach may not be relieved adequately by money compensation.

4.4 Real Estate Contracts Overview

Real estate contracts include the following:

- contracts for the sale of real property or any interest therein;
- agreements for leasing real property for a longer period than one year; and
- agreements authorizing an agent or broker to locate real estate for sale (Buyer Agency Agreement) or sell real estate (Seller Agency/Listing Agreement) for compensation or a commission.

These contracts are essentially like any other contract except that they must be in writing and signed by the authorizing party to make them valid under the Statute of Frauds.

In the usual real estate sales transaction, the prospective buyer states the terms and conditions under which they are willing to purchase the property. These terms and conditions constitute the offer. If the owner of the property agrees to all of the terms and conditions of the offer, it is an acceptance and results in the creation of a contract. It does not make a difference whether the offer comes from the seller or the buyer. If the negotiation ultimately leads to a definite offer on the one side and unconditional acceptance on the other side, the parties must express the agreed terms and conditions to writing and sign the contract.

Provisions in Real Estate Contracts

Forms such as listing agreements (authorization to sell), deposit receipts, and other real estate contracts for the sale of real estate should contain the following provisions:

- The date of the agreement;
- The names and addresses of the parties to the contract;
- A description of the property;
- The consideration (offer or purchase price);
- Reference to obtaining mortgages and the terms thereof or the terms and conditions of existing mortgages, if any;
- Any other provisions which may be required or requested by either of the parties;
- The date and place of closing the contract.

A contract of sale normally calls for the preparation of a deed to convey the property. It is executory because when the deed is properly signed and delivered to the purchaser the contract is executed.

Agent must give copies of contracts. The real estate license law requires that brokers and salespersons must give copies of documents and agreements to the persons signing them at the time the signature is obtained. The law not only applies to copies of listing contracts and deposit receipts, but to any document pertaining to any of the acts for which one is required to hold a real estate license.

4.5 Listing Agreements

Listing Defined

A listing is a written contract by which a principal (owner or someone legally authorized to act on behalf of owner) employs an agent (listing agent) to do certain duties (e.g., sell real property) for the principal. A listing agent is always bound by the law of agency and has fiduciary obligations to the principal.

Types of Listing Agreements

Exclusive Listings - must be for a definite term, with a specified time of termination. If a broker does not provide for this, the broker's license is subject to disciplinary action under the Real Estate Law.

- **Exclusive right to sell** - the listing broker has the "exclusive right" to sell the property. A commission is due to the broker named in the contract if the property is sold within a set time limit by the listing broker, by any other broker, **or by the owner**. Frequently, this listing also provides that the owner will be liable for a commission within a specified time after the listing expires, if a sale is made to a buyer introduced by the listing broker during the term of the listing. The real estate broker is usually obligated under the terms of the listing contract to furnish a list of persons with whom the broker has negotiated during the listing period, within a specified number of days after the expiration of the listing.

- **Exclusive agency** - the listing broker has the "exclusive agency" rights to sell the property. A commission is payable to the broker named in the contract, and if the broker or any other broker finds the buyer and effects the sale, the broker holding the exclusive listing is entitled to a commission. Because the listing refers to an agency and the owner is not an agent, **the owner may personally sell the property** without owing a commission to the broker holding the exclusive agency listing.

- **MLS listing** - an Exclusive Authorization and Right to Sell providing, among other things, that the agent member who takes the particular listing must submit the information to a central bureau to be distributed to all participants in the service. All members of the service are then authorized to sell the listing in cooperation with the listing agent. All commissions are shared between the cooperating agents according to a percentage assigned and disclosed by the listing agent.

Open listing - a written memorandum signed by the owner or their legal representative authorizing the broker to act as agent for the sale of the real property described. Usually, no time limit is specified for open listings. The property is identified and the general terms and conditions of sale are set forth in the open listing.

Open listings are the simplest form of written authorization to sell and may be given concurrently to more than one agent, making them **non-exclusive listings**. Usually, the seller is not required to notify the other agents in case of a sale to prevent liability of paying more than one commission.

Where open listings are given to several agents, the commission is considered to be earned by the broker who first finds a buyer who meets the terms of the listing, or whose offer is accepted by the seller. **If the owner personally sells the property, the owner is not obligated to pay a commission to any of the brokers** and the sale contract cancels all outstanding open listings.

Net listing - the compensation is not definitely determined in advance. Instead a clause in the contract usually permits the agent to retain (as compensation) all the money received in excess of the agreed upon selling price. Net listings can be **any type of exclusive listing or a non-exclusive listing**.

Under the Real Estate Law, failure of an agent to disclose the amount of an agent's compensation in connection with a net listing is cause for revocation or suspension of license. The disclosure must be done prior to or at the time the principal binds himself or herself to the transaction. The agent is also required to provide written notification within one month of the transactions' closing, to both buyer and seller, generally provided by the closing statement of the escrow holder.

A net listing is perfectly legitimate, but it may easily give rise to charges of fraud, misrepresentation and other abuses. Additionally, given the fiduciary duty to present all offers to the seller, if an offer were to be presented and accepted that is below the initial selling price on which the listing contract is based, the agent would not be entitled to a commission.

4.6 Exclusive Authorization and Right to Sell (MLS Listing Agreement)

The Residential Listing Agreement, Exclusive Authorization and Right to Sell are the most common type of listing.

Essential Objective

The property owner agrees to:

- exclusively authorize a single agent to represent the property for sale and
- pay a specified commission if a "ready, willing and able" Buyer presents an offer at the price and terms set forth within the timeframe of the contract, regardless of who introduces the buyer to the property and regardless if the sale is completed.

The broker is given authorization to:

- exclusively advertise and place a sign on the property (if applicable);
- submit property details to the appropriate multiple listing service (MLS);
- offer compensation to cooperating agents, (usually buyer's agents);
- Accept a good faith deposit from a prospective buyer on behalf of the seller.

Listing Form Overview

Below is a brief review of the form and terms for this contract.

Section 1.
- Parties - Names of all legal owners as "Seller" and Agency or Principal Broker as "Broker". NOTE: A salesperson is authorized to sign the contract as an agent of the Agency (or Principal Broker) only. The contract is between the Agency or Broker and property owner(s).
- Term of the Contract - The beginning date and expiration date and time. (NOTE: Most contracts in real estate are both dated and timed.)
- Property Description - Generally the address including the county, but if more description is required, as much information as necessary to clearly specify only this property.

Section 2.
- Listing Price
- Terms (if any). For instance: Cash only, details of assumable mortgage or seller financing.

Section 3.

- Broker Compensation - Discloses that commissions are negotiable by law and sets the amount of commission as a % or flat fee, etc.
- Details Seller's obligations to pay commissions, including the "Safety Clause" which states the Buyer must have physically entered the property with the broker/cooperating broker and have submitted the offer through said broker(s); both actions during the beginning/end dates of the contract.
- Authorization to offer compensation to cooperating Brokers
- Names any previous Listing Brokers (and prospective Buyers related to those Brokers) who could be entitled to commission if Buyers named were to purchase the property; and releases Seller from paying commission under this contract and Broker from their obligation to represent them.

Section 4.
- Declares that all fixtures and fittings that are attached are included in the transfer with the sale and all personal property is excluded from transfer.
- Specifically lists any additional fixtures or items that will excluded from sale (e.g., refrigerators, clothes washer/dryers) and additional items included with sale.
- Discloses any fixtures that are leased (propane tanks, solar panels) and any fixtures for which a lien has been placed to secure an outstanding amount due.

Section 5.
- Declares Broker as a subscriber to MLS and the rules, benefits and obligations of using the service.
- Allows Seller to opt out of MLS

Section 6.
- Seller represents there are no delinquencies, defaults or pending litigation or bankruptcies except as set forth.

Section 7.
- Details the specific duties both Seller and Broker exchange to perform the (bilateral) contract.

    The broker agrees to use due diligence to sell the property.

    The seller agrees to consider all offers, act in good faith and hold broker harmless from claims arising out of incorrect or incomplete information provided by seller.

    (**NOTE:** In California, Brokers have a separate legal obligation to be both diligent and sufficiently knowledgeable to verify or discover certain information relating to listed properties and to disclose this information to buyers. They cannot rely solely on information provided by seller if reasonable diligence or expertise would reveal it to be incorrect or incomplete.)

Section 8.
- Authorizes Broker to accept good faith deposits on behalf of Seller.

Section 9.

- Discloses Agency Relationship to Seller.
- Acknowledges receipt of additional Agency Disclosure forms required by law.

Section 10.

- Sets forth the obligations for maintaining liability (personal injury) and personal property insurance during the contract term.

Section 11.

- Authorizes Broker to photograph and distribute media of the property to market the property or promote the Broker in the future.

Section 12.

- Authorizes Broker to install a lockbox and permission for use by cooperating Brokers.

Section 13.

- Authorizes Broker to install for sale sign (or not).

Section 14.

- Declares that marketing and sale is in compliance with all state and federal Equal Housing Opportunity Laws and specifically local anti-discrimination laws.

Section 15.

- States that in the event of legal action relating to payment of the commission, the prevailing party will be entitled to reasonable attorney fees, except as stated in Section 19 below. (NOTE: California law doesn't provide for automatic recovery of attorney's fees unless specified in contract.)

Section 16.

- Additional Terms - For instance: the seller will paint the house prior to marketing or the Broker agrees to hold a certain number of open houses per month, etc.

Section 17.

- States that if an associate licensee (salesperson or Broker Associate) is signing the contract as an agent of the Broker, the Principal Broker or manager has the right to review the terms and cancel the contract by written notification within 5 days of execution.

Section 18.

- States that the contract is binding on Seller's successors and assignees.

Section 19.

- Sets forth the process for resolving disputes between the parties.

Section 20.

- Declares this to be the only and complete agreement. This contract supersedes any previous or oral agreements not reflected herein.

Section 21

- Declares "Seller" from Section 1 has the sole authority to transfer property and names any exceptions.
- Declares signatory is signing as a Representative of Property Owner.

Owner's signature - All owners must sign the contract. If the property is owned by a partnership or a corporation, all partners or corporate officers must sign.

Agent's signature When the listing is signed by salesperson member of the broker's staff or by the broker himself, it becomes a (bilateral) contract, with a 5-day management approval contingency. Broker (or broker's agent) must give the seller a copy of the agreement at the time of signing.

4.7 Real Estate Purchase Agreements and Receipt for Deposit

Function and Purpose

There is any number of pre-printed Purchase Agreements available; however, the California Association of REALTORS® provides many of the forms used and user guides associated with a typical transaction. Most agents use the standard C.A.R. form, Residential Purchase Agreement and Joint Escrow Instructions – RPA CA.

The RPA CA details the proposed terms of the purchase agreement and after be filled out, signed and accompanied by a money deposit; serves as an offer to purchase real property. These contracts are often referred to as a **"deposit receipt"**. A deposit receipt constitutes the receipt for the (earnest money) deposit, which must accompany the offer of a prospective Buyer as the consideration for a valid, binding contract. When the broker accepts this deposit, they acknowledge receipt by signing the form.

When both seller and buyer reach an agreement, express the contractual intention, declare their mutual acceptance by signing and receive a fully-executed copy of the contract, the RPA CA becomes the "real estate purchase contract" and contains the preliminary joint escrow instructions.

Unlawful Practice of Law

Sections 6125 and 6126 of the California Business and Professions Code prohibit the practice of law "by persons who are not active members of the State Bar". It goes on to quote California Jurisprudence saying "… an established business custom sanctions the activities of real estate and insurance agents in drawing certain agreements in business transactions in which they take part in their respective professional capacities."

The editors then quote an article by Robert L. Lancefield (29 California Law Review 602) which states: "While these actions are technically within the usual definition of practice of law, they are generally recognized as proper where:

- the instrument is simple or standardized;

- the draftsman or intermediary does not charge any fee for such work (other than his regular commission for the transaction); and,

- the drafting is incidental to his other activities in the transaction."

In short - **a licensee is not an attorney**. This prohibition is not limited to contracts; advising clients beyond the scope matters directly related to your role as a real estate agent is also prohibited. Always refer your clients to the appropriate legal, tax, lending and construction/inspection professionals.

Purchase Form Overview

Below is a brief review of the form and terms for this contract.

Section 1. - Offer
- Names the Buyer.
- Property Description - Generally the address including the county, but if more description is required to differentiate it from another property, as much information as necessary to clearly specify only this property.
- Purchase Price - The price being offered.
- Close of Escrow - Identifies a time for executing the paperwork required to transfer ownership.
- Identifies Buyer and Seller as "parties" of the contract and that Brokers are not.

Section 2. - Agency
- Discloses and confirms all agency relationships between any brokers and the parties.

Section 3. - Finance Terms
- Buyer represents that the deposit funds will be good when deposited with Escrow Holder.
- Details the amounts and timing of additional deposits due from Buyer.
- Discloses the purchase price as "All Cash" or details all financing involved in the purchase.
- Discloses the balance due as the financing down payment (less earnest money and any other deposits previously given).
- Totals all of the amounts in this section to equal the previously stated Purchase Price.
- Details the timing and process for verifying Buyer's downpayment and closing costs.
- Declares the offer is or is not contingent on an appraisal and the timing thereof.
- Details the mortgage contingency (if any) and the timing of application, etc.

Section 4. - Sale of Buyer's Property
- Declares that Offer is or is not contingent upon Buyer's sale of other property as a source of funds required for purchase.

Section 5. - Addenda and Advisories
- Details all pertinent Addenda and Advisories that are attached to the contract.

Section 6. - Other Terms
- Write in for any other duties or acts required to perform the contract (seller will paint the house; Buyer will be entitled to measure for drapes prior to closing etc.)

Section 7. - Allocation of Costs
- Sets forth who will pay for:
    - Inspections, Reports and Certificates (i.e., structural inspections, pest reports etc.)

- o Government Requirements and Retrofits (i.e., smoke detectors, water heater bracing)
- o Escrow and Title Costs
- o Any other costs (i.e., transfer tax, Homeowner Association Fees, etc.)

Section 8. - Items Included in Excluded from Sale

- Notes that items (generally fixtures as defined in Chapter 1) listed in MLS are not included or excluded from sale unless specified below.
- Details existing fixtures and additional items to be included.
- Identifies Leased or liened Items or systems.
- Details any items specifically excluded.

Section 9. - Closing and Possession

- Declares that Buyer will or will not occupy property.
- Sets a date and time that possession of the property will be turned over to Buyer.
- Sets forth the details for possession if the Seller remains after closing or if property is leased.
- Requires seller to turn over any keys, passwords, relevant internet devices, garage door openers, etc.

Section 10. - Statutory and Other Disclosures and Cancellation Rights

- Details the Seller obligations and Buyer's rights regarding Lead Based Paint Hazards.
- Details the Seller obligations and Buyer's Rights regarding other Natural and Environmental Hazard Disclosures and Booklets (i.e., Earthquake, Flood or Fire Zones etc.).
- Details obligations regarding Withholding Taxes.
- Details obligations regarding Megan's Law Database (sex offenders).
- Gives notice of any Gas and Hazardous Liquid Transmission Pipelines.
- Details obligations regarding condominium/planned developments.

Section 11. - Condition of Property

- Declares that property is sold in "as-is" condition.
- Details sellers' obligation to disclose defects and advises buyers of their rights to investigations/inspections of property and condition.

Section 12. - Buyer's Investigation of Property and Matters Affecting Property

- Details the contingency of purchase upon investigations and inspections that are satisfactory to buyer and details the permissions and access required to accommodate inspections.

Section 13. - Title and Vesting

- Details the matters relating to Title and Title Insurance.

Section 14. - Time Periods; Removal of Contingencies; Cancellation Rights

- Details time frames for delivery of Reports and Disclosures.
- Details time frames for completion of Inspections and Removal of Contingencies.
- Details each parties rights to termination related to each these matters and recourse regarding the expiration of time.
- Details the Effect of Cancellation on Deposits.

Section 15.- Final Verification of Condition

- Provides for Buyer to make a final verification that the property has been maintained, any repairs detailed herein are complete and seller has complied with other obligations (i.e., has vacated or vacated tenants, etc.)

Section 16. - Repairs

- Details the requirements for satisfactory verification of repairs.

Section 17. - Proration of Property Taxes and Other Items

- Details the formula by which any property taxes, Homeowner Association Fees, rents, special assessments, etc. will be prorated and what portion will be paid or credited to each party.

Section 18. - Brokers

- Acknowledges that any compensation Seller and Buyer may owe to their respective Brokers under other contracts is payable at the close of escrow.
- Acknowledges the limited scope of duties of the Brokers with respect to purchase price, validity of property inspections etc.

Section 19. - Representative Capacity

- Details the requirements if any person is acting in a Representative Capacity for either party to the contract.

Section 20. - Joint Escrow Instructions to Escrow Holder

- Declares the following paragraphs to be the Escrow Instructions and goes on to detail such instructions. (NOTE: Individual Escrow companies often add their own supplemental provisions.)

Section 21 - Remedies for Buyer's Breach of Contract

- Declares that any clauses added regarding remedies for Breach of Contract must satisfy the statutory regulations for Liquidated Damages under California Civil Code.
- Defines Liquidated Damages.
- Declares Mutual Consent for the release of any funds as damages.

Section 22 - Dispute Resolution

- Details processes for Mediation and Arbitration of Disputes.

Section 23 - Selection of Service Providers

- Declares that Brokers are not liable for the performance of any vendors or inspector they may refer to either party.
- Declares that both parties are entitled hire vendors, inspectors etc. of their choosing.

Section 24 - Multiple Listing Service

- Declares that upon the close of escrow, Brokers are authorized to report the details of the sale to the appropriate Multiple Listing Service which will be published and disseminated to authorized members of the service.

Section 25 - Attorneys Fees

- Declares the prevailing party will be entitled to any attorney's fees arising out of any court action or arbitration of this agreement.

Section 26 - Assignment

- Declares that the Buyer may not assign this contract without separate written consent of the Seller.

Section 27 - Equal Housing Opportunity

- Declares that the property is sold in compliance with all state and federal Equal Housing Opportunity Laws and specifically local anti-discrimination laws.

Section 28 - Terms and Conditions

- Affirms that this is an Offer to Purchase Real Estate on the foregoing terms and conditions and that until all parties have fully initialed and signed, a counteroffer will be required until an agreement is reached.
- Declares the seller has the right to continue to market the property and accept other offers prior to notification of Acceptance.
- The parties acknowledge they have read and received a copy of this agreement and acknowledge their agency relationships.

Section 29 - Time of Essence; Entire Contract Changes

- Declares that time is of the essence.
- Affirms that this document is intended to be the complete and final agreement between the parties and may not be contradicted by prior agreements.
- Declares no provision may be extended or amended except by agreement of both parties in writing.

Section 30 - Definitions

- Provides definitions of pertinent terms in the document.

Section 31 - Expiration of Offer

- Sets for the exact time and date of the Expiration of this Offer.

Buyer Signature Lines

Section 32 - Acceptance of Offer

- Warrants that Seller is the sole owner of the property and authorized to execute this agreement.

- Provides for Acceptance subject to an attached Counteroffer.

Seller Signature Lines

Confirmation of Acceptance by Buyer Agent

Contingencies - Removal and Notice to Perform

Several sections of the Purchase Agreement detail contingencies, usually related to property condition inspections, pest inspections, mortgages, appraisals etc. Additionally, the Seller is required to provide documentation relating to various disclosures.

Essentially an amount of time is allotted to a prospective buyer to ascertain the property condition and secure the funds required for purchase among other things. If the property exhibits structural defects or the Buyer is unable to obtain financing or the Seller fails to provide proper disclosure documentations, the contract may be rescinded and the deposit returned.

Before initiating a rescission of the agreement and escrow a "Notice to Perform" is typically required to be served. If the party receiving the Notice does not perform (typically within 24 hours), the other party has the option rescind. However, the disposition of the earnest money deposit must be agreed upon by both parties.

Liquidated Damages

The offer to purchase is accompanied by an earnest money deposit, held in escrow and in a successful transaction, applied towards the purchase price. If the Buyer defaults on the contract (for instance failing to make a mortgage application to secure purchase money), the earnest money is then treated as liquidated damages. Below are the major points to consider:

- California law requires that Liquidated Damages can only be applied to money prepaid as a deposit, downpayment, etc.

- the purchase of a residential dwelling of **no more than four units, one of which the Buyer intends to occupy,** liquidated damages retained by the seller may not exceed 3% of the purchase price unless the seller can establish a larger percentage (or the full amount) is reasonable.

- The balance of any money on deposit after damages have been established must be returned to the buyer.

For properties consisting of more than 4 units or commercial properties, liquidated damages can be any amount deemed to reasonably reflect damages.

4.8 Option Contracts

Sale or Lease Option Contracts

An option to purchase real property is a written agreement under which the owner grants a potential buyer the right to purchase the property at a fixed price within a certain time. The buyer, in effect, purchases an amount of time during which they can accept or reject the seller's offer. In these contracts the Seller becomes the Optionor and Buyer, the Optionee.

The option may be given alone or in connection with a lease of the property, commonly known as a "lease/option". It may be written in the form of an exclusive right to purchase or lease, or in the form of a privilege of first right of refusal to purchase or lease. The option automatically terminates at the expiration of the time specified unless exercised by the optionee.

Options create a unilateral contract that is irrevocable for the period of time specified since only the Seller is required to act in the event the Buyer exercises their option. The Option does not bind the optionee to any performance, but rather gives them the right to demand performance (sale) from the Seller.

As with all valid contracts, the Buyer must offer consideration for the Option. The optionor promises to sell in exchange for the optionee giving payment for the consideration of the option. Unlike a deposit, the consideration offered for the option is a payment and may be applied toward a future purchase price, but is not refundable if the option is not exercised.

Options can be recorded and when recorded, become a "cloud on the title" to the property in that the owner cannot sell to another party during the option period. Upon expiration, the seller should file a quitclaim deed to remove the option from record.

Exercising the Option

If the Option is exercised, the unilateral contract evolves into a bilateral, executory contract. Now both parties to the contract are legally bound to the terms and conditions of the contract, and either party can sue for specific performance should any future default arise.

Assigning the Option

Options can be legally transferred or the rights to the option sold to a third party without the optionor's consent. Any assignment or sale of the Option must take place during the valid time period of the original option agreement.

First Right of Refusal

Option Contracts should not be confused with a First Right of Refusal. The holder of a First Right of Refusal merely has the first right to purchase or refuse to purchase based on the Owner's desire to sell. If the owner ultimately decides not to sell, unlike the Option, the buyer cannot compel the owner to sell. The holder of the first right of refusal has merely the right to match any other offer the seller may be considering. For obvious reasons, the existence of a First Right of Refusal must be disclosed to all prospective buyers.

Installment Contracts

Installment or Real Property Sales Contracts have two unique elements: the Seller of the property in effect acts as the lender; and legal title to the property is not required to pass within one year. In these cases, the Seller is referred to as the "vendor" and the Buyer, the "vendee".

Essentially, at the closing of this transaction, rather than receiving the full purchase price, the Seller (vendor) agrees to grant "equitable title" (the right to possession only) to the Buyer (vendee) in exchange for some agreed upon number of installment payments. When the full purchase price is paid, the Seller grants the deed conveying full title to the property to the buyer.

4.9 Negotiating Contracts

As previously discussed, a valid, bilateral contract must contain a specific offer and mutual consent. Rarely in a real estate transaction is this accomplished in a single offer and acceptance. Rather, the offering process generally goes as follows:

1. A prospective buyer communicates the offer to their Buyer broker who fills in the RPA CA form and collects the earnest money deposit;
2. The Buyer Broker in turn presents the offer to the Seller Broker, sometimes in the presence of the Seller;
3. The Seller agent reviews the contract with the Seller and accepts, rejects or formulates a counter offer;
4. The Seller agent communicates the Seller's response to the Buyer Broker;
5. Buyer Broker reviews the response and any newly proposed terms to the prospective buyer; and
6. The Buyer accepts, rejects or counter offers.

This process is repeated until there is a mutual consent to the terms and conditions of the Purchase Agreement (or not).

Acceptance and Termination of Offers

- **Acceptance:** Either Buyer or Seller can accept the terms of the proposed contract. Acceptance generally goes into effect when it is communicated to the other party.
- **Rejection:** Either party can reject the proposed contract. Rejection terminates the offer and goes into effect when it is communicated.
- **Counteroffer:** Either party can counteroffer (propose new or different terms). A counteroffer effectively both rejects the earlier offer and creates a new one. If a buyer or seller later changes their mind and wants to accept an earlier offer or counteroffer, it must be renewed by the offering party to be valid. Counteroffers become the new offer when they are received.
- **Revocation:** Either Buyer or seller can revoke (terminate) their offer at any time before acceptance is received. Revocation becomes effective when it is communicated to the other party.
- **Time Lapse:** As previously mentioned, most real estate contracts are dated and timed. If acceptance of an offer or counteroffer is not communicated before the specified expiration, it is terminated. If no time is given, it is still considered terminated if acceptance is not communicated within a "reasonable" amount of time. It should be mentioned that extensions of time can be granted, but must be requested and granted before the expiration of time.
- **Death or Insanity:** If either party dies or becomes insane or incompetent prior to mutual acceptance, the offer is terminated.

4.10 Disclosures

There are several important disclosure requirements attached to the sale of residential real property of one-to-four units. The preparation and delivery disclosures falls on the seller and the seller's agent and all cooperating agents. If more than one agent is involved in the transaction, typically the agent obtaining the offer is required to deliver the disclosures to the prospective buyer.

Typically the seller (and/or agent) has 7 days to provide all required disclosures (or before the executing a lease option, sales contract, or ground lease coupled with improvements). If the seller delivers or amends certain disclosures after executing the offer, the buyer may have three days after delivery in person (or five days, if mailed) to terminate the offer or agreement to purchase by delivering a written notice of termination to the seller or seller's agent.

The required disclosures and disclosure requirements change and it is important to stay informed. State and local associations publish advisories regarding required disclosures as well as the CalBRE.

Smoke detector and Water Heater Bracing Statement Compliance

In California it is required to provide a compliance form for smoke detectors and water heating equipment bracing. Called a 'Smoke detector and Water Heater Bracing Statement Compliance" form this written statement reports the installation of smoke detectors per applicable California Fire and Building Codes as well as earthquake proofing the water heater with bracing as required by California Fire and Building Codes.

Carbon Monoxide detectors

For all dwellings using fossil fuel burning appliances and/or heating units, a fireplace, or having an attached garage, as of July 1, 2011 carbon monoxide detectors are required by law to be installed in all single family homes, and from January 1, 2011 carbon monoxide detectors are required by law to be installed in hotel and motel dwelling units that are intended for occupancy. On January 1, 2016 all other dwelling units, existing and new, are required by law to comply with the installation of carbon monoxide detectors.

The California Association of Realtors (CAR) offers a form that includes the smoke detectors and water heating equipment bracing statement and the carbon monoxide detectors installation in one statement. Additionally, the CAR TDS form incorporates the required disclosure and it no longer needs to be given separately.

Disclosure Regarding Lead-Based Paint Hazards
Much of the housing stock in California contains lead-based paint, which was banned for residential use in 1978. In the course of normal use, when lead-based paint peels and chips, it deteriorates into contaminated dust, creating a lead-based paint hazard. Children ingesting lead chips or dust may develop learning disabilities, delayed development or behavior disorders.

The federal Real Estate Disclosure and Notification Rule requires that owners of "residential dwellings" built before 1978 disclose to their agents and to prospective buyers or lessees/renters the presence of lead-based paint and/or lead-based paint hazards, as well as providing any known information and copies of reports about lead-based paint and lead-based paint hazards. This rule defines a residential dwelling as a single-family dwelling or a single-family dwelling unit in a structure that contains more than one separate residential dwelling unit, and in which each such unit is used or occupied, or intended to be used or occupied, in whole or in part, as the residence of one or more persons.

The federal Environmental Protection Agency (EPA) publishes a pamphlet titled *"Protect Your Family From Lead In Your Home."* describing ways to recognize and reduce lead hazards. The rule requires that a seller (or lessor) of deliver this pamphlet to a prospective buyer (or tenant) before a contract is formed and allow a ten-day inspection period. If the seller fails to disclose, deliver the pamphlet and allow for inspections during the proper time periods, the buyer can elect to cancel. The inspection process is typically paid by the buyer and can be waived by mutual written consent between buyer and seller.

Transfer Disclosure Statement

Sales of real estate property from 1 to 4 units and manufactured homes require the disclosure of any known defects to the buyer which are embodied in what is known as a 'Real Estate Transfer Disclosure Statement' (TDS). The TDS must be signed by all parties, including: the Seller, Seller's agent, Buyer and Buyer's agent.

The TDS is given in writing to the buyers when they sign the purchase agreement. If for any reason the TDS is given after the purchase agreement, the buyer has from three days after receiving the TDS to rescind the sale. The words sold "as is" do not mean that the seller need not disclose defects. Furthermore, sales that include an 'as is' statement do not displace or remedy the agent's duty to inspect and report defects.

Following is a sample of the format of the Transfer Disclosure Statement:

REAL ESTATE TRANSFER DISCLOSURE STATEMENT

THIS DISCLOSURE STATEMENT CONCERNS THE REAL PROPERTY SITUATED IN THE CITY OF _____, COUNTY OF _____, STATE OF CALIFORNIA, DESCRIBED AS _____. THIS STATEMENT IS A DISCLOSURE OF THE CONDITION OF THE ABOVE DESCRIBED PROPERTY IN COMPLIANCE WITH SECTION 1102 OF THE CIVIL CODE AS OF _____, 20___. IT IS NOT A WARRANTY OF ANY KIND BY THE SELLER(S) OR ANY AGENT(S) REPRESENTING ANY PRINCIPAL(S) IN THIS TRANSACTION, AND IS NOT A SUBSTITUTE FOR ANY INSPECTIONS OR WARRANTIES THE PRINCIPAL(S) MAY WISH TO OBTAIN.

COORDINATION WITH OTHER DISCLOSURE FORMS

This Real Estate Transfer Disclosure Statement is made pursuant to Section 1102 of the Civil Code. Other statutes require disclosures, depending upon the details of the particular real estate transaction (for example: special study zone and purchase-money liens on residential property).

Substituted Disclosures: The following disclosures have or will be made in connection with this real estate transfer, and are intended to satisfy the disclosure obligations on this form, where the subject matter is the same:

✎ Inspection reports completed pursuant to the contract of sale or receipt for deposit.

✎ Additional inspection reports or disclosures:

_____
_____
_____

II
SELLER'S INFORMATION

The Seller discloses the following information with the knowledge that even though this is not a warranty, prospective Buyers may rely on this information in deciding whether and on what terms to purchase the subject property. Seller hereby authorizes any agent(s) representing any principal(s) in this transaction to provide a copy of this statement to any person or entity in connection with any actual or anticipated sale of the property.

THE FOLLOWING ARE REPRESENTATIONS MADE BY THE SELLER(S) AND ARE NOT THE REPRESENTATIONS OF THE AGENT(S), IF ANY. THIS INFORMATION IS A DISCLOSURE AND IS NOT INTENDED TO BE PART OF ANY CONTRACT BETWEEN THE BUYER AND SELLER.

Seller ___ is ___ is not occupying the property.

A. The subject property has the items checked below (read across):

__Range	__Oven	__Microwave
__Dishwasher	__Trash Compactor	__Garbage Disposal
__Washer/Dryer Hookups		
__Burglar Alarms	__Smoke Detector(s)	__Fire Alarm
__TV Antenna	__Satellite Dish	__Intercom
__Central Heating	__Central Air Cndtng.	__Evaporative Cooler(s)
__Wall/Window Air Cndtng.	__Sprinklers	__Public Sewer System
__Septic Tank	__Sump Pump	__Water Softener
__Patio/Decking	__Built-in Barbecue	__Gazebo
__Sauna		
__Hot Tub __ Locking Safety Cover*	__Pool __ Child Resistant Barrier*	__Spa__ Locking Safety Cover*
__Security Gate(s)	__Automatic Garage Door Opener(s)*	__Number Remote Controls
Garage: __Attached	__Not Attached	__Carport
Pool/Spa Heater: __Gas	__Solar	__Electric

104

Water Heater: __Gas   __Water Heater Anchored, Braced, or Strapped*   __Private Utility or Other _____

Water Supply: __City   __Well

Gas Supply: __Utility   __Bottled

__Window Screens   __Window Security Bars

__Quick Release Mechanism on Bedroom Windows*

B. Are you (Seller) aware of any significant defects/malfunctions in any of the following? __ Yes __ No If yes, check appropriate space(s) below.

___Interior Walls ___Ceilings ___Floors ___Exterior Walls ___Insulation ___Roof(s) ___Windows ___Doors ___Foundation ___Slab(s) ___Driveways ___Sidewalks ___Walls/Fences ___Electrical Systems ___Plumbing/Sewers/Septics ___Other

Structural Components (Describe: _____

_____)

If any of the above is checked, explain. (Attach additional sheets if necessary): _

_____

_____

_____

* This garage door opener or child resistant pool barrier may not be in compliance with the safety standards relating to automatic reversing devices as set forth in Chapter 12.5 (commencing with Section 19890) of Part 3 of Division 13 of, or with the pool safety standards of Article 2.5 (commencing with Section 115920) of Chapter 5 of Part 10 of Division 104 of, the Health and Safety Code. The water heater may not be anchored, braced, or strapped in accordance with Section 19211 of the Health and Safety Code. Window security bars may not have quick-release mechanisms in compliance with the 1995 Edition of the California Building Standards Code.

Are you (Seller) aware of any of the following:

Substances, materials or products which may be an environmental hazard such as, but not limited to, asbestos, formaldehyde, radon gas, lead-based paint, fuel or chemical storage tanks, and contaminated soil or water on the subject property..	__Yes	__No
Features of the property shared in common with adjoining landowners, such as walls, fences, and driveways, whose use or responsibility for maintenance may have an effect on the subject property..	__Yes	__No
3. Any encroachments, easements or similar matters that may affect your interest in the subject property............................	__Yes	__No
4. Room additions, structural modifications, or other alterations or repairs made without necessary permits.........	__Yes	__No
Room additions, structural modifications, or other alterations or repairs not in compliance with building codes.	__Yes	__No
Fill (compacted or otherwise) on the property or any portion thereof...	__Yes	__No
Any settling from any cause, or slippage, sliding, or other soil	__Yes	__No

problems..
Flooding, drainage or grading problems.............................. __Yes __No

Major damage to the property or any of the structures from fire, earthquake, floods, or landslides..................................... __Yes __No

Any zoning violations, nonconforming uses, violations of "setback" requirements... __Yes __No

Neighborhood noise problems or other nuisances................ __Yes __No

CC&R's or other deed restrictions or obligations................... __Yes __No

Homeowners' Association which has any authority over the subject property... __Yes __No

Any "common area" (facilities such as pools, tennis courts, walkways, or other areas co-owned in undivided interest with others)... __Yes __No

Any notices of abatement or citations against the property... __Yes __No

Any lawsuits by or against the seller threatening to or affecting this real property, including any lawsuits alleging a defect or deficiency in this real property or "common areas" (facilities such as pools, tennis courts, walkways, or other areas co-owned in undivided interest with others)................ __Yes __No

If the answer to any of these is yes, explain. (Attach additional sheets if necessary.)
_____
_____
_____

Seller certifies that the information herein is true and correct to the best of the Seller's knowledge as of the date signed by the Seller.

Seller _____ Date _____

Seller _____ Date _____

III

AGENT'S INSPECTION DISCLOSURE

(To be completed only if the Seller is represented by an agent in this transaction.)

THE UNDERSIGNED, BASED ON THE ABOVE INQUIRY OF THE SELLER(S) AS TO THE CONDITION OF THE PROPERTY AND BASED ON A REASONABLY COMPETENT AND DILIGENT VISUAL INSPECTION OF THE ACCESSIBLE AREAS OF THE PROPERTY IN CONJUNCTION WITH THAT INQUIRY, STATES THE FOLLOWING:

✎ Agent notes no items for disclosure.

✏ Agent notes the following items:

_____
_____
_____

Agent (Broker Representing Seller) _____ By _____ Date_____ (Please Print)
(Associate Licensee or Broker-Signature)

V

BUYER(S) AND SELLER(S) MAY WISH TO OBTAIN PROFESSIONAL ADVICE AND/OR INSPECTIONS OF THE PROPERTY AND TO PROVIDE FOR APPROPRIATE PROVISIONS IN A CONTRACT BETWEEN BUYER AND SELLER(S) WITH RESPECT TO ANY ADVICE/INSPECTIONS/DEFECTS

I/WE ACKNOWLEDGE RECEIPT OF A COPY OF THIS STATEMENT

Seller_____ Date_____ Buyer_____ Date_____
Seller_____ Date_____ Buyer_____ Date_____

Agent (Broker Representing Seller) _____ By _____ Date_____ (Please Print)
(Associate Licensee or Broker-Signature)

Agent (Broker Obtaining the Offer) _____ By _____ Date_____ (Please Print)
(Associate Licensee or Broker-Signature)

SECTION 1102.3 OF THE CIVIL CODE PROVIDES A BUYER WITH THE RIGHT TO RESCIND A PURCHASE CONTRACT FOR AT LEAST THREE DAYS AFTER THE DELIVERY OF THIS DISCLOSURE IF DELIVERY OCCURS AFTER THE SIGNING OF AN OFFER TO PURCHASE. IF YOU WISH TO RESCIND THE CONTRACT, YOU MUST ACT WITHIN THE PRESCRIBED PERIOD.

A REAL ESTATE BROKER IS QUALIFIED TO ADVISE ON REAL ESTATE. IF YOU DESIRE LEGAL ADVICE, CONSULT YOUR ATTORNEY.

(CAL. CIV. § 1102 et. seq.)

Natural Hazard Disclosure Statements

A separate "Natural Hazard Disclosure Statement" must be included that divulges if the property lies in the following hazard areas or zones;

- Area of potential flooding
- Flood zone
- Special Flood Hazard area
- High fire severity zone
- Wild-land are with a substantial fire risk
- Earthquake fault zone
- Seismic Hazard zone

Environmental Hazard Disclosure Booklet - this disclosure booklet, entitled "*Environmental Hazards: A Guide for Homeowners, Buyers, Landlords, and Tenants*" provides additional information regarding earthquake hazards as well as information regarding asbestos, mold radon, lead and formaldehyde.

Mold disclosure- The TDS addresses mold, however, some brokers double down on protecting themselves by providing this additional disclosure form.

Disclosure of Ordinance Location- Must be given if a property is within 1 mile of an area where the military trained with ordinance (bombs, shells, explosives).

Gas and Hazardous Liquid Transmission Pipelines- Since July 1, 2013 every contract for sale of residential real estate must contain notice leading the seller to the directory known as the National Pipeline Mapping System website so a buyer can find information about possible transmission pipelines near the property.

Megan's Law- The buyer must be given notice of the availability of information on this sex offender registry website www.meganslaw.ca.gov .

Mello-Roos Disclosure- must be provided to any buyer purchasing a property that is subject to an ongoing lien securing special tax levies under Mello-Roos Community Facilities Act or the Improvement Bond Act of 1915.

Seller Financing Disclosure Statement - Sellers financing the sale of their homes by extending credit to the buyer must ensure adequate disclosure. This statement must clearly outline the financing terms of the loan, and be signed by the seller, any real estate agents and the buyer prior to the buyer signing the note.

Disclosures For Subdivisions, Condominiums And Stock Cooperatives
The owner of a separate interest in a common interest development (condominium, planned development, or stock cooperative, etc.) must provide a prospective buyer with the following:

- a copy of the governing documents of the development;

- a copy of the most recent documents of the homeowners' association, including financial statements, budgets and insurance information;

- a written statement from the association stating the amount of the current regular and special assessments, any approved changes in those fees and assessments not yet due, as well as any unpaid assessment, late charges, interest, and costs of collection which are or may become a lien against the property;

- any unpaid assessment, late charges etc. assessed again the property; and
- (if applicable) an age restrictions.

Study Smart Guide

Contract - an agreement to do or not do a certain thing.

Express - parties "express" their intention in words, orally or in writing.

Implied - parties "imply" a contract by their actions; need not be in words.

Bilateral contract - Both *parties* have made a promise to each other.

Unilateral contract - *One party* offers an incentive to cause another to act.

Executed - the obligations under a contract have been completely fulfilled.

Executory - the obligations under a contract have not been completely fulfilled.

Valid - contract is legally binding and enforceable by law.

Void- agreement is not a legal contract and cannot be enforced.

Voidable- contract is valid and enforceable, but can be terminated by one (or both) parties
Unenforceable-contract is valid, but cannot be enforced by law.

Essential Requirements: legal capacity, mutual consent, lawful object and sufficient consideration.
Fraud - misrepresenting a material fact with the intent to induce the other to enter the contract.

Constructive fraud - **unintentional** breach of duty which gains an advantage over another

Mistake of fact - ignorance of a material fact or by a mistaken belief.

Mistake of law - misunderstanding of the law.

Duress - coercion or confinement.

Menace - threat to commit duress.

Undue influence - unfair advantage taken by someone having the confidence of another or who holding authority over another.

Statute of Frauds - certain contracts are invalid, unless the contract is in writing and signed

Parol Evidence Rule - prohibits any outside oral or written evidence that would change or add to the terms of a written instrument.

Assignment - transfers all the interests, rights and remedies to the assignee.

Novation - substitutes a new obligation for an existing one, with the intent to satisfy the existing contract.

Statute of Limitations - the time allowed to file suit in a court of law.

Rescission - remedy for breach; must rescind promptly and restore everything of value.

Damages - monetary compensation for breach of contract.

Specific Performance - order for a defendant to perform the contract.

Listing - contract by which owner employs an agent to perform certain duties.

Exclusive Listings - contract for a definite term, with a specified time of termination; including Exclusive right to sell, Exclusive Agency, MLS listing.

Non-exclusive listing - contract given to more than one agent; includes, Open listing.

Net listing - contract for which agent's compensation is all money in excess of the sale price.

Residential Listing Agreement, Exclusive Authorization and Right to Sell (MLS Contract) - most common type of listing.

Residential Purchase Agreement and Joint Escrow Instructions – RPA CA - details the proposed terms of the purchase agreement. When accompanied by a money deposit, serves as an offer to purchase real property and **"deposit receipt"** for the (earnest money) deposit.

Option Contract - option to purchase from seller to buyer for certain price for a certain amount of time.

First Right of Refusal - offer of first right to purchase or refuse to purchase a piece of property.

Installment Contract - contract under which Seller acts as the lender. Transfers only right to possession until all agreed installment payments are complete.

Counteroffer - rejects an earlier offer and creates a new one.

Revocation - termination of an offer.

Transfer Disclosure Statement - required statement of known defects.

Chapter 4
Quiz & Answers

1) Which of the following is true:
   a) only written contracts are valid
   b) contracts are between 2 people
   c) contracts never expire
   d) contract is agreement to do or not do something

2) An "executed" contract means:
   a) the obligations are completed
   b) the obligations are ongoing
   c) the contract has been terminated
   d) a and c

3) Which of the following is NOT a "mistake of law":
   a) not knowing the law
   b) both parties not knowing the law
   c) misunderstanding the law
   d) being wrong about the law

4) The Statute of Frauds:
   a) protects all contracts from fraud
   b) determine whether a contract is lawful
   c) determines of a contract is enforceable
   d) lasts forever and never expires

5) Which of the following is true of contracts:
   a) they can never be changed
   b) they can be assigned
   c) they must be in writing
   d) are valid under parol evidence

6) Exclusive Agency refers to:
   a) a listing that can only be sold by the listing agent
   b) a listing that cannot be sold by the owner
   c) a listing that can only be sold by someone in the listing agent's office
   d) none of the above

7) Contingencies in a purchase agreement include:
   a) inspections of condition
   b) obtaining a mortgage
   c) having the property appraised
   d) all of the above

8) An Option Contract:
   a) is given by a buyer to a seller
   b) can be a right to purchase or lease
   c) can be revoked at any time
   d) is a unilateral contract

9) A buyer's offer is valid until:
   a) accepted by the seller
   b) until the stated time expires
   c) until a counteroffer is made
   d) until the other agent responds

10) Which of the following is true of lead based paint:
   a) it causes learning disabilties
   b) it is illegal and must be removed
   c) answer a only
   d) both a and b

ANSWERS:

| 1. d | 3. a | 5. b | 7. d | 9. b |
| 2. d | 4. c | 6. d | 8. b | 10. c |

Chapter 5

Chapter 5: Practice of Real Estate

To paraphrase the California Bureau of Real Estate Guide "... agency and fiduciary relationships between real estate brokers and their principals are among the most difficult concepts for licensees to understand ..." Different regulations define the nature of the licensees obligations differently depending on the context and the nature of the service being provided. Sometimes brokers are regulated under the laws of "Agent" or "Special Agent", sometimes "independent contractor" and sometimes "employee".

5.1 Responsibilities of Principal Broker to Salespeople

A real estate broker is responsible, and more importantly, legally liable for their agents (salespeople). As discussed in Chapter 3, a real estate salesperson or associated broker is an agent of the principal broker, regardless of their employment status.

There are three main types of relationships between Principal Brokers and their Salespeople:

1. **Principal and Agent** - can be as a general agent or special agent as defined in Chapter 3
2. **Employer-Employee** - performing service under the control and direction of Employer. All employees are agents, but not all agents are employees. Real Estate licensees are typically not employees, but the relationship of the Principal Broker and their Salespeople is often both as agents and employees. From a liability standpoint, it doesn't matter - the Principal Broker is liable for the actions of the Salespeople and has a responsibility to supervise and ensure full compliance with the law.
3. **Principal and independent contractor** - typically responsible for final results (closing the sale) rather than time and the methods of achieving those results (like an employee). Generally independent contractors are not subject to the daily control of the principal Broker. However, this does not diminish the Principal Broker's responsibility and liability for the conduct of the Salespeople. Independent Contractor is a status created to specifically relate to state and federal income tax reporting and other labor related purposes.

The relationship between the real estate broker and the salespeople is that of a principal and an agent/employee.

If the broker is a corporation, the salesperson or broker associate is an agent and employee of the corporation. The broker is indemnified from individual responsibility yet still responsible to guide the agents and employees of the corporation to adhere to all applicable Real Estate Law.

Broker's Duty to Supervise

An employer or broker/principal can be held liable in damages for the negligent conduct of their employees or agents, even if they may not have a direct hand in the negligence. This is known as "duty to supervise". In most cases the law assumes that the broker/principal should have known or made an effort to know about their employee/independent contractor actions and dealings. The independent contractor to broker relationship is unambiguous for all liability matters.

Certain actions require the supervision of the broker, examples include: seller "carry back" financing or a salesperson/ broker associate acting as a principal to make loans through the supervising real estate broker with the real estate broker coordinating the loan transaction.

Authority of Agents

California Civil Code provides that agents are authorized to do "everything necessary, proper or usual" in the course of performing under their contract. While the principal to the contract is liable for the actions of their agent, they are not responsible for actions beyond the scope of the agent's authority.

Agents do not have the authority to enter into contracts on their client's behalf, nor do they have authority to change or cancel contracts once all parties have reached an agreement.

Liability for Intentional Torts and Criminal Misconduct

In most instances the broker is not responsible for criminal misconduct or torts for their salespersons/independent contractors if the supervising broker has no hand in, or knowledge of, the improper actions. Yet the broker is nearly always found liable where the improper conduct of salespersons and partner brokers was foreseeable. Particularly when the supervising broker condones the misconduct or the broker knew or should have known of the misconduct but failed to act reasonably to prevent it. When a supervising broker knows a salesperson or broker partner has or intends to commit fraud, the broker must act to terminate the action, even if it means reporting the act to authorities.

5.2 Licensing and Continuing Education Requirements and Procedures

In California, there are many real estate activities for which a license is required when performed for a fee. The most common of these include:

- sales
- exchanges
- purchases
- rentals/leases
- negotiations
- offers
- listings
- options
- advertising real property
- prospecting
- loan negotiations
- apartment searches

Conversely, the following activities do not require a real estate license:

- Person acting on his own behalf
- Property manager employed by property owner
- licensed auctioneer
- Trustee
- Public servant executing official duties
- Attorney-in-fact under power of attorney
- Court appointee
- Financial institution employees (bank, insurance company or credit union)

Types of Licenses

There are two types of real estate licenses in California:

Real Estate Salesperson. A salesperson cannot be self-employed, but must work under the supervision of a licensed broker as an employee or independent contractor. Salespeople may only receive compensation from their supervising broker via payment, fee, or commissions. A California non-resident can hold a license, but is required to file a power of attorney designating the Commissioner of the Bureau of Real Estate as attorney-in-fact. This is necessary in the event the salesperson faces any legal actions.

Real Estate Broker. A real estate broker can be self employed operating as a sole proprietor. Brokerage offices must employ a designated Broker who is responsible for supervising salespeople. Brokers are responsible for maintaining a place of business. A copy of the broker's license and each associated agent must be displayed in an area of the office that is visible to the public. The broker must keep the Bureau of Real Estate apprised of the place of business and all agents associated with the office, with ongoing updates regarding any change of location and status of all associates.

For the purposes of supervision and regulation, the California Bureau of Real Estate considers the relationship between brokers and their salespeople as employer and employee. If a designated broker of a real estate agency dies, the broker's representative must apply to the Bureau for a temporary license. The completion of an exam is not necessary. The temporary license is non-renewable and valid for up to one year from the date of the original broker's death.

License Eligibility

Anyone interested in obtaining a real estate license must meet certain qualifications, take instruction and pass an exam and apply to and be approved by the California Bureau of Real Estate for the appropriate license.

Salesperson's license qualifications are:

- Be at least 18-years old

- Prove legal presence in the United States (i.e., birth certificate or resident alien card)

- Be honest and truthful

- Provide a complete history of any criminal convictions or violations and disciplinary actions (a conviction or failure to disclose can result in denial or a revocation of license)

- Successfully complete three college-level courses:
    - **Real Estate Principles**, and
    - **Real Estate Practice**, and
    - **One** course from the following list:
        - Real Estate Appraisal
        - Property Management
        - Real Estate Finance
        - Real Estate Economics
        - Legal Aspects of Real Estate
        - Real Estate Office Administration
        - General Accounting
        - Business Law
        - Escrows
        - Mortgage Loan Brokering and Lending
        - Computer Applications in Real Estate
        - Common Interest Developments
    - Courses must be completed at a private real estate school which has had its courses approved by the California Real Estate Commissioner or at an institution of higher learning accredited by the Western Association of Schools and Colleges or by a comparable regional accrediting agency recognized by the United States Department of

Education. Courses must be three semester-units or four quarter-units at the college level.
- Successfully complete the 150 question exam
- Apply to and be approved by the California Bureau of Real Estate (including a non-refundable application fee)
- provide a classifiable set of electronic fingerprints; and
- provide a social security number

Notes: -Members of the California State Bar are exempt from course requirements.
-Applicants submitting evidence of having completed the eight courses required for the broker exam are eligible to take the salesperson exam without submitting further evidence of experience or education.

Broker license qualifications are:

- Be at least 18-years old
- Prove legal presence in the United States (i.e., birth certificate or resident alien card)
- Be honest and truthful
- Provide a complete history of any criminal convictions or violations and disciplinary actions (a conviction or failure to disclose can result in denial or a revocation of license)
- Successfully complete eight college-level courses:
    - **Real Estate Practice**, and
    - **Legal Aspects of Real Estate**
    - **Real Estate Finance**
    - **Real Estate Appraisal**
    - **Real Estate Economics or General Accounting, and** *
    - **Three** course from the following list:
        - Real Estate Principals
        - Business Law
        - Property Management
        - Escrows
        - Real Estate Office Administration
        - Mortgage Loan Brokering and Lending
        - Advanced Legal Aspects of Real Estate
        - Advanced Real Estate Finance

- Advanced Real Estate Appraisal
- Computer Applications in Real Estate
- Common Interest Developments

*If **both** Real Estate Economics and General Accounting are completed, the applicant need only take **two** of the remaining courses.

  - Courses must be completed at a private real estate school which has had its courses approved by the California Real Estate Commissioner or at an institution of higher learning accredited by the Western Association of Schools and Colleges or by a comparable regional accrediting agency recognized by the United States Department of Education. Courses must be three semester-units or four quarter-units at the college level.
- Have completed a minimum of two years of full-time licensed salesperson experience or one of the following equivalents:

  - experience as an escrow/title officer or loan officer handling financing or real estate conveyancing

  - experience in the building trades that included the purchase, finance, development, and sale or lease of real estate

  - experience as a real estate appraiser

  - other experience the Bureau of Real Estate may consider equivalent; or

  - evidence of a 4-year degree from an accredited institution, provided the coursework included a minor or major in real estate.

- Successfully complete the 200 question exam

- Apply to and be approved by the California Bureau of Real Estate (including a non-refundable application fee)

- provide a classifiable set of electronic fingerprints; and

- provide a social security number

Note: -Members of the California State Bar **may** be exempt from course requirements. As of January 2013, a J.D. Degree alone may not be sufficient for an exemption from all coursework.

License Terms and Renewal

Both licenses are valid for 4 years and must be renewed prior to their expiration. Eligibility for renewal requires completing required Continuing Education coursework. Applications along with evidence of having completed the required coursework must be submitted to the California Bureau of Real Estate no earlier than 90 days prior to expiration.

Continuing Education

As of January 1, 2016, the following continuing education coursework is required:

- Salespersons renewing **an original license for the first time** must complete each of the following three-hour courses:

    o Agency

    o Ethics

    o Fair Housing

    o Trust Fund Handling

    o Risk Management

  AND

    o a minimum of 18 hours of consumer protection courses

  AND

    o the remaining course hours may be made up of either Consumer Services or Consumer Protection Courses.

- Brokers renewing **for the first time or renewing late** must complete the following continuing education courses, for a total of 45 hours:

    o Agency

    o Ethics

    o Fair Housing

    o Trust Fund Handling

    o Risk Management and

    o Management and Supervision

  AND

    o a minimum of 18 hours of consumer protection courses

  AND

    o the remaining course hours may be made up of either Consumer Services or Consumer Protection Courses.

For subsequent renewals, both salespersons and brokers must complete the 45 hours of continuing education courses as follows:

- One eight-hour survey course covering the six mandatory topics (Agency, Ethics, Fair Housing, Risk Management, Trust Fund Handling and Management and Supervision)

OR

- One course in each of the six mandatory topics

AND

- a minimum of 18 hours of Consumer Protection Courses

AND

- the remaining course hours made up of Consumer Service or Consumer Protection Courses

Brokers and salespersons who fail to complete the continuing education requirement will have their licenses put in an "inactive status." With an "inactive" license, individuals can earn and collect referral fees, but cannot practice real estate.

The 70/30 Exemption. Individuals who have had a California real estate license in good standing for 30 continuous years **and** who are more than 70 years old are exempt from the continuing education requirement.

5.3 Permitted Activities of Unlicensed Sales Assistants

The Principal broker is explicitly responsible for the supervision and control of the activities performed by their associates and employees to secure full compliance with the Real Estate Law. The broker is similarly charged with the responsibility to supervise and control all activities performed by their employees and agents during the course of a transaction **whether or not the activities performed require a real estate license.**

It is important for the broker to know and identify those activities which do and do not require a real estate license. The responsibility to supervise further extends to the employees or associates of any agent associated with the Principal Broker's office. The following is a general guideline of defined activities that can be performed by unlicensed employees or associates.

Cold Calling. Making telephone calls to canvass for interest in using the services of a real estate broker. The calls may only be used to develop general information about the interest of the person answering.

Should the person answering show an interest in using the services of a broker, they must immediately be referred to a real estate licensee. At no time may the cold caller attempt to persuade the person called to use a broker's services. Discussion must never be for solicitation purposes with respect to a specific property or transaction.

An appointment may be scheduled to enable the prospect to meet with a broker or an associate licensee.

Open Houses. Unlicensed employees can attend an open house by greeting the public, placing signs, handing out preprinted materials prepared by the licensee, or arranging appointments with the licensee.

An unlicensed person shall not:

- show or exhibit the property
- discuss terms and conditions of a possible sale
- discuss features of the property including the location, neighborhood services or schools
- Engage in any other conduct which is used, designed or structured for solicitation purposes with respect to the property.

Comparative Market Analysis. An unlicensed employee can make or prepare a comparative market analysis.

Communicating With the Public. A non-licensee can provide factual information to others from writings prepared by the licensee.

Arranging Appointments. Non-licensees may make or schedule appointments for licensees. In addition, they can order and arrange for reports and services from a third party, for example:

- a pest control inspection and report
- a roof inspection and report
- a title inspection and/or a preliminary report
- an appraisal and report
- a credit check and report
- Repair or other work to be performed to the property as a part of the sale.

Access to Property. An unlicensed employee can arrange access for a person inspecting the property for the purpose of preparing a report or performing repairs or other work to the property in connection with the transaction.

Advertising. Preparing and designing advertising if the advertising is reviewed and approved by the broker or associate licensee prior to its publication and properly identifies the Broker.

Preparation of Documents. Preparing and completing documents and instruments under the supervision and direction of the licensee.

Delivery and Signing Documents. Mailing, delivering, picking up documents or instruments related to the transaction. Obtaining signatures to the documents or instruments from principals, parties or service providers in connection with the transaction.

Note: The activity shall not include a discussion of the content, importance, relevance, or significance of the document with a principal or party to the transaction.

Trust Funds. Accepting and providing a receipt for trust funds received from a principal or a party to the transaction.

Communicating With Principals. Unlicensed employees can communicate with a principal in connection with a transaction about the timing for delivery of reports or other information needed concerning any aspect of the transaction or when services will be started or completed.

Document Review. Reviewing transaction documentation for completeness or compliance. Reviewing transaction documentation for the purpose of making recommendations to the broker on a course of action.

5.4 Compensation and Related Regulations

Commissions

Brokers are compensated for services according to terms of the listing agreement or buyer representation agreement. As discussed in Chapter 3, the principal Real Estate Broker or Agency is the party to that contract. Salespeople/Associated Brokers generally have a separate contract (or some agreement) with the Agency or Principal Broker.

Because Brokers are required to supervise, the Real Estate Commissioner treats the relationship between Agent and Agency/Broker as employer/employee for the purposes of regulation. As such, salespeople may not accept compensation from anyone other than their Principal Broker.

Commission Splits

When properties are sold, the commission paid for the sale is divided among several parties. This can include a cooperating agent (from MLS), franchise owners, principal broker-owner of the office and finally, the agent. Different real estate offices choose various ways to split commissions. For example, some offices may take a significant set percentage of each commission to cover operating and other expenses. Others may charge the agent a set monthly fee (often called "desk fees") and only a nominal percentage of each sale.

Workers' Compensation

From the perspective of California Labor and Workforce, the relationship between Salesperson/Broker is also employer/employee. The Principal broker is required to carry workers compensation insurance for salespersons and broker partners under the California Workers' Compensation Act.

Taxes and Social Security

All income, Federal Insurance Contributions, Federal Unemployment Taxes are the responsibility of the agents so long as the contract between Principal Broker and Agent is specified as an independent contractor. If the relationship is undefined, these contributions may be required. A determination is made by supplying detailed documents (work contracts and the like) and other data to obtain a ruling by the IRS as to whether the salespersons or broker associates are considered employees under these Acts.

5.5 Consumer Protections

California Consumer Protection Law

Consumer Protection Laws forbids deceptive and unfair trade practices. You must be familiar with the laws for two simple reasons: it's very easy to unintentionally violate the rules and the punishment can include imprisonment, severe fines and monetary damages.

Anti-Trust Laws

Anti-Trust Acts govern the laws of free enterprise and create restrictions on allowable behaviors between real estate brokers and their competitors and clients.

> **Sherman Antitrust Act** - The Sherman Antitrust Act of 1890 is the Federal prohibition of many business practices that could unfairly restrict free competition. "Anti-trust Conspiracies" happen when: 2 or more people agree to a "group action" and that action has the effect of restricting free enterprise. The relevant practices for real estate brokers fall into four main categories:
>
> - Price Fixing - an agreement between competitors to set property prices or commission rates.
>
> - Group boycotts - an agreement between two or more brokers not to do business with another broker. A single broker can refuse, but they cannot encourage others to so.
>
> - Tied-In Arrangements - the sale of one product cannot be tied to the purchase of another. These rules are quite complicated. The most common violation for real estate brokers would be the purchase of a property cannot be tied to the brokers' benefitting from future sales (i.e., "I'll make sure your offer for the land is accepted only if you list the houses you build with me.")
>
> - Market Allocation - Competitors cannot agree to divide up a particular area among themselves to exclude outside competition. This is considered a form of price fixing.
>
> **Cartwright Act** - California's State Antitrust laws are enshrined in the Cartwright Act and closely mirror the prohibitions of the federal act.

Truth in Advertising

The California Code's unfair competition rules include any unfair or deceptive advertising. Some examples are:

- Misleading or false advertising, including "puffing" (as previous discussed).

- Failing to disclose the ad is a solicitation by a real estate broker rather than the owner, known as a "blind ad".

- Advertising property under the salesperson's name is not allowed. While it can name the salesperson, only a licensed Broker may advertise property and must include the office name and information.

- Advertising that directly or indirectly discriminates against any group.

- Advertising goods or services with the intent not to sell them as advertised, commonly referred to as "bait and switch".

Some of the penalties that fraudulent or deceptive advertisers may suffer in California include: injunction, up to $2,500 fine for each violation and/or up to six months in jail for each violation.

Blind Advertising and Solicitation Materials

California Business and Professional Code declares that no agent can "publish, circulate or distribute" in any "newspaper, periodical or by mail..." a solicitation for any act for which a real estate license is required without a disclosure that they are performing an act for which a license is required. It goes on to declare that all solicitations must include the licensee's license ID Number "...on all solicitation materials intended to be the first point of contact with the consumer..." For the purposes of this regulation, "solicitation materials" include:

- business cards

- stationary

- advertising flyers

- other materials designed to solicit a professional relationship

While all advertising and materials must disclosure they are generated by a real estate broker, the inclusion of the License ID Number is NOT required on: advertising in print, advertising on electronic media and for sale signs.

5.6 Servicing Diverse Populations

Fair Housing and Anti-Discrimination

Laws at both the state and federal level prohibit discrimination in every type of real estate transaction. It is important to note that the information offered here applies specifically to business practices related to real estate transactions.

There is vigorous investigation and enforcement of these laws and regulations by the Bureau of Real Estate. Any complaint filed based on alleged discriminatory activities is pursued with the full support and backing of state and federal authorities. If a real estate agent or supervising real estate broker is found to be in violation, they will likely have their license suspended or permanently revoked.

As with antitrust laws, actually, even more so, familiarize yourself with these laws for the same two reasons: it's very easy to unintentionally violate the rules; and the punishment can include imprisonment, severe fines and monetary damages.

Federal Laws

Federal anti discrimination law encompasses a wide array of business and real property situations, including products and services offered by banks, insurance companies, corporations and small businesses, construction divisions, multiple listing services and real estate organizations. Enforcement and administration of the Federal Fair Housing Act is headed by the Secretary of Housing and Urban Development, a cabinet position reporting directly to the President. The Attorney General has the right to bring action against anyone suspected of engaging in the practice of denying access or the "full enjoyment" protected by these Acts. The court can issue a temporary restraining order, permanent injunction or other legal remedy against the person or persons denying others any protected civil rights.

Civil Rights Act of 1866: Predominately prohibits discrimination based on "race and color" in the sale and rental of property. This is the first of the anti-discrimination laws. It grants the rights to "make and enforce contracts, to sue, be parties and give evidence, to inherit, purchase, lease, sell, hold and convey real and personal property ..."

Civil Rights Act of 1968 (Title VIII): Specifically prohibits discrimination in housing based on race and color and expands it to include religion and national origin.

Housing and Community Development Act of 1974: Expands prohibitions to include sex.

Fair Housing Amendment Act of 1988: Further expands prohibitions to include persons with disabilities and familial status.

> Discriminating against disabled (mentally or physically) persons is characterized by not making reasonable accommodations regarding policies or necessary changes. Since 1991, homes that are four units or more are required to be accessible for people with disabilities for first floor units. In dwellings where elevators are present, units on upper floors must also be accessible for people with disabilities.

> Familial status relates to discrimination against pregnant women or families with children.

Federal Fair Housing Act - The Acts of 1968, 1974 and 1988 taken together constitute the Federal Fair Housing Act (FFHA) which specifically prohibits discrimination in the sale, rental and advertising of residential housing.

Some of the most relevant prohibited acts are:

- Choosing not to sell or rent to someone who is in a protected class, based on color, race, religion/creed, ancestry/national origin, gender, mental or physical disability, and familial status.

- **Redlining:** Modifying services or conditions for different people as a way of discriminating against someone in a protected class, such as refusal or special terms of a home loan based on protected class status.

- Discriminatory advertising directed toward someone in a protected class to discourage or prevent the sale or rental of a residence.

- Dishonestly regarding the availability of property for sale or rent with the intention of discriminating.

- **Blockbusting or Panic Selling:** Coercing homeowners into selling by representing negative consequences occurring when protected classes move into a neighborhood (such as a decline in values and/or rise in crime).

- Preventing individuals from full participation in organizations that engage in the rental or sale of residences (e.g. multiple listing service).

- **Steering:** Encouraging individuals to gravitate toward or away from certain neighborhoods based on protected class status.

- Stating in an appraisal report that the value of a property is affected by any of the above prohibited activities.

- Including notes with discriminatory preferences.

- Negatively interfering or retaliating against anyone exercising their rights to file a complaint.

FFHA Exemptions:

Sale or rental of a single family home **by the owner** who:

- owns three or fewer properties, and

- does not use a broker, and

- does not engage in discriminatory advertising, and

- if not the current or most recent occupant, has not sold another property in the last two years.

Rental by an owner of apartments or rooms in a multi-unit dwelling of four units or less, providing:

- does not use a broker, and

- does not engage in discriminatory advertising, and
- is currently occupying one of the units.

The sale or rental of a property owned or controlled by a religious organization, society or non-profit to a person of the same religion, society or non-profit, providing membership is not restricted by race, color or nationality.

The rental of lodging by a private club to members, provided it is not open to the public.

Familial Status Exemptions:

- Properties occupied solely by people 62 or older.
- Properties with at least 80% occupancy by people 55 and older.

Familial Status exemptions are based solely on occupancy, not ownership. Anyone may purchase the property, but cannot occupy until they meet the age restrictions.

Discriminatory Advertising

The Department of Housing and Urban Development (HUD) has published a list of words, phrases and symbols considered discriminatory in advertising. For the full list, See HUD Part 109-Fair Housing Advertising. Some of the major sections include:

Words descriptive of dwelling (white, Jewish, adult)

Words indicative of race, color, religion, sex, handicap, familial status and national origin

Symbols or logos which imply race, color, religion, sex, handicap, familial status and national origin

Colloquialisms (regional catchphrases) which imply race, color, religion, sex, handicap, familial status and national origin

Area Descriptions -names of facilities which would imply a discriminatory preference or exclusion (i.e., a religious institution or establishments known as catering to or excluding a particular protected class)

California State Law

In addition to federal laws, California has enacted several state laws designed to enforce the rights of all people to adequate housing and access to buying, selling and leasing of all types of real property. California is recognized as the leader among all states in the regulation of real estate activities, the laws of agency and the enforcement of anti-discrimination laws.

Unruh Civil Rights Act

The Unruh Act of 1959 is a state law that regulates the activities of business owners. Since real estate brokers and salespeople work at a brokerage office, it governs their activities.

The Act provides that:

"All persons within the jurisdiction of this state are free and equal, and no matter what their sex, race, color, religion, ancestry, or national origin are entitled to the full and equal accommodations, advantages, facilities, privileges, or services in all business establishments of every kind whatsoever."

Although certain specific elements of discrimination are mentioned, the law does apply to all forms of arbitrary discrimination performed by business establishments. The prohibitions most germane to brokers would be the acts of blockbusting and steering (as previously discussed).

Violators are liable for damages for each and every offense as determined by a jury or if no jury, then "treble damages"; but in no case, less than $4,000 plus attorney's fees.

The Rumford Act (California Fair Employment and Housing Act)

The Rumford Act of 1963 is another state law that prohibiting discriminatory practices. This Act states its purpose to provide effective remedies that will eliminate discriminatory practices; and further, "be an exercise of police power for the protection of the order, safety, health, morals and general welfare, health and peace of the people of this State".

According to the Rumford Act:

"The practice of discrimination because of race, color, religion, sex, gender, gender identity, gender expression, sexual orientation, marital status, national origin, ancestry, familial status, source of income, disability or genetic information in housing accommodations is declared to be against public policy."

It goes on to:

- specifically prohibit landlords from discriminating against or harassing members of the protected classes, and
- declares it unlawful for the owner of any housing or accommodation to make or to cause to be made, any written or oral inquiry (relating to the protected classes listed) of any person seeking to purchase rent or lease and housing accommodation.

Enforcement

It is important to note that enforcement of these two state laws are performed in distinct and separate ways as follows:

The Unruh Act is enforced through judicial proceedings.

The Rumford Act is regulated by administrative procedure, meaning the aggrieved party files a complaint with the California Department of Fair Employment and Housing.

Anyone initiating action based on discrimination can only file under one or the other state laws, but not both.

California Civil Code (Sections 54-55.1) - forbids discrimination against people with disabilities in housing transactions, including those who are deaf or visually impaired.

The **Housing Financial Discrimination Act of 1977 (The Holden Act)** forbids discrimination by a funding institution based on the racial, ethnic, national origin or religious makeup of a property's location, neighborhood or other characteristic ("redlining" as previously discussed). The statute applies to all loans on owner occupied residences with 1-4 units, including financial assistance, refinancing and remodeling and home improvement to any dwelling 4 units or less.

This Act requires a Fair Lending Notice stating in part:

> It is illegal to discriminate in the availability of financial assistance based on:
>
> - trends or conditions in a neighborhood, unless it can be demonstrated in that particular instance this consideration avoids an unsafe or unsound business practice, or
>
> - racial, ethnic, religious or nation origin composition of the neighborhood, or whether or not the composition is changing or expected to change, in appraising housing or determining terms and conditions of financial assistance.

Real Estate Commissioner Regulations

In addition to the legislative authorities, the California Real Estate Commissioner has a set of regulations governing the activities of real estate practitioners. Sections 2780-2781 give descriptions of activities relating specifically to discriminatory practices by licensees. Violations are a basis for disciplinary action which can include fines and suspension, or even permanent revocation, of your license to practice real estate.

5.7 CalBRE Jurisdiction and Disciplinary Actions

The Bureau of Real Estate monitors and regulates the real estate industry in California, promoting public awareness and delivering services to consumers and licensees. The Bureau consists of 11 members. The Real Estate Commissioner is appointed by the governor and appoints the other 10 members of the Bureau. The Commissioner is charged issuing the Regulations of the Real Estate Commissioner (which are in effect law) and with overseeing and enforcing Real Estate Law and Subdivided Lands Law.

The Bureau has the authority to do many things:

- Carry out state law.
- Administer examinations.
- Review records.
- Enforce license law by holding hearings and if necessary, appeals.
- Grant, refuse, restrict, suspend and revoke licenses.

Common License Violations

Enforcement of Federal, State and Real Estate Law all fall under the purview of the CalBRE. Some of the more common violations include:

- Making misrepresentations
- Being an undisclosed principal in a transaction
- Serving as a dual agent without proper disclosures and permissions from buyer and seller
- Not accounting for Trust Funds within an acceptable timeframe
- Improper Trust Fund Shortages and Overages
- Compensating an unlicensed individual with commission funds
- Failing to disclose or report criminal convictions
- Providing false or incomplete information on the license application or renewal form
- Engaging in real estate activities with an expired license
- Engaging in real estate activities while in an impaired state
- Participating in discriminatory practices
- Failing to distribute copies of real estate documents to all of the appropriate parties

- Commingling business and personal funds
- Encouraging a party to make or break a contract for secret profit
- Failing to properly supervise associated licensees, non-licensees and employees

Hearings and Appeals

In the event of a violation or complaint, a hearing is held. The licensee must be informed about the hearing (in writing) a minimum of 10 days before the hearing is scheduled. If the licensee appears, they can be represented by counsel, ask questions of witnesses and present records.

If the licensee is not satisfied with the decision of the Bureau, they can appeal to the superior court within 20 days. Disciplinary actions can include restriction, suspension or revocation of the license and significant monetary fines. If a license is revoked, the (former) licensee must release it to the Bureau within seven days.

California Real Estate Recovery Account

Claimants against a licensed real estate professional who have been awarded a judgment or restitution order but have been unable to fully collect from the licensee may have recourse through the Real Estate Recovery Account. This account is funded by a portion of all licensure fees from the Real Estate Fund at the State Treasury.

Recovery amounts are limited by law to a maximum of $50,000 per transaction with an aggregate maximum of $250,000 against any single licensee. If a payout is made on behalf of a licensee, the licensee is automatically suspended until repayment, plus interest, is made to the Recovery Account.

5.8 Trust Account Management (Broker's Escrow)

Real estate agents receive trust funds in the normal course of doing business, for instance, earnest money deposits with the initial Purchase Contract. Do not confuse this with the title transfer process of Escrow as previously discussed. While the premise of receiving funds of behalf of others is the same, always consider the context to discern which escrow is being discussed. Generally, the funds are referred to as "trust funds" and the special accounts into which they are deposited are often referred to as "escrow accounts" or "trust funds accounts".

When brokers receive funds on behalf of others, they create a fiduciary responsibility to the funds' owners. Brokers must handle, control and account for these trust funds according to established legal standards. Improper handling of trust funds is cause for revocation or suspension of a real estate license, and financial liability for damages incurred by clients.

Trust Funds Defined

Trust funds are money or other things of value received by a broker or salesperson on behalf of a principal and held for the benefit of others in the performance of any acts for which a real estate license is required. Trust funds may be cash or non-cash items, such as:
- cash;
- a check used as a purchase deposit (whether made payable to the broker or to an escrow or title company);
- a personal note made payable to the seller;
- Or even an automobile's "pink slip" given as a deposit.

Trust or Escrow Accounts

A trust account is set up as a means to separate trust funds from non-trust funds. An important reason for designating a trust fund depository as a trust account is to protect the principals' funds in the event of legal action against the broker or if the broker becomes incapacitated or dies. Trust funds held in a true trust account cannot be "frozen" pending litigation against the broker or during probate.

Trust accounts also have better insurance protection. Funds of various owners placed in a custodial deposit (trust account) in an insured bank are recognized for insurance purposes to the same extent as if the owners' names and interests were individual accounts, provided the trust account is specifically designated as custodial and the name and interest of each owner of funds in the account are disclosed on the depositor's records. **Each client** with funds deposited in a trust account maintained with a federally insured bank **is insured by the FDIC up to $250,000, as opposed to just $250,000 for the entire account**, as long as the regulatory requirements are met.

Escrow Rules
- all funds received on behalf of clients/principals must be deposited in an authorized trust bank account no later than three business days following the receipt of the funds by the broker or the

broker's salespersons or broker associates. An exception exists when a check is received from an offeror in connection with an offer to purchase or lease real property.

As provided under Commissioner's Regulation 2832, a deposit check may be held uncashed by the broker until acceptance of the offer if:

    a) the check by its terms is not negotiable by the broker (written out to someone else),

    OR

    b) the offeror has given written instructions that the check shall not be deposited or cashed until acceptance of the offer; AND

    c) the offeree is informed, before or at the time the offer is presented for acceptance, that the check is being held.

- A salesperson or a broker associate must immediately deliver all client or principal funds to the broker.
- A real estate broker must place the client's or principal's funds with a "neutral" escrow depository for example, a title company or licensed public escrow.
- The broker must promptly deliver the funds to the client or principal who is entitled to receive them.
- Trust bank accounts of real estate brokers must be established and maintained in compliance with the Real Estate Law and are not available to real estate salespersons.

General Account Requirements

Trust funds, such as purchase money deposits not forwarded directly to the contract's principal or to a neutral escrow depository or for which the broker does not have authorization to hold uncashed, must be deposited to the broker's trust fund bank account.

Trust accounts must meet the following criteria:
- be designated as a trust account in the name of the broker as trustee;
- be maintained with a bank or recognized depository located in California; and
- not be an interest-bearing account requiring prior written notice as a condition of withdrawal (with some exceptions).

Trust Account Withdrawals

Withdrawals may only be made by:
- the broker named as account holder;
- the designated broker-officer named as the corporate account holder;
- a specifically authorized salesperson licensed to the broker; or
- a specifically authorized non-licensee carrying a bond equal to the maximum amount of funds to which they may have access.

Withdrawals made by authorized salespeople or non-licensees do not relieve the broker or broker-officer from a broker's trust fund liability in handling trust funds.

Identifying the Owner(s) of Trust Funds

A broker must always be able to identify a) who owns the trust funds and b) who is entitled to receive them, since these funds can only be disbursed by authorization of that person. As the transaction progresses, the person entitled to the funds can be different than the person who originally gave the funds to the broker or the salesperson. For instance, in a typical sale transaction, the party entitled to the funds received from the prospective buyer depends on whether or not the offer has been accepted by the seller.

Prior to acceptance, funds received from the prospective Buyer belong to that person and must be handled according to their instructions until acceptance of the offer.

After acceptance, funds must be handled according to mutual instructions from Buyer and Seller as follows:

- A Buyer's check held uncashed by the broker may continue to be held uncashed after acceptance of the offer, only upon written authorization from the Seller.

- The Buyer's check may only be given to the Seller if the Buyer and Seller expressly agree in writing.

- No part of the Buyer's purchase money deposit can be refunded by an agent or subagent of the seller without the *express written permission* of the Seller to make the refund.

In the event of a dispute between Buyer and Seller regarding the disposition of the deposit money, the broker must hold the funds and seek a ruling from the appropriate Court.

Commingling and Conversion

Funds belonging to a licensee may not be commingled with trust funds. Commingling is strictly prohibited by the Real Estate Law. It is grounds for the revocation or suspension of a real estate license.

Commingling occurs when personal or company funds are deposited into the trust fund escrow account. Even if separate records are kept, it is a violation of Real Estate Law.

Conversion is the unauthorized use or disbursement of trust funds and can result in imprisonment in addition to license revocation.

The essential reason to maintain a separate trust account is to avoid commingling and conversion. Two recognized exceptions are:
- $200 of the Broker's personal or corporate funds may be held in the account to cover fees and expenses related to the maintaining the account; and
- Commission monies remaining on deposit after the funds have been disbursed. Commissions must be withdrawn within 25 days.

Escrow record keeping

To maintain the integrity of the trust fund bank account, a broker must ensure that:
- his/her personal or general operating funds are not commingled with trust funds;
- the balance of the trust fund account is equal to the broker's trust fund liability to all owners of the funds; and
- the trust fund records are in an acceptable form and are current, complete and accurate.

Liability

Responsibility, and the financial liability associated with that responsibility, begins when funds are received either from or for the benefit of a principal. The aggregate (combined total) liability at any one time is equal to the total *positive* balances due to all beneficiaries of the account.

Trust Fund Shortages

Funds on deposit in the account must always equal the broker's aggregate trust fund liability. If the account balance is *less* than the total liability a *trust fund shortage* occurs. A shortage is in violation of Commissioner's Regulation 2832.1, which states that the written consent of every principal owning funds in the account must be obtained prior to each disbursement, if the disbursement reduces the balance of account to an amount less than the existing aggregate liability of the broker to all owners of the funds.

Trust Fund Overages

Conversely, if the trust account balance is *greater* than the total liability, there is a *trust fund overage*. This immediately calls into question the possibility of commingling.

Avoiding Discrepancies

A trust fund discrepancy of any kind is a serious violation of the Real Estate Law. To ensure that the balance of the trust account always equals the trust fund liabilities, a broker should implement the following procedures:

> I. Immediately deposit all funds that are not being forwarded to a Sale Escrow or to the funds owner intact (don't deduct any fees or reimbursements directly from trust funds prior to deposit).

2. Maintain supporting paperwork for any disbursement from the trust account. Record disbursements accurately in both a Bank Account Record and a Separate Beneficiary Record.

3. Disburse funds only when the disbursement will not result in a negative or deficit balance in the account. Many shortages are caused by disbursements in excess of funds received from or for a beneficiary. Any excess disbursements are, in effect, paid from monies belonging to other beneficiaries.

4. Ensure that a check deposited to the trust account has cleared before disbursing funds against that check. For instance, when an offer is rejected by the Seller and the broker must return the earnest money deposit.

5. Keep accurate, current and complete records of the trust account and a separate record for each beneficiary.

6. Reconcile the bank statement and with the separate record for each beneficiary or transaction on a monthly basis.

5.9 Accounting Records

General Requirements

As previously discussed, one of the broker's primary fiduciary obligations to the client is the accounting of funds, regardless of whether the funds are deposited to the trust fund bank account, forwarded to sale escrow, held uncashed or released to the owner(s) of the funds.

Maintaining proper records:
- Provides the basis for the broker preparing an accurate accounting for clients.
- States the amount of money the broker owes the account beneficiaries at any one time.
- Proves whether or not there is an imbalance in the trust account.
- Guarantees that beneficiary funds will be insured up to the maximum FDIC insurance coverage.

There are two types of accounting records that may be used for trust funds: columnar records and records compatible with generally accepted accounting practices. Regardless of the type of records used, they must include the following information:

- a chronological accounting of all trust fund receipts and disbursements, with pertinent details;
- the balance of the trust fund account, based on recorded transactions;
- a chronological accounting of all receipts and disbursements affecting each beneficiary's balance; and
- The balance owing to each beneficiary or for each transaction.

Columnar Records

If there is more than one trust fund bank account, a different columnar record must be maintained for each account.

A columnar record consists of three types of records:

1. Trust Funds Received and Paid Out. At a minimum, this record must show the following information in columnar form:
   a) date funds were received;
   b) name of payee or payor;
   c) amount received;
   d) date of deposit;
   e) amount paid out;
   f) check number and date; and
   g) the daily balance of the trust account.

138

All transactions affecting the trust account are entered in chronological order regardless of the nature of or parties to the transaction.

2. Separate Record for Each Beneficiary or Transaction. This record accounts for funds received either from or for each beneficiary, or for each transaction. This record must show the following in chronological order:
   a) date of deposit;
   b) amount of deposit;
   c) name of payee or payor;
   d) check number;
   e) date and amount; and
   f) daily balance of each account after posting transactions.

A separate record must be maintained for each beneficiary or transaction from for which the broker deposited funds to the trust account.

3. Record of All Trust Funds Received But Not Placed in Broker's Trust Account (required when funds are forward directly to an authorized person.) This record is used to keep track of funds received and not deposited to a trust fund bank account. While these funds don't go into the trust account, the broker is handling the funds and must keep records. Examples are:

- earnest money deposits forwarded directly to sale escrow holder;
- rents forwarded to landlords; and
- borrowers' payments forwarded to lenders.

This record must show:
   a) the date funds were received,
   b) the form of payment (check, note, etc.),
   c) amount received,
   d) description of property,
   e) identity of the person to whom funds were forwarded, and
   f) date of disposition.

Other Accounting Methods and Records
A broker using trust fund records other than the columnar method must keep records with generally accepted accounting principles. Whether prepared manually or by computer, they must include at least the following:

1. A *journal* recording the chronological details of all trust fund transactions. The journal is a daily record of receipts and disbursements and meet the following minimum requirements:

a) Record of all trust fund transactions in chronological sequence.
   b) Contain information to identify the transaction such as the date, amount received or disbursed, name of payee or payor, check number, and identification of the beneficiary.
   c) Show the total receipts and disbursements at least once a month.

2. A *cash ledger* showing debits and credits and periodic balance according to the transactions recorded in the journal.

3. A *beneficiary ledger* for each beneficiary account showing the chronological transactions affecting each beneficiary's account, as well as the balance of the account. This reflects the broker's liability to each beneficiary.

To comply with generally accepted accounting principles, there must be a single set of journal, cash ledger, and beneficiary ledger for each trust fund bank account. Entries in all of these ledgers must be based on entries recorded in the journal.

Chapter 5
Quiz & Answers

1) A broker is only responsible for:
   a) employees
   b) independent contractors
   c) salespeople
   d) all of the above

2) Agents are NOT authorized to:
   a) do everything possible to perform
   b) enter into contracts on behalf of clients
   c) change contract on behalf of clients
   d) b and c only

3) Which of the following is true of salespeople:
   a) they cannot be self-employed
   b) they cannot be independent contractors
   c) they must be a California resident
   d) they are paid by buyers and sellers

4) Real estate licenses are valid for:
   a) 2 years
   b) 3 years, if you do continuing education
   c) 4 years
   d) 5 years

5) Commission amounts are:
   a) set in advance
   b) negotiated each time
   c) set by law
   d) set by the principal broker

6) All advertising must include:
   a) the salesperson's name and contact information
   b) the broker's name and office contact information
   c) only offerings for property available for sale
   d) all of the above except a

7) The Federal Fair Housing Act (FFHA):
   a) combines Acts of 1968, 1974 and 1988
   b) prohibits discrimination in the sale, rental and advertising of residential property
   c) prohibits encouraging people to live in certain neighborhoods
   d) all of the above

8) Housing discrimination is NOT governed by:
   a) federal authority
   b) local authority
   c) state authority
   d) CalBRE authority

9) Which of the following is NOT a license violation:
   a) making an accidental misrepresentation
   b) buying property for personal gain
   c) not balancing the escrow account
   d) offering a friend a referral fee for new business

10) A broker's trust account is:
    a) the sale settlement escrow account
    b) an operating account for real estate business only
    c) an account for holding sale deposits
    d) the account where your gift bonds are held

ANSWERS:

1. d	3. a	5. b	7. d	9. b
2. d	4. c	6. d	8. b	10. c

Chapter 6

6. Leases, Landlord/Tenant Law and Specialty Areas

6.1 Leases

In Chapter One/Ownership, a distinction was made between freehold estates and less-than-freehold estates, or in more common terms, a lease or leasehold estate. The main characteristic of a leasehold interest is the right to exclusive possession and use of the property by the lessee (tenant) for a period of time. The lessor (landlord) maintains title (as an "estate in reversion") regaining the full rights of ownership at the expiration of the lease.

Leases Defined

A lease is a formal written contract granting exclusive use and possession to a parcel of land or space, along with the benefits and enjoyment of that use, in exchange for consideration (rent). The interest is conveyed for a specific length of time which can be anywhere from hours to 100 years.

Leases are legally referred to as "chattel real" and are an *executory contract* requiring all elements of a valid contract. Performance is ongoing and the lease cannot be orally modified. While the contractual intention creates an interest in real property, the lease itself is a form of personal property and subject to the laws of personal property (for instance, a lease automatically transfers with the transfer of title).

In addition to meeting the standards of a valid contract, a lease must also meet the rules under the Statute of Frauds. Leases must be in writing if: it has a term of longer than one year; OR it has a term of one year or less that expires more than one year from the date of signing. Leases for less than one year can be oral, in which case the contract is "implied" by the actions of the parties: the tenant pays rent and takes possession of the property and the landlord accepts the payment. An oral lease is automatically governed under the rules of a "tenancy at will".

Types of Leasehold Estates

As discussed in Chapter One, there are four types of estates created by leases:

- estate for years
- estate from period to period (fixed term)
- estate at will (tenancy at will)

- estate at sufferance (leftover tenant)

Types of Leases

Leases fall into the following five categories, generally relating to how the rent and building maintenance and operating expenses are calculated.

- **Fixed or Gross Lease** - tenant pays a "fixed" amount of rent and landlord is responsible for maintenance and operating expenses.
- **Graduated Lease** - tenant pays a fixed amount with an "escalator clause" detailing periodic increases and landlord is responsible for maintenance and operating expenses.
- **Net Lease** - Tenant pays a fixed amount plus certain of the landlord's expenses. The most common of these is "triple net" under which the tenant pays the landlord's property taxes, hazard insurance and maintenance costs.
- **Percentage Lease** - Most often used for retail leases. The tenant pays a base rent plus a percentage of the gross receipts from the business. The percentage is often calculated based on the mark-up percentage applied to the goods being sold.
- **Ground Lease** - Tenant leases land with the obligation to make significant improvements like the construction of a building. At the end of the term, the improvements revert to the landlord.

Basic Contractual Terms

Leases do not have specific language or standard forms, but must meet the standards of a valid contract: offer and acceptance, competent parties, lawful object and sufficient consideration. The most basic terms of a written lease must:

- identify landlord and tenant
- state the contractual intention to "rent"
- identify the property
- establish the length of the lease (generally referred to as the "term")
- establish the type of lease (whether it is monthly or a fixed term)
- establish the rent (consideration) and when and how it will be paid

Rights and Obligations of Parties to a Lease

An oral tenancy at will can be very simple, but a written lease agreement lays out the rights and obligations of the parties involved in considerable detail. Some of the more important aspects of a lease are:

- term of lease;
- rent;
- security deposit;
- possession, maintenance, and improvements;
- liability of parties for injuries resulting from condition of premises;

- transfer of interest in leased premises (assigning or subletting);
- special covenants, conditions and provisions; and,
- termination.

Term of lease. The lease term is the period of time during which the tenant may occupy the premises. Since the lease term is an essential, if the lease fails to specify a term, a specific period of time is implied as a matter of law, based on the nature and circumstances of the lease.

When the lease term is not specified, the following statutory guidelines apply depending on the type of rental property:

- **For lodgings, dwelling-houses, and residential properties**-the period of time adopted for the payment of rent. For example, if rental payments are due on a monthly basis, the lease term is equal to one month.
- **For agricultural or grazing properties**-one year.
- **For all other properties where there is no custom or usage**-the tenancy is for one month unless otherwise designated in writing.
- **For a lease owned by an emancipated minor or an incompetent person**-no longer than a probate court may authorize.

Lease Extension and Renewal
A *lease renewal creates a new and distinct tenancy* and should be executed as an entirely new lease. A *lease extension is a continuation under the original lease.* If a tenant remains after expiration of the lease term **and** the landlord accepts rental payments, the lease is considered to be extended. In this case, the parties are presumed to extend under the same terms and conditions on a month-to-month basis (or whatever period the rent payment covers), but in no event longer than one year.

A lease clause granting the right to extend or renew is an *irrevocable offer* by the landlord to lease the property in the future on specific terms. Under the Statue of Frauds, the renewal or extension must be in writing and must be reasonably specific to be enforceable. A provision on terms "to be mutually agreed upon" is generally unenforceable. The right to extend or renew must be exercised prior to expiration of the lease.

A residential lease providing for an **automatic** renewal or extension **if the tenant either fails to move after expiration or fails to give notice of intent not to renew,** is voidable by the party who did not prepare the lease **unless** the automatic renewal clause is printed in 8-point boldface type and a warning of the automatic renewal clause appears in 8-point boldface type immediately above the signature line.

Rent. Rent is the consideration paid for possession, use, and enjoyment of leased property. A tenant's obligation to pay rent arises from either the express terms of a lease (privity of contract) or a tenant's mere occupancy of the premises where no gift is intended (privity of estate).

- Through privity of contract, a tenant is obligated to pay rent even if the tenant never enters into possession of the premises.
- Through privity of estate, even if a lease does not specify the terms for payment of rent, an obligation to pay rent arises out of a tenant's occupancy of the premises (again, assuming no gift is intended).

By law, the term "rent" includes "charges equivalent to rent." Unless specified in the lease, rental payments need not be paid in money, but can be made in the form of goods, crops, and or other consideration agreed upon by the parties.

Unless otherwise specified, rental payments are due at the end of each period (e.g., at the end of the day, week, month, quarter, or year) and delivered to the property. Most commercial and residential leases specifically require *payment of rent in advance* and provide for payment to a specific address.

A ***late charge and fee for returned checks*** is enforceable by the landlord if the amount of the charges and fees are specified in the lease *and* reasonably related to anticipated administrative costs and loss of interest caused by the late payment.

Even though most rent is paid in advance, it is not apportionable. Meaning, rent is due for the full term of the contract and not eligible for rebate if the tenant moves earlier *except*: when the lease is terminated due to the fault of the landlord, or if the lease provides for apportionment of rent. If rent is not paid in advance and the lease is terminated prior to the expiration, the tenant is liable only for rent due during the time they had the right to occupy the premises.

Unless otherwise specified, a tenant must pay rent throughout the term of the lease until they return possession of the premises to the landlord. The obligation to pay rent is generally independent of the landlord's lease obligations. Even if the landlord fails to honor the lease (e.g., fails to perform maintenance), the tenant must continue to pay rent.

Security deposit. A security deposit assures a tenant's performance of the lease obligations. A security deposit cannot exceed:

- 2 months rent - in an unfurnished, residential unit
- 3 months rent - in a furnished, residential unit
- an extra 1/2 month's rent if the tenant has a waterbed
- an "advance fee" of not less than 6 months- in leases longer than 6 months

In a residential lease, regardless of how the deposit is labeled ("advance fee", etc.) or the stated purpose (e.g., a "cleaning" or "security" deposit), the money is a refundable security deposit. All security deposits are refundable, less allowable and proven deductions for a tenant's default, such as final month's rent or damage.

The landlord must give written notice to the tenant informing them of their right to an initial inspection prior to their moving. If the tenant requests this inspection, they may be present or not and the landlord must do the inspection at a reasonable time, no earlier than two weeks before the termination of the lease. Based on the initial inspection, the landlord must provide an itemized list of repairs and the proposed deductions from the security deposit. The tenant may then use the time between the inspection and the termination of the lease to make repairs to avoid deductions from their security deposit.

The landlord must return the deposit in full or return the balance of the deposit with an itemized statement stating the reason and showing the amount of any deductions with accompanying receipts no sooner than 60 days from the expiration of the lease or within three weeks after a tenant vacates and surrenders the property.

If the property is sold, the landlord may return the deposit (less deductions) or transfer the security deposit to the new landlord by giving notice to the tenant of the name, address and phone number of the new landlord. If the original landlord fails to properly transfer or return the deposit, both the original landlord and the new landlord remain liable to the tenant for the amount of the deposit (less any lawful deductions).

If the landlord retains any portion of the deposit in bad faith, the landlord is liable for actual damages, along with penalty of up to twice the amount of the security.

Notice of Entry and Possession. In a *commercial lease*, the landlord has a right of entry to perform maintenance obligations following reasonable advance notice, unless otherwise specified in the lease.

In a *residential lease* a landlord may only enter the premises in specific situations, at certain times, and after giving (or attempting) advance notice. A landlord may not abuse this right or use it to harass the tenant. Except in cases of emergency or the tenant consents, a landlord may only enter during normal business hours with reasonable notice, generally 24 hours in advance.

Specifically, a landlord may enter **only**:
- in case of emergency;
- to make necessary or agreed repairs, decorations, alterations, or improvements;
- to supply necessary or agreed services;
- to show the unit to prospective or actual purchasers, mortgagees, tenants, workers, or contractors;
- when the tenant has abandoned or surrendered the premises; or
- pursuant to court order.

Notice for agreed repairs or services can be made orally with 24 hours advance notice provided the repairs are made within one week of the arrangement. When entering for showings to prospective purchasers, notice may be given orally if the landlord or agent notifies the tenant in writing within 120 days of the oral notice that the property is for sale. Notice should be 24 hours in advance and include the date, approximate time, and reason for entering.

Breach of the entry statues can be pursued under either: breach of the implied warranty of quiet enjoyment, including invasion of privacy and intentional infliction of emotional distress; or the statutory remedy of relief from harassment. Similarly, a landlord can petition for a court order to enter if a tenant fails to grant lawful access.

Quiet Enjoyment and Constructive Eviction
The essential privilege of a lease is the right to possess the premises. In every lease, the law implies that the landlord provide the tenant with possession and "quiet enjoyment" of the premises. This "covenant of quiet enjoyment" creates a promise that the landlord will not take or withhold any action disturbing a tenant's right to possession and quiet enjoyment.

The landlord may not cause any disturbance within their control that would render the property unsuitable for the use for which it was leased, known as "constructive eviction". These actions are defined as:

- a landlord's attempt to lease the property to a third party;
- harassment or unwarranted threats of expulsion;
- making extensive and unwarranted alterations which significantly interfere with the tenant's use and enjoyment; or
- failing to make necessary repairs.

Constructive eviction cannot be established if the tenant wrongfully or negligently causes the defects. A tenant must have a legal right to possession in order to claim of a breach of quiet enjoyment. If a landlord lawfully evicts a tenant, the tenant no longer has a legal right to occupy and would not constitute a violation of the quiet enjoyment covenant.

Maintenance
A landlord of a residential dwelling has a legal duty to keep the dwelling in a habitable condition. California law defines this duty as follows:

1. Effective waterproofing and weather protection of roof and exterior walls, including unbroken windows and doors;
2. Plumbing or gas facilities which conformed to applicable law in effect at the time of installation, maintained in good working order;

3. A water supply approved under applicable law, which is under the control of the tenant, capable of producing hot and cold running water, or a system which is under the control of the landlord which produces hot and cold running water, furnished to appropriate fixtures and connected to a sewage disposal system approved under applicable law;
4. Heating facilities which conformed with applicable law at the time of installation, maintained in good working order;
5. Electrical lighting, with wiring and electrical equipment which conformed with applicable law at the time of installation, maintained in good working order;
6. Building, grounds, and appurtenances at the time of commencement of the lease or rental agreement in every part clean, sanitary, and free from all accumulations of debris, filth, rubbish, garbage, rodents, and vermin, and all areas under control of the landlord kept in every part clean, sanitary, and free from all accumulations of debris, filth, rubbish, garbage, rodents, and vermin;
7. An adequate number of appropriate receptacles for garbage and rubbish, in clean condition and good repair at the time of the commencement of the lease or rental agreement, with the landlord providing appropriate, serviceable receptacles thereafter, and being responsible for the clean condition and good repair of such receptacles under his control; and
8. Floors, stairways, and railings maintained in good repair.

and goes on to include:

1. Install and maintain an operable deadbolt lock on each main swinging entry door of a dwelling unit;
2. for doors that cannot be equipped with deadbolt locks, the landlord must equip the door with a metal strap affixed across the midsection of the door with a deadbolt that protrudes into the doorjamb;
3. install and maintain operable window security or locking devices for windows that are designed to be opened; and
4. install locking mechanisms that comply with applicable fire and safety codes on the exterior doors that provide ingress or egress to common areas with access to dwelling units in multifamily developments.

California Health and Safety Code requires every dwelling intended for human occupancy have an operable smoke detector. The landlord is responsible for installing and maintaining the smoke detector, but the tenant has a duty to inform the landlord if it becomes inoperable.

As of 2016, The Carbon Monoxide Poisoning Prevention Act requires that every owner of a dwelling meant for human occupancy must have a carbon monoxide detector approved and listed by the State Fire Marshall in each existing dwelling unit having a fossil fuel burning heater or appliance, fireplace or an attached garage (including hotels, motels and "all other dwelling units").

In addition to the covenant of habitability and the landlord's maintenance obligations, various state laws and local housing codes require the landlord to keep a dwelling in good condition in accordance with specified structural, plumbing, electrical sanitation, fire and safety standards. Local government is generally empowered to investigate complaints and require the landlord to make needed repairs and/or to impose fines.

If the landlord fails to maintain a residential property in a condition fit for human occupancy, the tenant may give the landlord notice to repair the premises. If, after receipt of tenant's notice, the landlord fails within a reasonable time (usually 30 days) to make the repairs necessary, the tenant has the statutory right to either:

- spend up to one month's rent in repairs (only twice in any twelve-month period); or
- abandon the premises, in which case the tenant is relieved from the requirement of paying additional rent and the performance of other conditions of the lease.

Before the tenant may be entirely or partially absolved from paying rent or vacate the premises, the landlord must have failed to make the repairs. Conditions making a residential unit partially or entirely uninhabitable *does not automatically* give the tenant the right to reduce or stop paying rent. If a tenant vacates or pays a reduced rent (even in a good faith), the court may deny the claim that the premises are totally or partially uninhabitable. The court can rule that the tenant violated the lease by failing to pay the full rent, entitling the landlord to the same remedies as if a tenant simply failed to pay rent, including ordering the tenant be evicted and awarding the landlord damages for the rental value for the remaining term of the lease.

It is not always clear that a landlord's failure to maintain constitutes an actual breach of the implied warranty of habitability. As with the covenant of quiet enjoyment, a tenant risks that the court will not agree that the warranty has been breached. Additionally the law provides that if a tenant "contributes substantially" to the property being uninhabitable or interferes with the landlord's repair obligations, the landlord has no duty to repair the condition.

The tenant's legal obligations are:
- Keep his/her part of the property as clean and sanitary as the condition of the property permits (unless the landlord has expressly agreed in writing to do so);
- Dispose of rubbish, garbage, and other waste from the dwelling in a clean and sanitary manner (unless the landlord has expressly agreed in writing to do so);
- Properly use the plumbing, electrical and gas fixtures and keep them as clean and sanitary as their condition permits;
- Not permit any person on the property with the tenant's permission to willfully or wantonly destroy, deface, damage, impair, or remove any part of the structure or dwelling unit or the facilities, equipment, or appurtenances thereto; nor may the tenant do any such thing; and

- Occupy the property as an abode, using for living, sleeping, cooking, or dining purposes only those portions which were designed or intended to be so used.

In essence, if a tenant fails to pay rent, the landlord must continue to maintain the property for human habitability; and if the landlord fails to maintain the property, the tenant must continue to pay rent. Each may pursue other legal remedies.

Generally in commercial leases, repair obligations are specifically addressed in the lease. Essentially the landlord has no obligation maintain the property in tenantable condition except as specifically noted in the lease. The tenant must surrender possession of the premises in order to escape the obligation to pay rent.

Transfer of Lease

A landlord may **assign** its interest in leased property to a third party unless the lease states otherwise. The lease remains in effect with the new landlord and the tenant has the same rights and obligations.

By law, the tenant may also:

- **assign**-transfer the entire the premises for the entire remainder of the lease term; or
- **sublease/sublet**- transfer a portion of the premises, or the entire premises for less than the remaining lease term.

However, nearly all leases prohibit the tenant from subleasing or assigning or prohibit it without the landlord's consent.

Obligations for Assignment
As previously discussed, the assignment of any contract does not relieve the assignor (in this case, the original tenant) from its liability under the lease, unless the landlord expressly agrees to do so. The original tenant will remain liable under the lease throughout the remainder of the lease term. Unless assignees (new tenant) specifically assume all obligations, they are only responsible to the new landlord for those obligations under "privity of contract" (i.e., payment of rent and their duty to maintain).

Obligations for Sublease
Likewise, in a sublease the original tenant remains liable to the landlord for all obligations under the lease and for all acts by the subtenant. However, because there is neither "privity of contract" nor "privity of estate" between a subtenant and a landlord, a subtenant generally has no direct obligation to the landlord. All of the subtenant's rights run entirely through the tenant. The landlord *can only* enforce the lease provisions against the original tenant. If the landlord terminates the tenant's lease for default, whether it was the tenant or the subtenant who defaulted, the subtenant's rights in the premises will be simultaneously terminated.

6.2 Lease Terminations

A lease automatically *expires* without notice by either party at the end of the term specified. Since a lease is a contract, it may be *rescinded* if either party enters into the lease based on the other party's fraud or by either party relying on a mutual mistake.

It should be noted, some cities have rent and eviction control ordinances. Any attempt to terminate or evict a tenant occupying a unit subject to these controls can be severely limited and must be in compliance with the local ordinances.

A lease is *terminated* only:
- when a landlord or tenant exercises a specific right set forth in the lease, for instance
    - by notice
    - exercising an option to terminate, or
- as prescribed by law, for instance
    - either party's breach
    - illegal use of premises, or
- when a lease-terminating event occurs that is beyond the control of either the landlord or the tenant, for instance
    - death of the tenant
    - destruction of the property
    - abandonment and surrender of the premises

No lease may be terminated for any reason by:
- retaliatory eviction (e.g., landlord's retaliation for tenant's reporting health or safety code violations);
- discrimination against children or physically disabled persons; or
- discrimination under fair housing laws.

Termination by notice. Either party to a tenancy at will may terminate a lease by giving notice as provided in the terms and of the lease (except in instances of non-payment of rent or breach). Notice is given by advance written notice according to the rental term or 30 days, whichever is less. For instance, if the rent is paid weekly, then 7 days advance written notice is sufficient. Exceptions are:

- if the tenant has occupied more than one year - 60 days notice is required.
- if the unit is subject to City rent or eviction control - termination is limited to local laws and ordinances.
- if the unit is government subsidized - 90 days notice and "just cause" are required.
- mobile home parks - Owner/managers may only terminate or refuse renewal with 60 days notice and for the causes listed below:
    - failure to remedy governmental violations within a reasonable time after notification

- substantially disturbing other tenant's quiet enjoyment
- being convicted of practicing prostitution or felony controlled substances in the mobile home park
- failure to abide by rental agreement related to obeying rules and regulations of the home park
- nonpayment of rent or other home park charges
- Condemnation or change of use of the home park.

A fixed term lease automatically terminates upon expiration with no notice required by either party.

If a tenant fails to pay rent or breaches any other obligation under the lease, the landlord can terminate the lease and receive damages resulting from the nonpayment or breach. In this case, if the tenant refuses to give up possession, the landlord normally serves an appropriate notice (discussed below) and files an unlawful detainer action as a means to regain possession of the premises. These actions constitute an eviction which has three distinct steps:

- proper service of a 3-, 30-,60- or 90-day notice (depending on the nature of the breach and type of lease);
- legally filing, serving and prevailing in and "unlawful detainer" action; and
- recovering possession of the unit. If the tenant has not vacated, it is the landlord's right to have a sheriff physically remove them and their possessions.

If the tenant abandons the property, the landlord usually retakes possession and re-leases to others. At the end of the original lease term, the landlord may sue the old tenant for damages in the amount of the difference between the original leases total value and the amount actually received under the new lease.

A tenant in a foreclosed property has special protections. In a tenancy at will, the tenant must receive a 90-day notice prior to the unlawful detainer action being filed. In a fixed term lease, the tenant's lease is in full force and effect through the end of the lease term, except a 90-day notice may be given under the following circumstances:

- the property is re-sold and the purchaser will owner occupy as a primary residence; or
- the leaseholder is an immediate relative (spouse, parent, child) of the default mortgagor; or
- the rent is substantially less than fair market value, (except as may be reduced by subsidy or law); or
- the lease was not an arm's length transaction (i.e., between friends or in exchange for some other service, etc.)

Proper Notices

Notices of breaches have different timeframes and performance requirements depending on the reason for the notice.

3-day Notices - Ironically, there are three types of 3-day Notices as follows:
- Notice to Pay or Quit-used when tenant has failed pay rent.
- Notice to Quit - used when the tenant has committed a breach other than non-payment, specifically: a) uses the property for an unlawful purpose; b) materially damages the property; c) creates a nuisance on the property; d) subleases or assigns the tenancy in violation of the lease terms.
- Notice to Perform Covenants or Quit - used when a tenant has failed to perform some action or condition written into the lease agreement.

Tenants have 3 full days (12:01am-midnight) to comply beginning with the first day after the Notice is served. However, if Day 3 falls on a weekend or holiday, the period does not expire until midnight of the following Monday (or non-holiday).

30- and 60-day Notices - Used to terminate tenancies at will (except in cases of non-payment of rent or direct breach of agreement).
- 30-day is used when the tenant has occupied the unit for less than 1 year
- 60-day is used when the tenant has occupied the unit for a year or more

90-day Notices - Used for tenants in government subsidized housing. This notice must include "just cause", meaning there has to be a good reason for termination.

Proper Service of Notices
The notice of default or termination may be served in the following three ways:

- personal service - by delivery to the tenant in person;
- substitute service - by leaving a copy with a person of suitable age and discretion at the tenant's residence or place of business *and* mailing a copy to the tenant at the tenant's residence (if the tenant is not at home or their usual place of business); or
- Posting and mailing - by posting a copy in a conspicuous place on the premises and delivering a copy to any person occupying the premises, *and* mailing a copy to the tenant at the premises (if the tenant's place of residence or business address cannot be found and a person of suitable age and discretion cannot be found).

Service of 30-,60-, and 90-day Notices can be served as above OR by mailing a copy by Certified or Registered Mail.

Unlawful Detainer Actions
Proper delivery of a notice does not automatically terminate the lease. If the tenant fails to pay, perform or quit the premises after notice expires, the landlord may file an unlawful detainer action in court.

A defendant/tenant in an unlawful detainer proceeding has five days from service of the summons to file an answer with the court, or judgment will be entered in favor of the landlord. In the tenant's answer, the tenant must raise any affirmative defenses or they will be deemed waived. The most common defenses to an unlawful detainer action are:

- the landlord has not complied with the procedural requirements (e.g., failure to properly serve notice);
- the landlord has breached the implied warranty of habitability;
- the unlawful detainer was brought in retaliation for some lawful exercise of the tenant's rights (e.g., tenant's reporting landlord for violation of building or health code); or
- the landlord is evicting the tenant on the basis of the tenant's race or some other form of prohibited discrimination.

If the landlord wins the proceeding, the court will issue a "writ of possession" authorizing the local sheriff to remove the tenant and the tenant's belongings from the premises. A landlord is not permitted to enter the premises and forcibly remove the tenant or the tenant's property.

The purpose of the unlawful detainer procedure is to provide a landlord with a relatively quick and direct means of regaining possession following a tenant default and the tenant refuses to vacate voluntarily. Because possession is the focus, if a tenant relinquishes possession prior to the trial, the case is converted into an ordinary civil suit for damages and will not receive priority on the court's calendar. Similarly, if the tenant countersues or raises anything other than an affirmative defense, the same conversion holds true.

If a landlord files an unlawful detainer within 180 day of a tenant exercising a lawful right or remedy for breach by landlord under the lease terms, the landlord may guilty of a "**retaliatory eviction**". Such evictions are illegal and can result the landlord being held liable for damages and attorney's fees.

Proper Service of the Complaint or Summons for the unlawful detainer are the same as with the service of Notices above.

Self-Help Evictions
It is illegal for a landlord to remove a tenant by any means other than those laid out above. Landlords are lawfully prohibited from:
- changing locks or otherwise preventing entry or possession
- physically removing a tenant
- removing a tenant's belongings
- terminating utility services

and can be held liable for:
- actual damages

- a fine of up to $100 per day for each day the tenant was denied possession;
- a minimum of $250 for each separate act to deny the tenant possession;
- an injunction to prevent further acts; and
- attorney's fees.

Abandonment

If a tenant moves out of the property prior to the expiration of a fixed lease term or without giving proper notice, they are considered to have abandoned the property. Abandonment without proper cause (landlord's specific breach of the lease) does not absolve the tenant of their obligation to: pay any rent due through the end of the lease; and/or pay any reasonable loss of rent due to the landlord's obligation to re-rent the unit as soon as possible.

If a tenant does not provide notice of where to contact them, the landlord may prove abandonment if:
- the tenant becomes at least 14 days late on rental payments
- the landlord reasonably believes the unit has been abandoned
- the landlord mails or delivers a Notice of Belief of Abandonment to the tenant's last known address
- the tenant does not respond to any of the above by not paying rent or providing a written notice of not abandoning the property.

When all four of these conditions have been met, the premises is considered to be legally abandoned 15 days after the Notice of Belief of Abandonment (if served in person) or 18 days if mailed, and the landlord can regain possession of the property.

Disposition of Tenant Belongings

When a tenant is removed by a Sheriff or abandons the property, their personal belongings must be removed by the Sheriff or stored by the landlord. If the landlord stores the belongings, they must give written notice to the tenant or anyone they reasonably believe to be the owner of the belongings describing the belongings and stating a reasonable storage charge may be due prior to return. The notice must:
- contain one of two specific statements - one indicating the intended sale of the belongings at auction; and the other indicating a value of less than $700 providing for the sale or destruction without further notice.
- contain a date until which the property can be redeemed, not less than 15 days after the notice is delivered or 18 days if mailed

6.3 Disclosures Required by Owner or Rental Agent to Tenant

Fee Disclosure - Agents must provide written notification of whether or not the tenant is responsible to pay a fee for their services at the first face-to-face meeting. The notification must include the following:
- the amount of the fee;
- when it is due;
- circumstance under which all or a portion of the fee is refunded in the event the tenancy is not established;
- include the Agent's license number; and
- be signed by the Agent and prospective tenant or an acknowledgement that the tenant declined to sign.

Lead Based Paint Disclosure - Landlords (and their agents) owning property built prior to 1978 are required by Federal Law to:
- notify the tenant that the property is built prior to 1978;
- disclose the presence of lead based paints (if known)
- provide information relating to the hazards of lead based paint; and
- give the tenant the pamphlet entitled "Disclosure of Information on Lead-based Paint and/or Lead Based Paint Hazards."

It should be noted, the landlord is under no obligation to ascertain whether lead-based paint is present or to remove it. However, they must make the proper disclosures, provide the pamphlet and provide any information within their knowledge or possession.

Megan's Law Database Disclosure -As of April 1, 2006, every lease for residential property must contain the following specific words in no less than 8 point type:
> " Notice: Pursuant to Section 290.46 of the Penal Code, information about specified registered sex offends is made available to the public via an Internet Web site maintained by the Department of Justice at www.meganslaw.ca.gov. Depending on an offender's criminal history, this information will include either the address at which the offender resides or the community of residence and zip code in which he or she resides. (Neither Landlord nor Brokers (if any) are required to check this website. If Tenant wants further information, Tenant should obtain information directly from website.)"

Methamphetamine Contamination - If the Board of Health (or other appropriate official) serves notice that a unit or property is uninhabitable because of contamination by the production of methamphetamine, all occupants must vacate the affected areas until receipt of a notice of no further action required. Landlords (and their agents) must give a copy of the contamination notice to any tenant making an application for lease until the landlord receives the additional notice of no further action required.

Ongoing Pest Control Disclosure - Pest control companies are required to provide landlords and tenants written notice of the type of pesticides used in pest control. The landlord (and their agents) must provide a copy to new tenants intending to move in.

Military Ordnance Disclosure- Landlords (and their agents) who know their units are within 1 mile of a closed military Ordnance in which live ammunition or explosives were used, they must disclose this fact prior to the tenant signing the lease.

Management Disclosure - The owner, or agent acting on behalf of the owner, must disclose the name, address and contact information for each person authorized to manage the premises and receive notices and demands on behalf of the owner. A printed or typed written notice must be placed in every elevator and in one other conspicuous place, or in a non elevator building, posted in at least two conspicuous places.

Further Guidance

The State of California, Department of Consumer Affairs annually publishes a booklet entitled "California Tenants, A Guide to Residential Tenants' and Landlords' Rights and Responsibilities". A copy of the booklet can be downloaded from the Department of Consumer Affairs' web site at www.dca.ca.gov

6.4 Specialty Areas

Property Management

All brokers and salespeople should have a working knowledge of the general responsibilities and principals of property management. Specifically, property management is a specialty in which real estate brokers manage individual homes, apartment buildings, condominiums, large office and industrial complexes and shopping centers.

An agent's knowledge of agency, contracts, fair housing, rentals and leases makes up a considerable portion of property management requirements. Additionally, a professional manager would have knowledge of business administration, marketing, purchasing, credit, accounting, advertising, insurance, repairs and maintenance, taxation and public relations.

Professional Organizations

The Institute of Real Estate Management (IREM) and the National Association of Residential Property Managers (NARPM) are professional organizations dedicated to the improvement of the operational and ethical standards of its members.

IREM

In 1933 to foster professionalism and provide a source of management experience, a group of property management firms organized the Institute of Real Estate Management (IREM). To be a member, a property management firm is required to certify that it would adhere to the following guidelines:

- Maintain separate bank accounts for its own funds and for the funds of its clients, with no commingling;

- Carry a satisfactory fidelity bond on all of its employees whose duties involved the handling of funds; and,

- Refrain from taking discounts or commissions from purchases, contracts, or uses of clients' funds without full disclosure to, and permission from, the property owner.

Now, individuals meeting the educational and experience requirements are designated as Certified Property Managers (CPM). A lesser degree of training and on-site experience qualifies an individual as an Accredited Residential Manager (ARM). A firm that meets IREM's guidelines and utilizes at least one CPM can be designated as an Accredited Management Organization (AMO).

NARPM

NARPM offers professional designations, including RMP (Residential Management Professional) and MPM (Master Property Manager). The Association also offers a designation (CRMC – Certified Residential Management Company) for firms that manage single-family homes, and one for support staff (CSS – Certified Support Specialist).

Like IREM, NARPM promotes a high standard of business ethics, professionalism and fair housing practices. NARPM's Code of Ethics and Standards of Professionalism educate the membership on how a professional property manager should conduct business.

Types of Property Managers

There are three types of property managers:

- the individual property manager,
- the individual building manager, and
- the resident manager.

Individual Property Manager. An individual property manager is a real estate broker who manages properties for one or more property owners. Individuals may own their own firm, be a member of a management firm devoted full time to property management or be one of a number of property management specialists in a large real estate organization. Some property managers are asset managers, making the decisions of an owner relative to change of use, refinancing and sale. Asset managers frequently supervise other property managers.

Individual Building Manager. An individual building manager typically manages a single large property and may be employed by a property manager or directly by an owner.

Resident Manager. A resident manager lives on the premises they manage and may be employed by a real estate broker, managing agent or an owner to manage an apartment building on a part or full-time basis. California Law requires that every apartment building containing 16 units or more and mobile home parks with 50 units or more must have a resident manager.

Functions of a Property Manager

The property manager has a dual responsibility: to the owner or client who is interested in the highest monetary return from the property; and to the tenants, who are interested in the best value for their money, including reasonable safety and compliance with fair housing laws.

The property manager must promptly rent the property/units at the highest market rent possible, keep operational and other costs within budget, and preserve and enhance the physical value and prestige of the property. Some specific duties include:

- establish the rental schedule that will bring the highest yield.
- merchandise the space and collect the rent.
- create and supervise maintenance schedules and repairs.
- develop a tenant/resident relations policy.
- hire, direct and supervise employees and building staff.
- audit and pay bills.
- maintain proper records and make regular reports to the owner.

- advertise and publicize vacancies through selected media and broker lists.
- qualify and investigate a prospective tenant's credit.
- prepare and execute leases.
- obtain decorating specifications and secure estimates.
- inspect vacant space and recommend alterations as the market dictates.
- keep abreast of the times and competitive market conditions.
- be knowledgeable about and comply with applicable Federal, State and local laws.

6.5 Development

Developers can be national, regional or local. Development is very high risk, generally due to long term carrying costs and the necessity to anticipate the real estate climate. There are no state licensing requirements for developers or subdividers; if you've got the courage and the financing, you can make (or break) your fortune.

"Land developers" specialize in converting raw land to finished lots, selling to builders who then construct and sell the individual properties. Often, the land developer will begin construction of improvements, installing off-site improvements and infrastructure (roads and utilities).

Other developer-builders plan and complete the entire subdivision from raw land through the construction and sale of homes. In the course of business, a developer often:

- carries inventory of raw land, semi-finished and/or finished products;
- has several ongoing projects both "spec" (for sale) and custom (pre-sold);
- uses personal funds or negotiates loans from land sellers, joint venture partners (private investors) or financial institutions; and
- assumes large risks due to planning uncertainties and misjudgment of the market resulting in delays and losses due to interest payments, carrying charges, overhead, and other costs.

Subdividing

A subdivider, builder or developer must understand the potential difficulties involved in subdividing and the potential market for the project. The development plan must take into account state and local government regulation (e.g., the Subdivided Lands Law, the Subdivision Map Act, the California Environmental Quality Act, zoning) and nearly as important, public opinion.

Zoning and planning regulations drastically reduce the potential of a property. Before a developer or builder purchases property, they must consult with the local planning agency and private land use specialists to evaluate the likelihood of final approval of a project and the time frames for the approval process.

To determine the profit yield, the developer must calculate:

- cost of the land;
- government fees;
- off-site improvements (e.g., water mains, sewers, streets, gutters, curbs, sidewalks, and street lighting);
- survey, legal, marketing, financing and office/overhead costs; and,

- the future sales price(s) of the lots or unit.

The developer's estimate of how quickly the lots will sell (the absorption rate) will impact the marketing, financing, and overhead costs, all adjusted for anticipated market fluctuations. The sum of all costs and expenses, subtracted from the estimated sale prices, derives the estimated profit, along with factoring in "soft costs" (promotion, financing and administrative costs) before profits are actually realized. In order to accurately calculate these costs, the developer must formulate a specific plan for:

- physical layout of project;
- land use processing and approval schedule;
- financing, from construction through the last sale;
- amenities to be provided;
- promotional advertising and sales management.

At times, developers subdivide a large tract of land according to a phased master plan, meaning a portion of the improvements are built and sold with the stipulation that additional units will then be built and sold at a later date. This alleviates some of the longer term financing and carry costs and avoids overstraining the market demand/absorption rates. These projects are more complex, with more governing restrictions and more obstacles to state and local approval.

Developer-Builder

Development and building requires financing for land acquisition, use approval and subdividing, construction, marketing, and carrying costs of properties until sale. Developer-builders may set up subsidiaries: one company to hold title and subdivide the property; another to conduct building operations; and another for sales and marketing.

Subdividing and building, like all real estate activities is cyclical; high productivity and profit may be followed by depressed sales and losses. The fluctuating nature of land costs, unpredictability of land use approvals, credit terms and property values must all be accurately factored into the process.

Home Construction

The details of home construction methods and pricing materials are not generally within the scope of the real estate licensee's role. However, an effective agent should have a working knowledge of the following general areas:

- Prices per square foot for varying styles of home and quality of construction
- Styles of architecture and how to identify them, along with common concerns and desirability of certain floor plans and specific room layouts, i.e. separate dining or family rooms?
- Maintenance and desirability of exterior surface materials

- Types of roofing, mechanical systems (heating/cooling, plumbing, electrical), windows, and general costs of installation and operation

- Prevention of dry rot, mold/fungus and insect infestations?

- What restrictions governing maintenance or improvements run with the property?

6.6 Sale and Leasing of Businesses (Business Opportunity)

Real Estate Law defines "business opportunity" as the sale or lease of the business and the goodwill of an existing business enterprise or opportunity. In 1966 California merged the licensing for business opportunities and real estate, essentially requiring real estate licensing for anyone negotiating the sale, purchase or lease of a business.

The sale of a business opportunity may involve only personal property and not the real property. Typical transactions involve retail stores, automotive service businesses, restaurants and bars, bakeries, etc. The sale generally includes the inventory, fixtures, non-competition agreement, lease assignment and goodwill.

If real property is involved in the sale, the agent must treat the sale of the business and sale of the land/building as two separate and concurrent transactions. The sale of the business being personal property, transferred by Bill of Sale and a separate sale of real property transferred by deed with two concurrent and contingent escrows.

Agency

In most business opportunity transactions, the real estate licensee will be acting as a dual agent, with the informed consent of the principals. Thus, the licensee is in a fiduciary relationship with both the buyer and seller.

A broker may be asked to counsel a business opportunity buyer. As previously discussed, it is imperative that this advice cannot be construed as legal advice or as representations regarding the future viability of the business.

Important topics for consideration include:

- money the buyer can invest, including necessary start-up costs, (inventory, deposits with utilities, licenses and permits, lease payment, advertising, etc.); and where additional funds, if needed, may be borrowed;

- expected credit terms from suppliers;

- buyer's net income expectations and unexpected expenses or losses; and,

- the likelihood that the current financial statement (balance sheet) and earnings statement (profit and loss) of the business and the buyer's financial statement will be adequate to obtain a direct loan from a bank or a loan through the SBA.

Listings

Listings should be taken with great care after evaluating the business location, operation and the seller's records and financial statements (profit and loss statements, balance sheets and business tax statements for at least the last three years). The seller, or seller's accountant or attorney, should cooperate in furnishing the broker with income and expense records and copies of leases, insurance policies, inventory records for resale items, equipment, furniture, sales tax reports, IRS schedules, etc., so that the agent can evaluate the quality of the business and its income stream to arrive at a fair market price and listing terms with the seller.

Most authorizations to sell require a good deal more information about the property than would be necessary in listing a residence. The Business Disclosure Statement (C.A.R. Form BDS) can assist in establishing the listing price, a disclosure of material facts regarding the operation of the Business and a proposal of items to be included in or excluded from sale; the BDS's relation to the purchase agreement; and the owner's warranty of the accuracy of the information provided and that the owner has good and marketable title to the Business and personal property being offered for sale. The BDS has provisions for the owner to provide the financial information for the most recent year-to-date and the preceding three years.

A business opportunity broker must ensure that all representations concerning a business are those of the owner or seller. A broker may be liable for any personal representations or projections that he or she makes.

Franchising

Franchising is a business plan whereby a firm (franchisor) agrees to provide a purchaser-investor (franchisee) the right to offer, sell or distribute goods or services under a marketing plan or system prescribed by the franchisor, for a franchise fee.

Franchising allows investors to benefit from the expert management, assistance, special training, and marketing and promotional know-how of the franchisor while being self-employed. Popular franchise are areas are: real estate, food services, hotels and motels, convenience stores, and fitness.

There are many risks to consider in purchasing a franchise and a real estate licensee should possess the required knowledge of the entire system before considering this type of specialty.

Escrow

The use of an escrow holder specializing in business bulk transfers is advisable for all business opportunity transactions. It is the escrow holder's responsibility to insure that both the obligations and benefits of the Bulk Sales Law and, if applicable, the Secured Transactions statutes concerning personal property transfers and security devices have been met and/or obtained.

Escrow instructions generally require the escrow holder to:

- conduct lien searches;
- publish, record, and mail to the tax collector the appropriate Notice(s) to Creditors of Bulk Transfer;

- obtain the designated tax releases from the government agencies who could otherwise impose successor tax liability upon the buyer; and,
- act as a general "clearing house" depository for funds, documents, instruments and delivery of same at close of escrow, at which time the escrow holder provides an accounting.

Business Opportunity Involving Liquor Licenses

The sale or lease of a business involving the manufacture, sale or distribution of alcohol is a specialty of its own, governed by the ever changing Alcoholic Beverage Control Act. The Department of Alcoholic Beverage Control issues licenses to qualified people or businesses at specific, approved locations.

The prospective purchaser must apply and receive approval for the license to be validly transferred. There are several factors involved in transfer approval and it should never be assumed the application will be successful. Before filing a license transfer application, the applicant and current licensee must file a notice of intended transfer with the county and establish an escrow. Escrow may not release any consideration before the ABC approves transfer of the license. Then, transfer of the business will occur simultaneously with transfer of the license.

Bulk Sales

A bulk sale is the selling off of more than half the value of a seller inventory (outside of the normal course of doing business) and is governed by the Uniform Commercial Code. In this case, at least 12 days in advance of the sale, the **buyer** must: record notice of the sale in each county where the inventory is stored; and publish at least one notice in a major newspaper in the appropriate judicial district.

The purpose of the notices is to alert any creditors to the sale and give them time to file any claims upon the proceeds, preventing the seller from absconding with the money. If the notice requirement is not properly met or intentionally concealed, the **buyer** becomes liable for valid claims brought by prior creditors.

Mineral, Oil and Gas Brokerage

As of 1994, a separate license is no longer required for a licensed real estate broker or salesperson to engage in Mineral, Oil and Gas transactions. All M.O.G. licenses may be renewed, but no new M.O.G. licenses are issued.

A real estate agent may now solicit, negotiate and broker the sale, purchase or exchange of mineral, oil or gas properties. A real estate license is also required to assist or offer to assist another in filing an application for the purchase or lease, or to locate or enter upon mineral, oil or gas properties owned by the state or federal government.

Anyone acting as a principal in the purchase, lease optioning mineral, oil or gas land *for the purpose of selling, leasing assigning, etc.* must obtain a real estate license. In addition, anyone acting as a principal who offers mining claims for sale or assignment must also have a real estate license.

STUDY SMART GUIDE

Lease - exclusive use and possession to a parcel of land or space, along with the benefits and enjoyment of that use, in exchange for consideration (rent), referred to as "chattel real". An *executory contract.*

Types of Leases - Fixed or Gross Lease, Graduated, Net Lease, Percentage Lease, Ground Lease.

Lease Term - period of time during which the tenant may occupy the premises.

Lease renewal - creates a new and distinct tenancy, executed as an entirely new lease.

Lease extension - continuation under the original lease.

Rent - consideration paid for possession, use, and enjoyment of leased property.
Privity of contract - a tenant is obligated to pay rent even if the tenant never enters into possession of the premises.
Privity of estate - obligation to pay rent resulting from a tenant's occupancy of the premises.
Security deposit - deposit assuring a tenant's performance of the lease obligations.
Quiet Enjoyment - essential privilege of a lease is the right to possession and "quiet enjoyment".
Constructive Eviction - any disturbance that would render the property unsuitable for use as intended.
Lease assignment - transfer of entire premises for the entire remainder of the lease term.
Sublease/sublet - transfer of a portion or the entire premises for less than the remaining lease term.
Eviction - an unlawful detainer action as a means for landlord to regain possession of the premises after a breach of the lease.
3-day Notices - *Notice to Pay or Quit*-for nonpayment of rent; *Notice to Quit*- for breach other than non-payment of rent; *Notice to Perform Covenants or Quit* - for failed to perform some action or condition of lease agreement.

30- and 60-day Notices - terminates tenancies at will - 30 days for less than 1 year occupancy; 60 days for more than one year.
90-day Notices - for tenants in government subsidized housing and must include "just cause".
Self-Help Evictions - Illegal eviction by changing locks, physically removing a tenant, removing a tenant's belongings and/or terminating utility services.
Abandonment - tenant moves prior to the expiration of lease or without proper notice.
Fee Disclosure - written notification of whether tenant is responsible to pay a fee for services, required at the first face-to-face meeting.

Property management - specialty in which real estate brokers manage individual homes, apartment buildings, condominiums, large office and industrial complexes and shopping centers.

Types of Property Managers - individual property manager, individual building manager, and the resident manager.

Developers - can be national, regional or local; no state licensing

Land developers - specialize in converting raw land to finished lots, selling to builders. Often constructs preliminary roads and utilities).

Developer-builders/Subdividers - plans and completes subdivisions from raw land through the construction and sale of finished homes.

Business opportunity - sale or lease of a business and the goodwill; requires a real estate license.

Franchise - a business plan whereby franchisor provides franchisee the right to offer, sell or distribute goods or services under a marketing system prescribed by the franchisor, for a franchise fee.

Business Opportunity Involving Liquor Licenses - sale or lease of a business involving the manufacture, sale or distribution of alcohol is a specialty of its own, governed by Alcoholic Beverage Control Act. Requires approval for license transfer.

Bulk Sales - selling off of more than half the value of inventory (outside of normal business) and governed by the Uniform Commercial Code.

Mineral, Oil and Gas Brokerage - No separate license required but anyone acting as a principal for the purpose of selling, leasing assigning, etc or offering mining claims for sale must obtain a real estate license.

Chapter 6
Quiz & Answers

1) Lease are:
   a) ongoing and executory
   b) personal property
   c) can be orally modified
   d) a and b only

2) When no lease term is specified:
   a) lease continue until one party gives notice
   b) the lease is invalid
   c) the lease can be terminated at any time
   d) lease terms are governed by law

3) Which of the following is true:
   a) the tenant must pay rent even if they never move in
   b) rent must always include some form of money
   c) excess rent must be promptly returned if the tenant moves early
   d) it is illegal to charge late fees on rent

4) Security Deposits:
   a) cannot exceed one month's rent
   b) are always fully refundable
   c) are used to assure tenant's compliance
   d) are required by law

5) In the event of non-payment, the landlord can:
   a) change the locks
   b) serve a 3-day notice
   c) begin showing the apartment to new tenants
   d) all of the above

6) An unlawful detainer is:
   a) the landlord's right to hold your belongings until the rent is paid
   b) a tenant who unlawfully occupies an apartment after the lease expires
   c) the landlord's right to change the locks
   d) the court action to begin the eviction process

7) An individual property manage:
   a) manages only one property
   b) owns an individual management company
   c) is the only property manager at their firm
   d) none of the above

8) Which of the following is true of Developers:
   a) they must be licensed in the state
   b) they can be regional or national
   c) they must specialize in either land or housing development
   d) they must oversee the entire project until completion

9) The sale or lease of a business:
   a) involves only the personal property of the business
   b) is called a business opportunity
   c) requires an agent to be an undisclosed dual agent
   d) requires the agent to provide legal and business advice

10) A liquor license:
    a) automatically passes with sale
    b) must be cancelled and re-issued after sale
    c) must be approved for transfer simultaneously with sale
    d) none of the above

ANSWERS:

1. d	3. a	5. b	7. d	9. b
2. d	4. c	6. d	8. b	10. c

Chapter 7

Chapter 7: Property Valuation and Appraisals

The ability to ascertain accurate values for real and personal property is among the most essential tools for success as a real estate agent. Only a thorough understanding of real estate values will enable agents to truly serve their clients and fulfill their obligations under the law. By far, the single question most frequently asked of a real estate agent is: "How much is my (or that) property worth?"

7.1 Values

Brokers and salespersons must have a commanding understanding of:
- the theoretical concepts of value;
- the conditions affecting value; and
- the most appropriate method of accurately estimating value.

Value Defined

Value is the current worth of all rights and future benefits of owning a particular piece of property, relative to the typical user or investors. For the purposes of property valuations and appraisals, you are generally dealing with two classes of value: *market value* and *subjective value*.

- **Market value** - the most probable price a property would bring when freely offered on the open market between a willing buyer and a willing seller. Market value should not be confused with market price. Market price is the *actual* sale price of a particular property and may or may not have been an arm's length transaction".

- **Subjective value** ("Utility Value" or "Value in Use") - the value of improvements or amenities to a specific person (i.e., a secluded property abutting conservation land may be more valuable to an outdoorsy person vs. someone who wants to walk to dining and nightlife; or installing an elaborate home gym may or may not have significant value to couch potatoes).

Elements of Value

There are basically four elements of value, all of which are essential. These are best remembered by the acronym DUST:

- **D**emand - relates to the public's desire for the property and is generally considered together with the financial ability to purchase.

- **U**tility-relates to usefulness or a property's ability to satisfy a need (i.e. shelter or income).

- **S**carcity-relates to the availability of property (or types of property).

- **T**ransferability- relates to the ability to transfer (sell, gift, lease) property.

None of these elements alone will create value. For example, something can be scarce but, without some desirable use (utility), there is no demand for it. By the same token, if something is not transferrable, it cannot be sold. Real estate cycles cause fluctuations in these elements of value. For example, when interest rates increase, fewer buyers are able to qualify for loans. This in turn reduces demand, usually leading to a lack of scarcity and eventually driving values downward.

External Forces Influencing Value

There are four external forces that create, expand or destroy value. Each of these factors changes constantly and when taken together essentially determines the value of a given location.

- **Environmental and physical characteristics**

    - Environmental - climate, earthquakes, ease of access to other areas and proximity to recreation or business centers.

    - Physical - amenities such as quality of schools, availability of local shopping and public transportation.

- **Social ideals and standards** such as population growth, age, birth and death rates; and attitudes toward education and recreation.

- **Economic influences** such as unemployment, wage levels; availability of credit, interest rates and rental prices.

- **Political or government regulations** such as zoning laws, building codes, rent controls and environmental legislation affecting new development.

7.2 Principals of Valuation

A basic knowledge of the underlying principals of valuation is essential to developing methods for understanding and evaluating value.

- **Principle of substitution.** This principle is the essence of property valuation. Value is set by the cost of an equally desirable substitute. The value of a property to its current owner generally cannot exceed the value of other similar properties. In short, when all else is equal, a buyer cannot be expected to pay more than the price of an equivalent substitute.

- **Principle of supply and demand.** Price variations relate directly to the balance between supply and demand. Increasing supply leads to decreased demand and tends to lower value; and conversely, increasing demand leads to reduced supply and tends to increase value.

- **Principle of competition.** Substantial profits lead to more competition to reap those profits. When there is increased demand for new construction, competition among builders can affect the balance between supply and demand. This in turn can result in lower prices, which may then create a renewed lack of supply, resulting in increasing prices.

- **Principle of highest and best use.** The most profitable use of a parcel of land is known as "highest and best use"; meaning the improvements to the land that produce the greatest net return. For instance, a single home on a parcel zoned for 25 apartment units is not considered the highest and best use and must be taken into consideration when determining value.

- **Principle of change.** Property values are in a constant state of change. Economic, environmental, government, and social forces all affect real estate values.

- **Principle of conformity.** Maximum value is realized when land uses are compatible and architecturally harmonious (picture a single house surrounded by high-rise office buildings).

- **Principle of balance.** Value is created and sustained when highest and best use is maintained. *Over-improvement* or *under-improvement* creates an imbalance. For instance, in a neighborhood undergoing revitalization, the value of the unrenovated (under-improved) home is not in balance with that of its bright and shiny neighbors.

- **Principle of progression.** The worth of a lesser-valued property is enhanced by proximity to properties of greater value.

- **Principle of regression.** The worth of a greater-valued property is diminished by proximity to properties of lesser value.

- **Principle of contribution.** Improvements to a property are valued relative to the increased value of the whole property or by the decreased value when they are absent (i.e., a new kitchen adds value; the immediate need for a new kitchen decreases value.)

- **Principle of anticipation.** Value is created by anticipated future benefits and future resale values. Past values are used to anticipate future benefits.

- **Principle of four-stage life cycle.** Property is characterized by four distinct stages: *growth, stability, decline, and revitalization.* Properties, neighborhoods, etc., generally follow this pattern of growth and decline, frequently followed by revitalization starting the process anew.

Appreciation and Depreciation in Value

Appreciation is any increase in value, most often due to factors such as increased demand or contribution.

Depreciation (as it relates to valuation) is any loss in value. Do not confuse "actual depreciation" (related to valuation) with the accounting /tax method of depreciation (usually "book depreciation"). It is considered that there are three main factors causing depreciation.

- **Deterioration** - the physical result of uncorrected wear and tear over time (often referred to as "deferred maintenance"), and natural causes such as flooding etc.

- **Functional Obsolescence** - the result of functional aspects of a property becoming outdated or obsolete. This occurs as styles (as in kitchens and bathrooms) and preferences (open floor plans, multiple baths, garages) change or as the result of an over-improvement not adding requisite value (remember the elaborate gym and the couch potato analogy).

- **Locational or External Obsolescence** - the result of outside influences such as neighborhood deterioration, proximity to undesirable areas (airports, high traffic) or even changes in zoning laws or environmental restrictions.

Depreciation can be:

- **curable** - when repairs and/or re-design and renovations can be made to overcome ("cure") the deterioration and/or functional obsolescence; and

- **incurable** - economic or locational obsolescence are beyond a homeowner's ability to control (incurable); or when the repairs or renovations necessary to cure functional obsolescence or deterioration would cost more than the value of the property once restored.

7.2 Appraisals

Appraisers in California must hold a valid Appraising License. At this point, it is important to distinguish between an appraisal and a Broker's Price Opinion or CMA. A BPO or CMA is a less formal, but educated, opinion of value designed to provide information necessary to establish and understand the range of values in a particular area over a certain period of time. This option is generally compiled for a homeowner (seller) or potential buyer considering the current real estate climate. To develop the opinion or analysis, the broker must follow the standards and principals for determining value.

Broker's Price Opinion (BPO) or Comparative Market Analysis (CMA)

A Comparative Market Analysis or BPO analyzes the asking prices of comparable properties that are currently listed, but not sold; the asking prices of properties that are in escrow, but not closed; as well as the selling prices of those that have recently sold and closed (ideally within 3-6 months) are all considered. This allows a homeowner or potential buyer to develop an accurate picture of the appropriate asking price and/or selling price for a given home.

As mentioned, clients will constantly ask you to evaluate a property's value. Your first response must be "I'm not a licensed appraiser, but I may be able to help you understand value. Why do you need the information?" Generally, a formal appraisal is needed for most legal purposes such as mortgages and estate or financial settlements.

Purposes and Uses of Appraisals

The basic purpose of an appraisal is to estimate value for a particular reason (i.e., supporting evidence of sales price, loan value, financial settlements, etc.). Some of the circumstances requiring the estimate of value are:

1. *Transfer of ownership of property.* Generally a BPO or CMA is used in discussing the listing and sale prices of property, however, there are instances when a formal appraisal can be helpful in contentious situations, or
    a) in the case of a trade, as an independent verification of competing opinions.
    b) a formal appraisal is required for estate or financial settlements.
2. *Financing and credit.* Lenders use the appraisal to determine if the property is of sufficient value to secure the mortgage or to measure the profit projections of real estate projects.
3. *Insurance Purposes.* Appraisals are required to settle claims if a property has been destroyed and for the replacement cost associated with the amount of coverage.
4. *Appraisal for taxation purposes.* Appraisals are used for reassessing value for property taxes; determining the amount of estate or gift taxes; and in the case of income property, the basis of depreciation for income tax purposes.
5. *Condemnation actions.* When the government takes property by eminent domain, appraisals are needed to estimate the price and damages to be awarded to the property owner.
6. *Other.*
    a) Estimating market rents in lease negotiations.

b) Fraud.
c) Damage awards.
d) Division-of-estates. A distribution of property under the terms of a will, in divorce proceedings, or between rival claimants usually requires the value of the property be determined by appraisal.

7.3 The Appraisal Process

Consistently and accurately valuating property is somewhat of an art form. While much of the final result is based on a depth of knowledge and understanding of the ever-changing marketplace, there is a process. Following are the steps to developing an appraisal:

1) Identify the purpose of the appraisal
    - Who is requesting the appraisal and for what purpose
    - What are the pertinent characteristics of the property for the intended use (land, building desirability, restrictions)
2) Identify the specific data relative to the pertinent characteristics and where to find the information
3) Collect and analyze the data
4) Apply the appropriate method(s) of valuation (see below) and establish an opinion of value
5) Reconcile the valuation methods and adjustments to confirm a final opinion of value and finalize the report with supporting documentation.

Methods of Valuation

There are three approaches to consider when estimating value. Many times, it's necessary to use the approaches in conjunction with one another; a process commonly referred to as "reconciliation". The basic approaches are:

- **Sales comparison approach.** Recent sales and listings of similar properties and locations are analyzed. This approach is the most common for real estate agents offering a BPO or CMA.

- **Cost approach.** This approach establishes the value of the land (as if vacant), added to the current cost of reproducing/purchasing the improvements, less depreciation. This approach is often *reconciled* with or used as an alternative to the Sales Comparison Approach when there is a lack of similar property data or when a property requires significant renovation in order to compare with similar properties.

- **Income approach.** The estimated potential or future income of a property is capitalized into value by this approach.

Just as nearly every property differs from another, the reasons for making an appraisal can also differ. A developer trying to establish the costs of a piece of land on which to develop lots and sell homes has radically different motivations, financial requirements and price points than the homebuyer looking for a long term home in which to raise a family. Additionally, the reason for the appraisal varies widely. The value of a home to a prospective purchaser is different than to the lender, the insurer and the tax collector. All of these influences affect both the approach to estimate value and ultimately, the consideration of that value.

As a result, the very first step in any appraisal is to be clear about the purpose of the appraisal and which value is needed. Another factor is the availability of sufficient data to formulate the opinion. A home in a subdivision with several recent sales lends itself perfectly to the straight sale comparison approach. A property that is radically dissimilar or in need of major renovation may require a combination of the sales comparison and cost approach. In this case, each approach is worked through independently and then reconciled against one another to reach a conclusion of value.

Factors Affecting Value

Once data is compiled and approaches are identified, it is necessary to reconcile the subject property and make positive and negative adjustments in value. The basic criteria to be considered are:

- location, neighborhood and nuisances (airports, railroads etc.);

- lot size, topography, desirability and improvements; and

- if site is improved; the age, architectural style, size, room arrangement and count, number of bedrooms and baths, general condition, superior/inferior repair and design, special features, higher/lower quality of construction and finishes.

7.4 Sales Comparison Approach

This approach compiles data using similar properties. Appraisers use the principle of substitution; using comparables as similar as possible to the subject relative to the factors in a given price range. Generally, if you can find 3-5 good comparable properties for sale, 3-5 pending escrow and 3-5 sales closed; the better the result. This data is laid out on a grid showing the adjustments and then reconciled for the final report.

Sample Sales Comparison Grid

The Grid shown here is a sample of the recent sales portion of the appraisal or BPO. It assumes the subject property is a 3-year old, 3-bedroom Colonial with a 2-car garage in good condition on an average to good- sized lot with no locational obsolescence.

	Comparables			Subject
	Data 1	Data 2	Data 3	
Sales Price	$862,000	$827,000	$878,000	?
Adjustments				
Financing	Conventional	Conventional	Conventional	
Conditions of Sale	None	None	None	
Sale Date	June	September	October	
Adjustments	None	None	None	
Location	.7 mi - similar	.5 mi - similar	1.2 mi - superior arts district -20,000	
Lot and Views	4500 - Some	3500 - Train nearby +10,000	5600 - Good -7,000	5200 - Some
Age/Style	3-Colonial	5-Colonial	5-Gambrel Colonial	3-Colonial
Square footage	2,400	2,430	2,550	2,450
Garage	2	1 +5000	2	2
Rooms	7	7	9 -2500	7
Bedrooms	3	3	4	3
Bathrooms	3	2.5 +5,000	3	3
Overall Condition	Excellent	Good	Excellent	Excellent

		+10,000		
Adjustments	None	*(inferior) +35,000	*(superior) -29,500	
Reconciliation				
Net Adjustments	None	+$35,000	-$29,500	
Adjusted Sale Price	$862,000	$862,000	$857,500	
Indicated Value				$860,000

7.5 Cost Approach

As discussed, the Cost Approach calculates value as the combination of: the value of the land (as if vacant); *and* the cost to reconstruct or reproduce any buildings as new, *less* the depreciation of the building due to age and/or deterioration and obsolescence compared to a new building. Once again, we apply principle of substitution: value is set by the price of an equivalent substitute.

The formula for determining value using this approach is:

Value = Land Value + Replacement or Reproduction Cost – Accrued Depreciation

Estimating Cost New

The Cost Approach views the value of the building at its cost of reconstruction as new. The two most common bases for calculating costs new are:

- **Replacement Cost New** - views the building as if reconstructed with modern methods, design and materials. The advantage of Replacement Cost is the availability of accurate current costs of modern methods, design and materials. Replacement Cost New is the most frequently used Cost Approach base.

- **Reproduction Cost New** - calculates the cost of reconstructing a replica ("reproduction") of the appraised building on date of valuation. This is a replica in both design and materials. Pricing labor and materials can sometimes prove difficult for materials no longer widely available or installed by hand labor. Reproduction Cost New is most useful for certain methods of calculating depreciation, unique or antique construction and some court proceedings.

Each of these bases can be valuable in estimating cost as new. But each is a distinct approach and they should not be confused.

Steps in the Cost Approach

1. Estimate the land's current market value, assumed vacant and available for improvement to its highest and best use. Land value is usually based on a market approach utilizing comparable market data of similar sites in the area. Find the per square foot costs to determine an average value per sq. ft. and apply those numbers to our lot.

Example

Sales	Price	Date	Size (feet)	Square Feet
1	$5,000	January	50 x 120	6,000
2	$4,750	June	40 x 130	5,200
3	$5,500	September	50 x 120	6,000
Opinion based on the above examples	$6,600	September	50 x 150	7,500

2. Estimate the cost new of reconstructing the buildings and other improvements.
    - Select the proper cost new base: *Reproduction Cost* of duplicating the replica of the appraised building using original materials and design on date of value; or *Replacement Cost* of replacing the building using modern materials, methods, and design on date of appraisal.
    - Do a property inspection, description, measurement, and plot plan of building improvements and equipment, noting the type, style, quality, and condition of building materials and workmanship.
    - Select method of cost new estimating. The **Square-Foot Method** is the most common method used on the West Coast to estimate construction costs. In this method, the property being appraised is compared with similar structures where costs are known. Standard building types whose costs are known are broken down to a cost per square foot of floor area. The building being appraised is compared with the most similar type of building and its cost per square foot is used for the subject property. Adjustments must be made for size and various exterior and interior features. Though adjustments cannot be made for all variables, this method is generally accurate enough for most real estate purposes.

Abstraction Method

The abstraction method is used to obtain land value where there are no vacant land sales. The steps are:

    a. Research property sales in the same neighborhood on lots with similar characteristics.

    b. Estimate of the cost new of the improvements is made.

  c. An amount is deducted from cost new for accrued depreciation.

  d. The depreciated cost of the improvements is deducted from the selling price of the property.

  e. The difference represents an approximation of land value.

Example:

Appraised lot size is 65' X 100' = 6,500 sq.ft. Sale property is 6,000 sq. ft. lot with a single family residence and sold for $83,000. The sale building has an estimated cost new of $61,000 and an accrued depreciation estimated at $20,000. Land value by abstraction:

Price of sale property $83,000

Less depreciated value of improvements:

Cost new $61,000

Less accrued depreciation $20,000

Depreciated value $41,000

Indicated land value $42,000

Divide by lot size .... ÷ 6000 sq.ft.

Indicated lot value/sq.ft. .... $7.00/sq.ft.

Multiply by subject lot size:

65' x 100' = 6,500 sq.ft. .... x 6,500

Indicated value of lot $45,500

Factors in Land analysis and valuation

As the old saying goes: the three most important factors in ascertaining value are; 'location, location, location'. The physical location of the property by street, block, neighborhood, and city is heavily weighted for the valuation of a particular site. Additionally, since sites are often unique in any number of ways including; dimensions, layout, topography (such as being flat or sloped); some, even though comparative in size, are simply superior to others. It is important that each site be analyzed individually.

Calculating Depreciation

Depreciation has two uses: one for the appraiser and another for a tax professional or owner concerned with tax deductions. The definitions and uses of depreciation are:

  Book depreciation - a tax accounting calculation of steady depreciation from owner's original purchase price or cost basis. This act of depreciating assets is an income tax deduction, allowing the owner to recover the cost of the investment over the "useful life" of the improvement. It is often the motivation to purchase or exchange income properties.

Actual depreciation - actual depreciation is just as it says. It is a building's loss of value due to factors previously discussed. Actual depreciation used by appraisers is:

- a loss in value;
- determined by market data, property condition, etc.; and
- deducted from current reconstruction cost new.

Accrued depreciation - depreciation which has already occurred up to the date of value. As previously discussed, it may be classified either as curable or incurable based on the economic feasibility.

Remainder depreciation - depreciation which will occur in the future.

Methods of Calculating Accrued Depreciation

There are two common methods of calculating accrued depreciation:

- straight line or age-life method - depreciation which occurs annually in proportion to the improvement's total estimated life; and
- cost-to-cure method - depreciation calculated by the cost of repairing curable depreciation.

Straight Line (Age-life) Method

The straight-line method requires two calculations be made:

- the annual rate of depreciation - For example, an improvement with an estimated total life of 50 years would be said to depreciate at an equal rate of 2 percent per year. (2 percent x 50 years equals 100 percent depreciation); and
- the effective age of the building - the effective age is generally considered rather than the actual age. Effective age is the age of typical, comparable buildings of equal condition, utility and life expectancy. For example, if a building is 50 years old and would sell for as much as adjoining 30-year-old properties, it would be said to have an effective age of 30 years.

Once these calculations have been made, the straight line method is easy to calculate. To continue our example:

If our building's original cost was $500,000 with an annual depreciation rate of 2% annually ($500,000 ÷ 50 = $10,000/yr and $10,000 ÷ %500,000 = .02); and

Because our building is in high demand and well-maintained, its effective life is 30 years; our accrued depreciation is $300,000 (Annual Depreciation of 2% x 30 years of effective life = $300,000 accrued depreciation

Cost-to Cure Method

In truth, buildings do not depreciate in a straight line due to the real estate market's changing demand and individual owner's diligence in maintaining properties; which bring us to the Cost-to-Cure Method.

This method is carried out by observing all factors of obsolescence (as previously defined, including: deferred maintenance, functional and external) and determining dollar values for these factors.

Cost to cure is the most accurate method of establishing value in older properties where replacement costs are not readily available.

7.6 Income Approach

The Income Approach calculates the present value of future benefits (income stream and return on investment). This method is predominantly used in the valuation of income property and is based on the appraisal principle of anticipation.

The Income Approach Method has a specific formula:

Value = Net income ÷ capitalization rate

It is important to recognize, as with all great formulas, if any two of the values are known, the third can be calculated (i.e., Capitalization rate = Value ÷ net income, etc.)

The steps to estimating value by this method are:

- calculate the net income of the property;
- calculate the capitalization rate; and
- apply the formula for the final opinion of value.

Determining Net Income

Net income is the amount of income remaining after operating expenses and rent losses have been deducted from the gross income of a property. The process of determining net annual income is:

- Estimate the potential gross income the property;
- Deduct an annual allowance for vacancies and rent collection losses from the gross income (the "effective gross income"); and
- Deduct annual expenses of operation (maintenance, utilities, real estate taxes, insurance along with reserves for capital improvements (replacement of building components) from the effective gross income to arrive at the net income of the property.

Calculating Capitalization Rates

Real estate investors expect a return of their capital invested (purchase price, etc.), plus a return on that capital. The *recapture* of capital occurs through income payments, the proceeds from the eventual sale of the property (known as *reversion*), and usually a combination of the two. Capitalization converts future income into an indication of present value (the cap or yield rate). This is accomplished through the analysis of comparable sales and the cap rate or yield percentage between net income and sales price. Ready?

So, using our newly acquired skills of comparing recent sales of income property and our trusty income formula from above:

- identify the sale prices for recently sold income properties;
- estimate each property's net income; and

- divide it into that property's sale price ... and voila - we have the capitalization rate for that property.

Gross Rent And Gross Income Multipliers

The Income Approach methods discussed rely on the capitalization of *net* income. As a real estate agent, you will be dealing with clients wishing to invest in real estate. For the typical investor, the GRM (Gross Rent Multiplier) or GIM (Gross Income Multiplier) are simpler methods of capitalizing income to arrive at an idea of value.

The Gross Rent Multiplier (GRM) analyzes the *gross* rents of a property. Some properties derive income from other sources beyond just rents (parking fees, etc.), in which case analyzing the *gross income* of the property is required. GRM and GIM can be calculated on either a monthly or annual basis, but must be applied consistently to the gross income of the property. Both rent and income multipliers must be applied to market rate income to be accurate. So, if the property you're evaluating has below market rents, you must calculate the income based on what the rents should be in the current market. The same is true when establishing the multiplier. If a comparable property had below market rents, you must adjust the income to reflect current pricing.

Calculating Rent and Income Multipliers

The Gross Rent Multiplier is found by dividing the sales price of an income property by its monthly rent. For example: a $500,000 sales price divided by a monthly rent of $2500 results in a gross rent multiplier of 200. If homes in the area are selling at prices equivalent to 200 times the monthly rental, then the 200 multiplier would apply to other comparable homes in the area. This formula can also be used to project appropriate rents. If homes in the area are selling for $500,000, we can divide the multiplier of 200 into the selling price to get our projected rental amount of $2500.

Reconciliation

As mentioned, there are occasions where a lack of relevant data may require more than one approach be applied in order to form a final opinion of value. It is important to note, the final opinion is not just an average of the approaches.

After each approach to value has been calculated, it is necessary to *reconcile* all the approaches to arrive at a final opinion. Consider the purpose of the appraisal; whether one approach is more appropriate to the purpose; which approach is based on the strongest data; and lastly, use your judgment and experience to reach a final conclusion.

7.7 Appraisal Licensing and Regulation

In California, appraisers are regulated by the California Office of Real Estate Appraisers (OREA) under the California Real Estate Appraisers' Licensing and Certification Law. OREA regulates licensing and investigates complaints.

License Levels

There are four levels of licenses, each with its own requirements and restrictions.

Trainee License

- Minimum of 150 hours of education, including at least 15 hours of the Uniform Standards of Professional Appraisal Practice (USPAP) coursework within the past five years.

- Successful completion of AQB endorsed Uniform State Residential Licensed Real Property Appraiser Examination.

- Trainee licensees must work under a supervising appraiser and may work on any appraisal that is within the scope of the supervising appraiser's license.

Residential License

- Minimum of 150 hours of education, including at least 15 hours of the Uniform Standards of Professional Appraisal Practice (USPAP) coursework.

- 2,000 hours of experience in the field with a minimum of 12 months of relevant experience.

- Successful completion of AQB endorsed Uniform State Residential Licensed Real Property Appraiser Examination.

- Residential licensees are limited to appraising simple (non-complex) residential properties of 1-4 units valued at less than $1,000,000, and non-residential properties valued at less than $250,000.

Certified Residential License

- Minimum of 200 hours of education, including at least 15 hours on USPAP

AND

- An Associates Degree or 21 semester credits in the specified areas

- 2,500 hours of experience in the field with a minimum of 30 months of relevant experience.

- Successful completion of AQB endorsed Uniform State Residential Licensed Real Property Appraiser Examination.

- Certified Residential licensees are limited to appraising properties of 1-4 units of any value or complexity, and non-residential properties valued at less than $250,000.

Certified General License

- Minimum of 300 hours of education, including at least 15 hours on USPAP

AND

- A Bachelors Degree or 30 semester credits in the specified areas

- 3,000 hours of experience in the field with a minimum of 30 months of relevant experience and a minimum of 15 hours of experience earned with non-residential property.

- Successful completion of AQB endorsed Uniform State General Licensed Real Property Appraiser Examination.

- Certified General licensees are not limited in appraising properties regardless of type, value or complexity.

License Terms and Renewal

Appraisal licenses are good for two years. Licensees are required show evidence of completing of 56 hours of continuing education *every four years* for continued renewal.

Federal, State and CalBRE Regulations

Congress enacted the Financial Institutions Reform, Recovery and Enforcement Act (FIRREA) in 1989. Title XI of FIRREA contains the *Real Estate Appraisal Reform Amendments* requiring states to establish a program to license and certify real estate appraisers for federally related transactions. Title XI requires states to adhere to the qualifications criteria set by the Appraiser Qualifications Board (AQB) of The Appraisal Foundation. Additionally, the Uniform Standards of Professional Appraisal Practice (USPAP), created by the Appraisals Standards Board of the Appraisal Foundation, sets the minimum standards for property appraisals.

Federal Regulations

The essence of FIRREA requires that appraisers be able to form an opinion of value independent of the requesting authority or client. All parties related to a transaction involving a federally-related institution are prohibited from:

- withholding or threatening to withhold payment for a report;

- either promising, withholding or threatening to withhold future business to an appraiser;

- requiring a preliminary estimate of value as a condition to ordering an appraisal or conditioning an order or payment on the appraiser's valuation;

- requesting or providing an appraiser with a desired value in advance of the appraisal, except for providing the copy of the sales contract;
- any attempt to influence an appraiser's independence, impartiality, or objectivity; and
- any act that violates any law or regulation, including the Truth and Lending Act, Regulation Z and USPAP.

Lenders must provide all borrowers with a copy of any appraisals related to their transaction no less than 3 days prior to the closing.

State Regulation

The Enforcement Division is OREA's investigative and enforcement division. It provides consumers with protection against unlawful and fraudulent conduct by appraisers by: examining past conduct of applicants for licensure, investigating complaints and denying licenses or imposing disciplinary sanctions. Upon approval from the Chief Deputy Director and the Director, the Division may seek deny, restrict or revoke a license and/or impose a fine of up to $10,000 for each violation of state law.

CalBRE Regulations

The Real Estate Commissioner has issued additional regulations specific to real estate licensees' behavior and relationship to appraisers. These regulations prohibit licensees from improperly influencing or attempting to improperly influence the development, reporting, result or review of an appraisal in connection with a mortgage loan. "Improper influence" is defined, but not limited to:

(NOTE: all prohibited acts below include the act of threatening same)

- withholding timely or partial payment for a completed report, regardless of whether the transaction closes;
- withholding future business, terminating or demoting an appraiser;
- the express or implied promise of future business, promotion or increased compensation;
- conditioning the order of an appraisal report or payment/bonus for same on the opinion, conclusion or valuation reached or on a preliminary estimate of value in advance of the appraisal.
- requesting an appraiser provide an estimated, predetermined or desired valuation prior to the completion of the report or requesting that an appraiser provide estimated values or comparable sales prior to the completed report;
- providing an anticipated, estimated, encouraged or desired value for the subject of an appraisal or a proposed or target amount to be loaned, except for providing a copy of the sales contract;

- requesting the removal of language noted in a report related to observed physical, functional or economic obsolescence or adverse property conditions;

- providing an appraiser, appraisal company or appraisal management company with stock or other financial or non-financial benefits.

Provided the request does not violate existing laws, licensees are expressly NOT prohibited from requesting the appraiser:

- consider additional, appropriate property information;

- provide further detail, substantiation or explanation for the value conclusion;

- correct errors in a report.

Study Smart Guide

Value - current worth of all rights and future benefits of ownership to users or investors.

Market value - most *probable* price a property would bring when freely offered on the open market between a willing buyer and a willing seller.

Market price - actual sale price of a property; may or may not have been an arm's length transaction".

Subjective value ("Utility Value" or "Value in Use") - value of improvements or amenities to a specific person

Elements of Value - Demand, Utility, Scarcity, Transferability (DUST)

External Forces Influencing Value - Environmental characteristics, Physical characteristics, Social ideals and standards, Economic influences, Political/government regulations.

Principals of Valuation - substitution, supply and demand, competition, highest and best use, change, conformity, balance, progression, regression, contribution, anticipation and four-stage life cycle.

Appreciation - increase in value.

Depreciation - loss in value. Do not confuse "actual depreciation" (related to valuation) with the accounting /tax method of depreciation (usually "book depreciation").

Deterioration - the physical result of uncorrected wear and tear over time ("deferred maintenance") and natural causes.

Functional Obsolescence - functional aspects of a property are outdated or obsolete.

Locational or External Obsolescence - outside influences such as neighborhood deterioration, proximity to undesirable areas

Curable depreciation - repairs and/or re-designs and renovations can cure deterioration and/or functional obsolescence.

Incurable depreciation - economic or locational obsolescence beyond a homeowner's ability cure or repairs or renovations necessary to cure functional obsolescence or deterioration would cost more than the value of the property once restored.

Broker's Price Opinion (BPO) or Comparative Market Analysis (CMA) - report analyzing the asking prices of comparable properties currently listed, but not sold; the asking prices of properties in escrow, but not closed; and selling prices of properties recently sold and closed. (ideally within 3-6 months) are all considered. Prepared by real estate agents for homeowners/ buyers to develop an accurate asking price and/or selling prices.

Purposes and Uses of Appraisals - Transfer of ownership, Financing and credit, Insurance, Taxation, Condemnation and estimating rents, fraud, damages and estate divisions

Methods of Valuation - Sales comparison, Cost approach and Income approach.

Sales Comparison Approach - compiles data using similar properties.

Cost Approach - calculates value as the combination of: land value (as if vacant) **plus** reconstruction/reproduction costs of any buildings as new, **less** depreciation.

Cost Approach Formula: Value = Land Value + Replacement or Reproduction Cost – Accrued Depreciation

Square-Foot Method - most common method used on the West Coast. Subject property is compared to similar structures where costs are known and broken down to a cost per square foot of floor area.

Abstraction Method - used to obtain land value where there are no vacant land sales.

Actual depreciation - actual depreciation is just as it says. It is a building's loss of value due to factors previously discussed.

Accrued depreciation - depreciation which has already occurred up to the date of value.

Remainder depreciation - depreciation which will occur in the future.

Methods of Calculating Accrued Depreciation - straight line or age-life method and cost-to-cure method

Straight Line (Age-life) Method - requires two calculations be made: annual rate of depreciation effective age of the building.

Cost-to Cure Method - observing all factors of obsolescence, assigning dollar values and deducting those values from comparable properties. Most accurate for older properties where replacement costs are not available.

Income Approach - calculates the present value of future benefits (income stream and return on investment), used in the valuation of income property.

Income Approach formula: Value = Net income ÷ capitalization rate

Net income - gross income less operating expenses and rent losses.

Capitalization Rates - converts future income into present value (the cap or yield rate).

Gross Rent Multiplier (GRM) - analyzes the gross rents of a property.

Gross Income Multiplier (GIM) - analyzes gross rents and income from other sources (parking fees, etc.).

Reconciliation - used when a lack of relevant data requires more than one approach need to form opinion of value.

License Levels - Trainee, Residential, Certified Residential, Certified General

License Terms and Renewal - two years. Renewal requires evidence of 56 hours of continuing education *every four years*.

FIRREA - requires that appraisers be able to form an opinion of value independent of the requesting authority or client.

Chapter 7
Quiz & Answers

1) Market value is:
    a) the actual price of a property being sold
    b) the value to a particular class of people
    c) the value of future rights and benefits
    d) the probable value if offered for sale

2) Demand refers to:
    a) the usefulness of property to most people
    b) the availability of types of property
    c) the scarcity of availability
    d) the public desire for a property

3) An increasing supply leads to:
    a) decreased demand
    b) increased competition for profits
    c) the principal of balance
    d) devalued anticipated benefits

4) A property that is outdated:
    a) is unsalable
    b) is subject to condemnation
    c) is functionally obsolete
    d) all of the above

5) Appraisers must:
    a) hold valid real estate licenses
    b) hold valid appraiser's licenses
    c) hold no special license
    d) none of the above

6) Appraisals are used for:
   a) transfers of property
   b) settling estates
   c) resolving disputes
   d) all of the above

7) A valuation considering the cost of recent sales:
   a) uses the cost approach
   b) uses the sale comparison approach
   c) uses the cost of replacement
   d) b only

8) Appraisers must:
   a) provide an estimated value in advance
   b) give an independent valuation
   c) match the value to the mortgage amount
   d) a and b

9) An appraisal:
   a) is an average of all value methods
   b) is subject to reconciliation
   c) is a disclosure of market value
   d) none of the above

10) Net income is:
    a) income derived from rents
    b) total income
    c) income after expenses
    d) income before expenses

ANSWERS:

1. d   3. a   5. b   7. d   9. b

2. d   4. c   6. d   8. b   10. c

Chapter 8

Chapter 8: Financing Concepts and Regulations

8.1 General Financing Concepts

Affordable, readily-available financing is the linchpin around which our system of real estate revolves. A comprehensive understanding of this industry is essential for any competent real estate professional.

Traditionally loans and mortgages were secured from "depository institutions" such as banks, savings and loans and credit unions. Over the past couple of decades, the rise of non-institutional lenders ("non-banks") as sources of loan funds has expanded rapidly. These non-banks include mortgage bankers, finance lenders, pension and hedge funds, mortgage and investment trusts, and private parties. In addition, insurance companies (neither depository institutions nor non-banks) invest some of the premium dollars from policyholders in real estate and mortgage loans.

California legislation now characterizes these non-depository institutions and non-banks as institutional and supervised lenders for purposes of regulation. This legislation includes mortgage bankers (now licensed under the Residential Mortgage Lending Act), finance lenders (now licensed under the California Finance Lender Law), certain pension funds, mortgage and investment trusts, and hedge funds.

Mortgage Markets

Since the 1980s, mortgage loan brokers (MLBs) have become a major source of residential mortgages, originating from 50 to 70% of residential loans. The expansion of non-depositories and non-banks and their increasing share of the residential mortgage market resulted in the expansion of the secondary mortgage market to accommodate mortgage backed securities.

California MLBs also make and arrange residential loans on behalf of private parties, known as private investors/lenders. These loans rely to a large extent on the equity held by the borrower and to a lesser extent on the credit worthiness and finances of the borrower. In the early 1990s, banks and lenders began expanding their loan offerings to include these non-traditional loans, which had been previously almost an exclusive market for private investors/lenders funding loans through MLBs.

The investors/lenders and the MLBs through whom these loans were funded could not compete with the loan products now being offered by banks and non-banks. At the time, the secondary market would not purchase the bulk of these alternative mortgage products. To create the cash flow necessary to fund these loan products, a new secondary market was born, relying primarily on mortgage backed securities.

There are essentially two markets for the sale of mortgages: primary and secondary.

Primary Mortgage Market - Banks and lenders create mortgages sold directly to the borrower.

Secondary Mortgage Market - Primary lenders package a portfolio of mortgages sold to government-related agencies and investors, including insurance companies and hedge funds.

The Primary Mortgage Market

The traditional primary mortgage market consisted banks and lenders funding loans from their own capital and making loans directly to consumers/borrowers. They replenished their capital by selling loans in the secondary mortgage market.

Historically, loans sold into the secondary market were either insured by the Federal Housing Administration (FHA) or guaranteed by the Veteran's Administration (VA). Mortgage bankers with sizeable assets and the mortgage experience required by government agencies qualified as "approved lenders/mortgagees".

Primary Market Insurers and Guarantors

- **Federal Housing Administration (FHA)** - This federal agency insures loans made by its approved lenders/mortgagees nationwide.

- **California Housing Finance Agency (CalFHA)** - This agency is California's affordable housing agency. It purchases the low-interest loans made to first-time homebuyers in the state through its approved lenders.

- **Veterans Administration (VA)** - This federal agency currently indemnifies loans made to qualifying veterans nationwide.

- **Department of Veterans Affairs (DVA)** - California established its own program for California Veterans. This agency assists qualified California veterans with the purchase of housing and farms. The DVA does not fund loans directly, but rather purchases properties selected by veterans to be "sold back" to the veterans over time under a land contract of sale using the selected property as security. These contracts are retained by the DVA and not typically sold into the secondary market.

The Secondary Mortgage Market

Lenders originating mortgage loans traditionally replenished their capital by: selling the loans to U.S. and foreign banks, to investors willing to hold loans on a long-term basis, or to Fannie Mae or Freddie Mac. More recently, the secondary mortgage market expanded to include investment banks and international investors packaging loans as mortgage backed securities (MBS). This expansion was created specifically to facilitate the sale of alternative and non-traditional mortgages previously unsalable in the secondary market.

Secondary Market Insurers and Guarantors

These quasi-government mortgage insurers and guarantors were established to purchase mortgages from primary lender for the purposes of freeing up funds for lenders to make more loans and to alleviate the lender's financial risk in owning these loans.

- **Federal National Mortgage Association (FNMA or Fannie Mae)** - FNMA initially provided a secondary market for FHA and VA loans, later expanding to include conventional mortgages insured by a private mortgage insurer. In the early 2000s, FNMA expanded again by including non-traditional and alternative loan products in their portfolio. Their mortgage back securities plan included their lenders selling pools of mortgages in exchange for securities with an undivided interest in a designated pool of loans that could then be sold or retained by qualifying lenders. Now, here's the great part, FNMA provides a 100% guaranty of full and timely payment of interest and principal to the holders of their securities.

    In 2008, Fannie Mae was placed into receivership by the federal government and continues its operation under the governmental conservatorship of the Federal Housing Finance Agency (FHFA). They also continue to maintain a resale/refinance program enabling approved lenders to allow borrowers to convert adjustable rate mortgages (ARMs) to fixed rate loans or obtain new mortgages at competitive interest rates.

- **Government National Mortgage Association (GNMA or Ginnie Mae)** - Ginnie Mae is a government corporation administering mortgage support programs unavailable in the private market place. GNMA increases liquidity in the secondary mortgage market and attracts new sources of funds for residential loans. Ginnie Mae differs from FNMA in that they do not purchase mortgages, but like FNMA, guarantees mortgage-backed securities issued by approved lenders. GNMA's three major activities include: a Mortgage-backed securities (MBS) Program; special assistance functions; and management and liquidation functions.

    Through the MBS Program, GNMA guarantees mortgage backed securities issued by mortgage bankers, savings institutions, commercial banks and other approved financial intermediaries. Ginnie Mae guarantees that security holders will receive payments of principal and interest as scheduled, less servicing costs and GNMA fees. Because of the federal guaranty, GNMA backed securities are considered by many to be as safe, as liquid, and as easy to hold as those issued directly by the U. S. Treasury.

    Under the special assistance functions, GNMA purchases certain types of mortgages to provide support for low-income housing and to counter declines in mortgage lending and in housing construction. Under the management and liquidation functions, GNMA manages and sells portfolios of federally-owned mortgages.

The President of the United States appoints the President of GNMA, who acts under the direction of the Secretary of the Department of Housing and Urban Development (HUD).

- **Federal Home Loan Mortgage Corporation (FHLMC or Freddie Mac)** - Freddie Mac was established to increase the availability of mortgage credit to finance housing by developing, expanding and maintaining a nationwide secondary market primarily for conventional loans originated by HUD-approved lenders. Freddie Mac finances most of its mortgage purchases through the sale of mortgage participation certificates (PCs) that require issuance and acquisition by qualified investment buyers (QIBs).

    Until 2008, Freddie Mac was an independent stock company and functioning in direct competition with FNMA; but like FNMA, was placed into receivership and operates as a governmental conservatorship under the Federal Housing Finance Agency (FHFA) to continue its residential mortgage loan programs.

Secondary Market for Non-Traditional Mortgage Products

As previously discussed Wall Street bankers began underwriting securities backed by non-traditional mortgage products and other "subprime" loans. These loan products would not have historically qualified for sale to FNMA or FHLMC and still cannot be guaranteed by GNMA.

Beginning in the early 2000's, FNMA and Freddie Mac lowered their standards and began including these loan products in portfolios owned and/or securitized by these quasi- government enterprises. This expansion of the secondary market resulted in the growth of these types of loans made available to residential borrowers previously unable to qualify for purchase or refinance their homes. This allowed conventional lenders to grant mortgages to borrowers they would normally have declined; and then sell these alternative and subprime loan products to FNMA and FHLMC, as well as directly to investment bankers for securitization through Wall Street.

In response to the major increase in these "exotic" loans and the consumer protection issues they created, in 2006 and '07, the Fed developed the "Interagency Guidance on Non-Traditional Mortgage Product Risks" and issued the "Statement on Subprime Mortgage Lending". These guidelines were adopted and applied to all federally-related mortgage loans as well as to guide all state supervised lenders and mortgage brokers.

These documents established risk management practices, consumer protection principles and control systems for lenders and brokers when offering or advertising alternative mortgage and non-traditional loan products. They address the particular risks associated with ARMs, stated income, limited documentation and other loan products related to borrowers with a low credit score. One major objective was to ensure that borrowers received full and complete disclosures of all material terms for these loans.

As an aside, following these decrees, the Wall Street market for alternative mortgages or non-traditional loan products stagnated relatively immediately. By the fall of '07, the pipeline for these securities dried up and the secondary market for these products almost entirely shut down.

On January 1, 2008, California law was amended and the Legislature authorized the Commissioners of the Department of Real Estate (DRE), Department of Corporations (DOC), and of the Department of Financial Institutions (DFI) to adopt regulations ensuring licensee compliance with the '06 and '07 federal mandates. The DRE further promulgated regulations requiring increased disclosure of loan terms and requiring specific underwriting guidelines for DRE licensed lenders when making these loans. The DOC and DFI also adopted regulations in regard to their licensees.

8.2 Lenders, Mortgage Loan Brokers (MLB) and Mortgage Loan Originators (MLO)

Traditionally, lenders "originated" (made or funded) a loan directly. In the late 1980s, authorities expanded the term "originate" to include third parties who arrange loans for lenders. Third party "originators" are known as mortgage loan brokers (MLBs). Recently, the definition of "originating" has been extended to all employees acting as loan representatives for banks and lenders. For the purposes of regulation, MLBs and lender representatives soliciting and negotiating residential loans are known as Mortgage Loan Originators (MLOs).

- **Lenders** make or originate and provide funds for mortgage loans.

- **Mortgage Bankers** are privately-owned companies, often subsidiaries or affiliates of banks and other lenders. They act as authorized agents and representatives originating and providing funds for mortgage loans.

- **Mortgage Loan Brokers (MLB)** are third parties who find and match borrowers with lenders for a fee

- **Mortgage Loan Originators (MLO)** are anyone who offers or takes a mortgage loan application or offers to negotiate terms for a fee. For the purposes of regulation, Originators include direct lenders, third party brokers and all associated employees acting as representatives.

The Safe Mortgage Licensing Act (SAFE Act)

The Secure and Fair Enforcement for Mortgage Licensing Act of 2008 (SAFE Act), required states to pass laws to comply with SAFE or HUD (Federal Housing and Urban Development) would take over the regulation of mortgage loan originators. The SAFE Act is designed to enhance consumer protection and reduce mortgage loan fraud by setting national minimum standards for the licensing and registration of state-licensed mortgage loan originators (MLOs).

The SAFE Act established a Nationwide Mortgage Licensing System and Registry (NMLS) in which states are required to participate. California law was amended expanding the authority of the DRE to participate in the NMLS, including the licensing and registering of MLOs. The amendment includes requirements for doing business as an MLO; establishes a one year term for the license endorsement; authorizes application forms; imposes record keeping and transaction fees; and defines violations of the law and the penalties to be imposed.

Licensure is now required in California when MLOs engage in the making or arranging of loans primarily for personal, family, or household use that are secured by deeds of trust or mortgages through a lien on real property when the security property is a dwelling consisting of 1 to 4 residential units. The MLO licensure/registration also applies when the financing arranged is to construct on the security property the intended dwelling of the borrower. In lay terms: making or arranging any residential mortgage loans.

The SAFE Act requires:

- state-licensed MLOs to pass a written qualifying test,

- to complete pre-licensure education courses,
- to take annual continuing education courses,
- to submit fingerprints to NMLS for submission to the FBI for criminal background checks, and
- to authorize the NMLS to obtain independent credit reports and examine the credit worthiness and financial standing/responsibility of applicants (for both licensure and subsequent renewals).

Real Estate Licensees as MLB/MLO

In California, a real estate broker is authorized to make or arrange mortgage loans secured by real property. These activities are characterized as mortgage loan brokerage and licensees known as mortgage loan brokers (MLBs). California law requires loan processors and underwriters to either function as employees of the real estate broker (MLB/MLO) or to be separately licensed if providing services as an independent contractor.

As of 2011, all companies and licensees must apply to become licensed or registered as an MLO. Prerequisite requirements for the endorsement to act as an MLO is consideration of previous license discipline, a review of criminal records where the applicant was convicted of a felony, and whether the felony involved fraud, dishonesty, a breach of trust, or money laundering. Further, an applicant for the endorsement to act as an MLO must undergo a qualifying written examination, demonstrate financial responsibility and meet new educational requirements.

8.3 Conventional and Alternative Financing

A residential mortgage loan is generally obtained by homeowners for personal and family use. These mortgages are secured by a 1-4 unit dwelling, which can include a condominium or cooperative, mobile homes and trailers that are personal residences. Marketplace competition, including FHA insured or VA indemnified loans, contributes to the continued availability of fully-amortized, long-term, fixed interest rate mortgages. Fannie Mae and Freddie Mac's secondary purchase and resale of these loans also contributes to the availability of these mortgages.

Conventional Fixed-Rate Financing

Conventional fixed-rate loans have no insured backing from FHA or guarantee from VA. They are generally long term (amortized over 30 years) with a fixed rate of interest over the course of the loan. Depending on the current economic confidence (which often relaxes or constrains the qualifying guidelines for borrowers), long-term, fixed-rate financing is usually the first choice for the average homebuyer due to the stability of monthly payments over the life of the loan.

Alternative Financing

In a stable economy (i.e., low inflation and steady, low interest rates), the long-term, fixed-rate conventional loan is generally the financing option of choice for purchasing residential property. However, as interest rates rise and/or qualification guidelines get tighter and more difficult for the average homeowners to meet, homebuyers may turn to alternatives to long-term, fixed-rate loans.

These loans can be invaluable when used properly. However, alternative mortgages have ramifications that must be fully understood by the borrower. It should be noted, as a real estate licensee acting as a MLB/MLO, the explanation and ensuing assurance of the borrower's full understanding of the issues surrounding the use of these loan products falls within the context of fiduciary duties owed a client, in this case, to the intended borrower. Below are some of the more common forms of alternative financing.

Adjustable Rate Mortgages (ARMs)
An ARM is just as it says - a loan in which the interest rate fluctuates (adjusts). Generally, there is an advantageous initial (or "teaser") interest rate for a period of time, after which the rate of interest adjusts on a predetermined, periodic schedule (monthly, quarterly, etc.). The amount of the adjustment is tied to a specified margin added to current short term market rates and remains in effect until the next adjustment period. There is usually a cap on how high the rate can go and a "floor" on how low it can drop. Generally the initial "teaser" rate makes monthly payments more affordable during the initial period; but borrowers bear the risk that interest rates will generally increase over the life of the loan, causing their monthly payments to rise.

Reverse Mortgages (RMs)

Most older homeowners live on some form of fixed income and often own their homes outright or with relatively small mortgage loan balances. For those wanting or needing to supplement their income, the choice is either selling the home to access the equity or considering a reverse mortgage.

The reverse mortgage loan is a FHA insured product also known as a Home Equity Conversion Mortgage (HECM). Under a HECM reverse mortgage, older homeowners need not make loan payments; but instead can receive monthly income or a lump sum from the lender. HECMs are due and payable when the borrower permanently leaves the property, upon sale of the property or upon death of the age-qualifying homeowner.

The fees, costs, and expenses to originate a reverse mortgage are typically much higher than conventional loans. It would be ill-advised to consider a reverse mortgage for a short period; therefore, reverse mortgages should only be considered by a homeowner with a long-term commitment to occupy the property.

Rollover Mortgages (ROMs)
ROMs are a renegotiated loan with monthly payments amortized over 25-30 years. Basically, the interest rate (and monthly payments) is adjusted to the prevailing market rate usually every five years. Monthly payments are calculated by the same formula as conventional mortgages, with the term of the loan decreasing in increments of five years, with full payment at the maturity date specified at loan origination.

Graduated Payment Mortgages (GPMs)

GPM's allow partially deferred payments of principal usually during the first five years of the loan term. Thereafter, the principal and interest paid monthly increase greatly. These types of loans are for borrowers whose income will increase in the future.

8.4 Primary Financing Documents and Instruments

A negotiable instrument is a written, unconditional promise to pay a specific amount of money at a defined time or on demand. A check drawn on a bank is an example of a negotiable instrument; it is subject to the promise to pay to the payee or to the order of the bearer. Bank checks are the most common type of negotiable instrument. The real estate financing process involves essentially two documents in tandem: a promissory note and the accompanying security instrument (the mortgage or deed of trust). The promissory note is the evidence of the debt and the deed of trust or mortgage is the instrument making the real property described the security (collateral) for the debt/loan or other obligations.

Promissory Notes

The promissory note (or "Note") is the evidence of the debt owed by the borrower to the lender. It is the contract by which the borrower promises to pay the lender under the agreed terms. The note may also include future obligations such as home equity lines of credit or other additional advances laid out in the mortgage or deed of trust (the "security instrument"). The promissory note is the overriding document. If there are conflicts in the provisions of the note and the mortgage document, generally the terms of the promissory note are controlling.

Promissory notes constitute "two-party paper" - the maker and payee. The maker promises to pay the payee a specified amount of money on a certain date, upon demand, or under the agreed terms. There are several basic kinds of promissory notes, generally characterized by the schedule for payment of the principal and interest. Below are several of the most common:

- **Installment note** - periodic payments of some principal and some interest in a fixed amount until the loan is fully paid (known as "amortized" or "fully amortized" - meaning spread out over the term of the loan). This is the most common note and there are several variations: payments in a fixed amount as described is known as a "level payment note".
- **Balloon note** - payments of the full amount of interest due and only some or no principal. At the end of the term, the remaining unpaid principal is due in full in the form of a "balloon" payment.
- **Adjustable rate note** - payments fluctuate on a prescribed schedule based on the prevailing market interest rate.
- **Renegotiable note** - equal payments of principal and interest made for a specified term, (often five years), after which the full loan amount is due or renegotiated at the prevailing interest rate based on a preset margin relative to an authorized standard (index).
- **Straight note** - payment of interest only during the term of the note, with the principal sum becoming due and payable on a certain date;
- **Demand note** - no payments are made until the holder makes demand for its payment in full.

Security Instruments

A "security interest" refers to the interests of the lender/creditor in the property of the borrower/debtor, in this case, the mortgage on real property. The property of the borrower is set aside so that the lender/creditor can sell it if the borrower defaults on the debt or other obligations. The document describing both the rights and obligations of the lender and the borrower is called a security instrument. Deeds of trust and mortgages are security instruments.

Deed of Trust vs. Mortgage

The deed of trust is most frequently used in California real estate loan transactions. Changes in the laws have removed many of the differences between a mortgage and a deed of trust. However, there are a few important differences that remain. One major difference is the procedure in the event of a default, which we will cover shortly in the Foreclosure section.

> **Deed of Trust** - an instrument drawn between three parties; a trustor (the borrower), a beneficiary (the lender), and a neutral third party (the trustee). Under a deed of trust, the borrower holds equitable title to the property and the trustee holds legal title. The deed of trust can only be dissolved by the trustee issuing a deed of reconveyance. Once the loan obligations have been satisfied, the trustee reconveys the property to the trustor.
>
> **Mortgage** - an instrument drawn between two parties; the mortgagor (the borrower) and mortgagee (the lender). Under a mortgage, the borrower retains title to the property subject to the lien imposed by the mortgage. A mortgage is discharged by a certificate of discharge.

Elements of Security Instruments

Negotiation is the transfer of an instrument whereby the recipient becomes a subsequent holder. If the instrument is payable to order, it is negotiated by delivery and acceptance with proper endorsement. If payable to bearer, it is negotiated by delivery and acceptance. Negotiable instruments are generally freely transferable. To be considered negotiable, the document must be:

- Signed by the maker or drawer;

- Include the unconditional promise or order to pay a certain amount in U.S. dollars;

- Payable on demand or at a specified time; and

- Be payable to the holder or bearer.

There is no specified standard form for mortgages and deeds of trust. However, most contain the following basic clauses or provisions:

(NOTE: Although Deeds of Trust are by far the more common security instrument used in California, the term used overwhelmingly by lay people and professional alike is mortgage. For simplicity sake, unless otherwise specified, consider the word "mortgage" to refer to deeds of trust and/or mortgages.)

Acceleration Clause - In the event of a default or failure to observe other obligations (i.e., lack of appropriate maintenance or insurance), the lender can demand immediate full payment of the outstanding balance of principal and interest due.

Alienation Clause (also known as a "due-on-sale" clause) - In the event of a sale or any transfer of interest, the lender can demand immediate full payment of the outstanding balance of principal and interest due. With or without an alienation clause, the sale of the property does not discharge the obligation of the security instrument. Potential buyers can take title to the property in two ways:

- By assumption - the buyer becomes primary in the obligation to repay the debt and the seller remains secondarily responsible; or

- Subject to - the original borrower remains fully liable for the debt, but in the event of default, the property is subject to foreclosure.

In 1982, the federal government enacted the **Garn-St. Germain Act** which provides for certain exemptions to the alienation clause:

- transfers by will or law upon the death of a joint tenant;
- transfers as a result of a divorce decree or legal separation;
- transfers to relatives upon the death of the borrower;
- transfers to a family trust;
- transfers involving a spouse or child becoming the owner of the property; and
- granting of a lease for three years or less, without an option to buy.

Late Payment Clause - Under California Civil Code, late fees on conventional loans secured by single family, owner-occupied homes cannot exceed 6% of the payment or $5, whichever is greater. Late charges cannot be levied: if the payment is made in full within 10 days of its due date; until the borrower has been notified in writing and given 10 days to pay; and the billing statement clearly states that late fees will be imposed after 10 days. FHA & VA loans impose a late fee of 4% of the payment after 15 days; and CalVet imposes a fee of $4 if payment is made after the 10th day of the month.

Prepayment Clause - The terms under which a loan may be paid off earlier than agreed without a "prepayment penalty." Most loans secured by owner-occupied, residential property (4 units or fewer) contain a clause stating that during the initial five years, up to 20% of the original principal can be repaid without penalty in any or each 12-month period. Regardless, prepayment penalties cannot exceed an amount equal to 6 month's advance interest on the prepaid principal. California law prohibits any prepayment penalty after the initial 5 years for owner-occupied, residential property and CalVet prohibits prepayment penalties completely. There are varying federal guidelines that will be addressed as they come up later in this text.

Subordination Clause - Declares the mortgage will be of a lower priority than another mortgage yet to come. This clause often comes into play when developers mortgage unimproved land with the intention of obtaining a later construction loan with which to build the houses. In this instance, the construction loan holder would be paid first and the land loan would be "subordinated or junior" to the construction loan, even though it was obtained and recorded first. (See Junior and Senior Mortgages below)

Defeasance Clause - In the case of a deed of trust, the lender is required to submit the "request of reconveyance" to the trustee within 30 days of payment in full. The trustee must then execute and record the new deed within 21 days. In the case of a mortgage, the lender must record a "certificate of discharge" of the lien within 30 days following payment in full.

8.5 Types and Purposes of Secured Loans

There are many types of loans that cover an array of circumstances under which a potential borrower may choose to obtain funds for financing real property. Below are several of the most common along with some of the associated terms.

Purchase Loan - obtained to finance the costs of purchasing a property. Whether or not the borrower intends to live in the property affects both the type of loan available and the amount of the downpayment required. Generally, lower rates and better terms are offered the higher the down payment.

Refinance Loan - replaces an existing loan. Generally used to: lower interest rates; access additional credit ("cash out"); and change to a different type of mortgage (i.e., discharge an adjustable rate mortgage in favor of a fixed rate mortgage).

First Mortgage - the loan in the first position for repayment. In the event of a sale or default, this mortgage is the first to be paid. First mortgages generally have lower interest rates and better terms due to the security of being first in line.

Second Mortgage - the loan in the second position for repayment; second to be paid. "Seconds" generally have higher interest rates due to the increased risk of being second in line.

Junior and Senior Mortgages - these terms refers to any mortgages in relation to one another. For instance, the second mortgage is "junior" to the first mortgage (considered senior). However, that same second mortgage would be considered "senior" to a third mortgage were one to exist.

Bridge or Swing Loan - this is a short term loan used by buyers purchasing a new home prior to the sale and closing of their existing home. The funds are used for the downpayment and closing costs of the new purchase and secured by the equity in the buyer's existing home. When the existing home closes, proceeds from the sale are used to pay off the "bridge". These are generally quite expensive.

Home Equity Mortgage (HELOC) - more commonly referred to as a "home equity line of credit". HELOCS allow homeowners to establish a revolving line of credit secured by the equity in their home. Since it is a revolving line of credit, they can spend (and pay for) only the amount needed at a particular time, rather than obtaining a second mortgage, borrowing (and paying for) the full lump sum. These loans are often used for capital improvements (new kitchens, small additions, etc.) and can sometimes be used in lieu of the more expensive bridge loan. Lenders typically limit the credit amount to a percentage of the current property value minus existing liens and mortgages.

Construction Mortgage - used to finance major improvements to a property, whether it be an existing improvement or unimproved land. Construction loans are generally short term and include a schedule of payments from the lender to the borrower, referred to as "advances" or "draw downs". The schedule for advances is usually based on certain benchmarks achieved over the stages of construction. For instance, when the excavation is complete and the foundation poured, a predetermined amount of money would be released to the borrower. These loans are often expensive and when construction is complete, the borrower obtains permanent financing on the now improved property (referred to as a "take-out" loan).

Blanket Mortgage - these loans are secured by more than one piece of property. When the equity of a single property is not enough to cover the amount being borrowed, the borrower offers another property (in which they have equity) as further collateral. Often developers buying land for subdivision and sale will use this financing. Blanket Mortgages generally contain a "partial release" clause; meaning in the case of the subdivider, a single lot or house can be sold and the proportionate amount of the blanket mortgage is released. This allows the mortgage amount to be reduced incrementally without having to reset the financing to allow for individual sales.

Seller Financing - In some instances, the seller of a property may choose to finance a portion of the purchase money, rather than receive a lump sum. These types of loans are referred to as "seller carry back loans". There are any number of ways to structure these mortgages. Generally, a seller who grants a mortgage for some portion of the purchase money essentially acts as a second mortgagee. Buyer and seller agree on a rate of interest, payment schedules and terms. The carry back loan is junior to any conventional financing and often requires the approval of the primary lender. Real estate licencees arranging seller financing should take particular care to fully understand and comply with the many additional disclosures and fiduciary responsibilities involved in such a transaction.

Private Financing - generally referred to as "hard money" or "private money" loans. Most often these loans are used by developers intending to purchase and improve a property rather than obtain a construction loan. Because private investors/lenders are usually motivated by higher returns on their investments, these loans are generally quite expensive. As above, a licensee arranging these loans should take caution to comply with all additional responsibilities and disclosures.

8.6 Foreclosures

When a borrower defaults or breeches the terms of a mortgage, the lender is generally entitled to recover the debt by the process of foreclosure. This procedure is used to terminate the rights, title, and interests of a trustor/mortgagor in the property through sale of the property and use of the proceeds to satisfy the debt/loan. Defaults or breeches can occur in a variety of ways, such as failure to make payments, pay property taxes, maintain proper insurance or any other non-compliance with the terms of the security documents.

California has a "one-action" foreclosure policy; meaning, the lender may choose only one of two avenues to foreclosure: Judicial or Non-Judicial. A mortgage without a *power of sale* can only be foreclosed judicially (by court proceeding). A deed of trust or mortgage that contains a *power of sale* may be foreclosed non-judicially by trustee's sale (without the direction/supervision of the court). Most security instruments used in California expressly provide for *power of sale,* offering the choice of a non-judicial or judicial foreclosure sale. As a result, judicial foreclosures in California are rare.

Deficiency Judgments

Beyond the power of sale, the choice of non-judicial or judicial foreclosures involves the decision to pursue a *deficiency judgment.* A deficiency judgment is a personal judgment against a debtor/borrower for any difference between the unpaid balance of the debt/loan (plus interest, authorized fees, costs, and expenses of sale) and the actual proceeds from the sale.

As of 2013, California revised the lawful definition of "purchase money loan" to include "...repayment of a loan which was in fact used to pay all or part of the purchase price ..." In essence, this means anyone who obtained both a first and second mortgage (after 2012) that was used for the initial purchase of property is protected from a deficiency judgment on the second mortgage as well as the first. This includes any refinance loans used to pay down the original purchase loan. Generally speaking, this new definition renders deficiency judgments difficult to obtain.

Judicial vs. Non-Judicial Foreclosure

Beyond the fact that nearly all security instruments in California contain a power of sale (which allows for a non-judicial foreclosure), other considerations include:

- the difficulty of obtaining a deficiency judgment;

- because of the court proceeding (rather than private sale under a non-judicial foreclosure), judicial foreclosures take much longer to conclude and are much more expensive to pursue;

- borrowers have a right to redeem their property at several junctures during any foreclosure process. Redemption is achieved by paying the entire debt, plus any court or sale costs. After a trustee's sale, the borrower has no right to redeem the property. Under a court-ordered Sheriff's sale, the borrower has three months if there was no deficiency and one year if the lender pursues a deficiency judgment; and

- The distribution of the proceeds from a sheriff's sale go first to the court costs and attorney's fees; then to the expenses of sale; then to the foreclosing mortgagee, junior lienholders and finally borrower. Because there is no court proceeding for a trustee's sale, the funds are applied directly to the expenses of sale, the foreclosing mortgagee, junior lienholders and borrower.

Judicial Foreclosure
A judicial foreclosure is usually sought when a beneficiary or mortgagee wants to obtain a deficiency judgment. The judicial sale process involves:

- filing a complaint and notice of action (lis pendens);

- a summons served on all parties whose interests are to be eliminated, such as the trustor and junior lien holders;

- a trial, after which the decree of foreclosure and order of sale are entered; and,

- a sheriff records and serves (delivers) the Notice of Levy followed by the Notice of Sale.

When there is a successful bidder, the sheriff issues a Certificate of Sale stating the title is subject to any redemption privilege of the debtor/borrower. When a deficiency judgment is available, the property is sold subject to the one-year redemption period. This certificate transfers title to the highest successful bidder. The bidder receives no rights to possession over the redemption period, but does have the right to receive and/or impose rents from tenants occupying the property. The title is subject to any senior liens but all junior liens have been eliminated. The Certificate of Sale is recorded, but the title is not cleared until the Sheriff issues a Deed of Conveyance after the redemption periods.

Sale proceeds are applied to costs of the lawsuit and attorney fees; to selling expenses; to the amount due the foreclosing beneficiary/mortgagee; to junior lien holders in order of priority; and finally, any excess to the debtor/borrower. If the borrower does not redeem the property within the 3-month or l-year redemption period, the Sheriff will issue a Deed of Conveyance. At that point, the successful bidder receives all rights, title and interest back to the date of the foreclosed borrower' initial purchase. The successful bidder, as new owner, may now evict the foreclosed borrower or any tenants in possession of the property.

A lender or creditor seeking a deficiency judgment must file an application with the court case within three months of the sale for a determination of the deficiency.

Non-Judicial Foreclosure
When the security instrument includes a *power of sale*, the alternative remedy for a creditor/lender to recover the debt is through a non-judicial foreclosure. Given most security instruments in California contain a power of sale clause, most foreclosures are pursued under these procedures. A non-judicial foreclosure requires the lender to direct the Trustee named in the security instrument to hold a public trustee's sale". The non-judicial sale process is as follows:

- Lender notifies the trustee to issue and record a Notice of Default and provides evidence of the amounts in delinquency or breech.

- copies of the recorded Notices and evidentiary documentation must be mailed to the trustor (borrower) and anyone who has requested special notice within 10 days. Additional copies must be provided to any party with a recorded interest in the property (junior or other lienholders) within 30 days.

- after 3 months of recording the Notice of Default, the trustee must issue a Notice of Sale. The trustee will conduct the public sale no sooner than 3 months and 20 days after recording the original Notice of Default.

Unless the borrower contests the trustee's sale by obtaining a temporary restraining order (TRO) and/or a preliminary injunction, no court proceeding is required in non-judicial foreclosures. The passing of time required between filing of the Notice of Default, the Notice of Sale and the actual sale date affords the borrower the opportunity to pursue relief through court proceedings.

Contact Requirements Prior to Filing a Notice of Default

As of 2013, the mortgage servicer is required to contact the borrower at least 30 days prior to the recording of a Notice of Default to ensure "...*borrowers are considered for, and have a meaningful opportunity to obtain available loss mitigation options, if any, offered by or through the borrower's loan servicer such as loan modifications or other alternatives to foreclosure.*" Due diligence requires the beneficiary/lender/mortgagee, its servicing agent, or another lawfully authorized agent make contact either in person or by telephone, advising the borrower of the availability of a United States Department of Housing and Urban Development (HUD) certified housing counseling agency and the toll free telephone numbers of agencies providing counseling services for borrowers.

The contact requirement provides an opportunity to assess the borrower's financial situation and explore options to avoid foreclosure. The borrower can designate a HUD-certified counseling agency, an attorney, or another advisor to discuss their finances, options to avoid foreclosure, or any loan modification or workout plan offered by the beneficiary/lender/mortgagee. (NOTE: foreclosure alternatives are discussed later in this chapter.)

As a result, no Notice of Default can be filed until:

- copies of certain documents pertaining to security instruments and assignments have been provided;

- 30 days have passed since contact with the borrower or a diligent effort to contact the borrower has failed;

- a borrower requesting foreclosure prevention has been provided with a **single point of contact** (SPOC) to assess their ability to avail themselves of foreclosure prevention alternatives;

- a borrower's application for a loan modification or other alternative has been reviewed and approved or rejected.

Also in 2013, the federal government issued rules requiring a "continuity of contact" similar to California's single point of contact; however, federal rules require a 120-day wait period, rather than California's 30 days. In some cases, the federal timeline may override California's 30-day period. Essentially, this means that lenders may not offer foreclosure prevention alternatives while simultaneously proceeding with foreclosure, referred to as "dual tracking."

Notice of Default and Election to Sell

The Notice of Default must declare the entire debt amount due resulting from the breach and/or default. Unless the default is non-curable, the Notice must clearly state the borrower's right to cure the default any time until 5 business days prior to the trustee's sale date (or any postponed sale date).

If the borrower makes no request for notice or provides no address, the Notice of Default must be personally delivered or published weekly for four weeks in a general newspaper in the judicial jurisdiction starting within ten days. If these procedures (and all other requirements) are followed, the Notices are valid regardless of whether the borrower has actual knowledge of them.

Notice of Sale

If the loan is not reinstated, the trustee issues a Notice of Sale. The Notice of Sale sets the sale date no sooner than twenty days after the recording date of the notice. The sale date is set to allow time for the required recording, publication, posting, and mailing of the Notice.

The Notice of Sale must be recorded and mailed to the borrower at least fourteen days, and others requesting/receiving the Notice of Default at least twenty days, before the sale. The Notice must also be published once a week over a period of at least twenty days in a general newspaper in the city, county, or judicial district where the property is located. Three publications are required, no more than seven days apart. Additionally, the notice must be posted in at least one public place where the property is located and in a conspicuous place on the property. These posted notices must include the property address being sold as well as the date, time and place the sale will be held.

Lastly, a copy of the Notice must be send to any state taxing agency that has recorded a lien within 20 days and to the IRS within 25 days.

The Trustee's Sale

The sale is conducted by public auction by the trustee, or a named auctioneer. The trustee may state that the property is being sold "as is"; however, they have a duty to disclose any known material facts that affect the property and its condition or value.

All bids must be cash, cashier's check or equivalent from a financial institution authorized to do business in California. Any person may bid at the trustee's sale, including the borrower, lender/creditor, or a junior lien holder. The foreclosing beneficiary/lender/mortgagee (who holds the debt/loan evidenced by the promissory note and the security instrument being foreclosed) may offer a "*credit-bid*" up to the amount owed.

A trustee may reject all bids and postpone the sale if they reasonably believe the bids to be inadequate. Generally, the trustee receives prior instruction from the security holder relative to rejecting bids and postponing the sale. When postponing, the trustee must disclosure the reason and declare the date, place and time of the new sale. Bid fixing, restraining from bidding, or the offering or accepting of consideration for not bidding at a trustee's sale ("chilling the bidding process") is unlawful and subjects the participants to fine, imprisonment, or both.

After the Sale

The successful bidder receives a trustee's deed to the property containing specific language giving notice of compliance with the foreclosure statutes to protect this bidder and subsequent purchasers of the security property. The title conveyed does not warranty that no title defects exist, and, in fact, remains subject to the following liens and conditions:

- any liens that were senior to the foreclosed security;
- Federal tax liens filed more than thirty days before the date of the trustee's sale unless the proper twenty-five day notice has been given the Internal Revenue Service;
- Real property taxes and assessments;
- Valid mechanic's liens; and
- possible rights of existing tenants to remain in possession through the end of their lease term or any rights of tenants under local rent control ordinances.

Even with proper notice to the IRS, the federal government may have the right for 120 days following the trustee's sale to redeem the security property by paying the amount advanced by the successful bidder/purchaser.

The successful bidder is generally entitled to immediate possession of the property and may evict the former debtor/trustor/mortgagor by delivering a three-day Notice to Quit and filing an Unlawful Detainer action.

The trustee distributes the sale proceeds in the following order: first to fees, costs and sale expenses; to beneficiary/lender/mortgagee to satisfy unpaid principal and interest in full and any lawful charges, penalties, costs, expenses, attorney's fees and advances; to junior lien holders in order of priority; and any surplus to the debtor/trustor/mortgagor.

Foreclosure Alternatives

There can be several reasons a homeowner may need or seek to stop paying their mortgage. In some instances, property values have declined at such a rate that the mortgage amount is significantly higher than the current property value (known as "being underwater" or "upside down"). In other cases, initial teaser rates for adjustable rate mortgages have reset to significantly higher rates the borrower can no longer afford. There are several alternatives to foreclosure. Among the most common are:

- **Loan modification** - adjusting terms of the mortgage to relative to a borrower's ability to pay
- **Short sale** - a lender approved sale whose proceeds equal less than mortgage balance
- **Deed in lieu of foreclosure** - just as it says; the borrower offers and the lender accepts conveyance of the deed (along with any liens) instead of foreclosure proceedings

- **Bankruptcy** - the court proceeding during which a debtor declares their inability to pay their debts.

Loan Modification

Loan modifications attempt to keep borrowers in their homes and paying their mortgage rather than foreclosing. The modification program targets a ratio of not more than about 30% of the borrower's gross income going to housing related expenses (i.e., new principal and interest payment, taxes and insurance). The object of resetting the terms of a modification is buyer's long-term ability to stay in the home and sustain the payments. It should be noted that lenders are not required to accept the new terms of a modification. However, it is often financially advantageous when considering the time and expense associated with foreclosure proceedings combined with the reality of foreclosed properties often selling far below their outstanding mortgage balances and often market values.

The loan modification should include some combination of:

- a reduction in interest rates for a fixed term of at least five years;

- an extension of the amortization period to no more than 40 years from the original date of the loan (spreading the principal out longer reduces the monthly payment);

- a reduction of the principal amount owed;

- compliance with the applicable federally mandated loan modification guidelines; and,

- any other factors that have resulted in a reduction in foreclosures.

Short Sales

A short sale allows the borrower to sell the property for an amount less than that outstanding debt, averting the foreclosure proceeding. The terms and conditions of purchase are set and the sale is supervised by the lender. Lenders waive their rights to any deficiencies provided the title was voluntarily transferred, conveyancing documents duly recorded and the proceeds of sale have been tendered to the mortgagee/beneficiary as agreed. Short Sales are attractive to lenders for several reasons; proceeds are often higher than would be gained from the sale of a foreclosed property; costs and risks associated with maintenance/ownership of a foreclosed property; as well as the time and expense of foreclosure proceedings.

Deed in Lieu of Foreclosure

A Deed in Lieu of Foreclosure is just that: the borrower surrenders the deed (with encumbrances) to the borrower to avoid a foreclosure proceeding. The lender is under no obligation to accept the deed, but there are benefits to each. For the borrower, this is the fastest way out from under the financial burden of making payments and likely the least damaging to their credit rating. For the lender, they gain immediate access to the property and eliminate the time and expense of foreclosure. Since title transferred after foreclosure is generally free of additional liens, a borrower with outstanding liens beyond the outstanding mortgage would not likely qualify for this option.

Bankruptcy

The United States Bankruptcy Court conducts these proceedings for the purpose of discharging or restructuring outstanding debt. There are three distinct options:

- **Chapter 7** - the debtor's assets are sold and the proceeds applied to discharge outstanding debts. This is the least expensive and fastest option, making it the most common for personal bankruptcies. Most personal belongings, cars, pensions and any homestead protections are exempt from liquidation. Additionally, not all debts can be discharged, such as some taxes, child support or alimony. Chapter 7 is not available to individuals deemed to earn sufficient income for a Chapter 13 proceeding.

- **Chapter 13** - The court and debtor structure a repayment plan for the outstanding debt. Chapter 13 can be used as a limited form of loan modification in that borrowers may be able to include past due payments in the repayment plan. In addition, under the Chapter 13 rules, debtors with multiple liens can sometimes eliminate junior liens on their property (called "lien stripping"). Qualification for Chapter 13 includes both secured and unsecured debt limits which reset every 3 years.

- **Chapter 11** - most commonly used by business for restructuring debt; but, can apply to individuals who own several non-exempt properties.

Mortgage Foreclosure Consultants

Since 1979, several pieces of legislation have been passed providing protections for homeowners occupying 1-4 unit dwellings that are subject to a Notice of Default. The law specifically acknowledges that these homeowners are subject to "fraud, deception, harassment and unfair dealing" by foreclosure consultants. The Mortgage Foreclosure Consultants Law addresses the problem of consultants representing that they can assist homeowners who are in foreclosure, often charging high fees, frequently exacting payment of their fees by an lien on the property, and knowingly perform an essentially worthless service to the homeowner.

Foreclosure consultant is defined as "any person who makes any solicitation, representation, or an offer to any owner to perform for compensation, or who for compensation, performs any service the person in any manner represents he or she will do including any of the following:

- Stop or postpone the foreclosure sale;

- Obtain any forbearance from any beneficiary/lender/mortgagee;

- Assist the owner in the right of reinstatement;

- Obtain any extension of the period within which the owner may reinstate his or her debt/loan or obligations;

- Obtain any waiver of an acceleration clause contained in the promissory note or in a deed of trust or mortgage on a residence in foreclosure (or in both the evidence of debt/loan and the security instrument);

- Assist the owner to obtain a loan or advance of funds;

- Avoid or ameliorate the impairment of the owner's credit rating resulting from the recording of a Notice of Default or through the conduct of a foreclosure sale;

- Save the owners residence from foreclosure; or,

- Assist the owner in obtaining from the beneficiary/lender/mortgagee or trustee acting under a *power of sale* or from a counsel acting for the beneficiary/lender/trustee the remaining proceeds from the foreclosure sale of the owner's residence (surpluses due to the owner as the borrower upon whom the foreclosure was conducted)."

Licensed attorneys providing these services in the course of their practice and real estate licensees are exempt from the definition as mortgage consultants. Unless specifically exempt, foreclosure consultants must register with the California Department of Justice and maintain a surety bond in the amount of $100,000. A violation of these laws may be punished by a fine of not more than $10,000 or imprisonment in the county jail or state prison for not more than one year, or both. Finally, any provision in a contract with a foreclosure consultant that purports to limit the liability of the foreclosure consultant under these laws is void and, at the option of the homeowner, would render the contract void.

These provisions go on to declare that "any person, *including attorneys and real estate agents*, may not collect advance fees for loan modification services related to mortgage or deeds of trust secured by a residential property containing four or fewer dwelling units." These provisions specifically declare it unlawful for any person negotiating, arranging or otherwise offering (or attempting any of same) to perform loan modification or other mortgage loan forbearance for a fee to be paid by the borrower to:

- charge or collect any compensation until they have fully performed each and every service they represented or contracted to perform;

- accept any wage assignment or lien/security of any type on real or personal property as compensation; or

- take any form of power of attorney from the borrower for any purpose.

8.7 Real Estate Finance Regulations

"Predatory Lending" describes a myriad of abusive lending practices by some banks, lenders, and even some MLBs that have been construed as preying upon unsophisticated consumers and borrowers. The U.S. Congress and California legislature have each enacted legislation adding substantial new laws related to making and arranging residential mortgage loans, with a primary focus on owner-occupied properties. Additionally, new federal regulations have been adopted as guidance for lenders and MLBs/MLOs engaged in making and arranging alternative mortgage instruments or non-traditional mortgage products. Following are some of the major regulations.

Equal Credit Opportunity Act (ECOA)
The ECOA was enacted by the federal government to promote the availability of credit without regard to race, color, religion, national origin, sex, marital status, or age (other than minors) and whether all or part of the applicant's income is derived from a public assistance program. The law requires creditors/lenders to:

- notify applicants of actions taken on their applications (including credit denials) within 30 days;
- to report credit histories in the names of both spouses on an account;
- to retain records of credit applications;
- to collect information about the applicant's race and other personal characteristics in applications for dwelling-related loans; and
- to provide applicants with copies of appraisal reports prepared and used in connection with credit transactions.

These laws apply to anyone participating in the decision making process of extending revolving credit, including, retailers, credit card companies, banks and mortgage lenders and their representatives. *Of particular concern to real estate licensees is the 30-day notice requirement.* Real estate brokers (MLBs/MLOs) may have primary responsibility for providing this notice when they engage in pre-screening functions on behalf of a particular lender. If an adverse action was taken (denial), the lender or MLB must send the applicant an ECOA Notice reiterating the prohibitions against discrimination, provide the name of the enforcement agency and the specific reason(s) for denial.

In 1974, this was breakthrough legislation for women. Nearly as important as the new requirements were the prohibitions introduced by the legislation. These prohibitions include:

- asking about birth control or future child-bearing;
- asking about alimony or child support income, except when that income is used for qualifying; and
- income discrimination based on sex or marital status.

Failure to comply with ECOA may result in damages up to $10,000 for individuals and the lesser of $500,000 or 1% of the creditor's net worth for class actions suits.

Truth In Lending Act (TILA) And Regulation Z

Enacted in 1969, the principal purpose of TILA was to increase consumer understanding of the true costs of financing and credit along with significant new protections. The Federal Reserve Board (FRB) adopted Regulation Z as the vehicle to implement TILA. TILA requires extenders of credit to disclose the credit terms in a standardized way that allows consumers/borrowers to make meaningful comparisons among various creditors/lenders.

TILA requires standardized disclosures about loan terms and the fees, costs, and expenses of obtaining/using credit. Lenders must disclose the cost of credit as a dollar amount (the finance charge) and as an annual percentage rate (APR). APR is the effective interest rate when costs, fees and expenses are factored into the payment amount. Because finance charges can vary widely, APR can be significantly higher from one lender to another.

Under certain circumstances, Regulation Z also provides the borrower the opportunity to rescind acceptance of credit terms for up to 3 days ("3-day right of rescission"). The 3-day right applies to refinance loans or other junior liens, but not primary or seller financing.

One aspect of Regulation Z of particular note for real estate professionals relates to advertising practices. Because TILA posits that certain credit terms must be considered together for a full understanding, Reg Z requires that when advertising contains a "triggering term", then other credit terms must also be disclosed for a complete picture. It should be noted that the APR alone is not considered a triggering term.

Under Reg Z, "triggering terms" are:

- the amount of any payment,
- the amount or percentage of downpayment required,
- the number of payments or timeline for repayment, and
- the amount of any finance charges.

which in turn then requires the disclosure of:

- all repayment terms, specifically the payment amounts over the life of the loan and any balloon payments required;
- the amount or percentage of downpayment; and
- the APR

These rules apply to anyone (including real estate agents, developers, landlords and lenders) advertising credit terms for real and personal property and commercial leases.

Ability to Repay and Qualified Mortgage Rules (ATR/QM)

As of January, 2014, nearly all applications for owner-occupied residential loans (1-4 units) require lenders to make a good-faith effort to demonstrate the borrower's ability to repay. Exceptions to the new rules include: timeshares, HELOCs, some bridge loans and some reverse mortgages. At a minimum, lenders/creditors must now consider:

- current or reasonably anticipated income/assets and employment status;
- current debt, alimony and child support obligations;
- the monthly payment amount, including the monthly payment amount of any simultaneous loans;
- the monthly payment for any mortgage-related obligations;
- the monthly debt-to-income ratio; and
- credit history.

Included in the ATR/QM Rules, FNMA and Freddie Mac can no longer purchase loans that: are not fully-amortizing, have a term exceeding 30 years or include points and fees in excess of 3% of the total loan amount or other loan limits under the Ability-to-Repay Rule.

Real Estate Settlement Procedures Act (RESPA) Regulation X

The federal government enacted the Real Estate Settlement Procedures Act (RESPA) in 1974 requiring up-front estimates of closing costs and prepaid expenses (fees, points etc.) be provided to consumers/borrowers for any transaction with a federally-regulated institution. The purpose of this regulation was to prevent bait-and-switch tactics and eliminate the practice of real estate agents, developers, lenders, appraisers (essentially everyone involved in the settlement of a real property transaction) of paying kick-backs or referral fees to one another in exchange for service. Significant amendments to RESPA became effective over a period of several months prior to January 1, 2010. Major disclosure and timing requirements under RESPA are:

- mortgage loan applicants must be provided with a special information booklet entitled, "Shopping for Your Home Loan, HUD's Settlement Cost Booklet", at the earliest possible time;
- a Good Faith Estimate (GFE) must be completed and delivered within 3 days of the loan application. The GFE includes an estimate of settlement charges, closing costs and prepaid expenses as well as the prospective material loan terms;
- a Servicing Disclosure statement within 3 days. This statement discloses whether the lender intends to service the loan or transfer servicing elsewhere; and
- a HUD-1 or HUD-1A (for refinance loans) must be completed and made available to the borrower one business day prior to closing or settlement. The HUD-1 (discussed further below) provides the *actual* settlement charges, closing costs and prepaid expenses for comparison with the GFE.

HUD-1 or HUD-1A (Uniform Settlement Statement)

A major new regulation under RESPA was the required use of a standardized settlement statement (HUD-1 or HUD-1A). The settlement statement details every amount paid to (credited to) and every amount paid by (debited from) the buyer and seller at the closing of escrow. Generally, the HUD-1 is used for property purchases and the HUD-1A for refinances or junior encumbrances. The settlement agent/escrow holder is required to use the HUD-1 or HUD-1A settlement statement in every settlement/escrow of a mortgage loan involving a federally regulated institution.

- **HUD-1** - a standardized, three-page document detailing all monies exchanged/paid at settlement and used to compare the *estimates* given in the GFE to the *actual* final charges and amounts.

- **HUD-1A** - a similar two-page document, generally used for refinances showing only amounts debited from (paid by) the borrower.

Seller Financing Disclosure Law

Most seller financing is exempt from much of the borrower protection regulation. However, any professional arranging financing for a fee, is responsible to provide the borrower with a Residential Purchase Money Loan Disclosure. It should be noted, this law applies to a real estate licensee receiving any fee for arranging credit (including negotiating terms, preparing loan documents, etc.) unless the transaction is otherwise covered under Federal or State laws.

Study Smart Guide

Primary Mortgage Market - Banks and lenders create mortgages sold directly to the borrower.

Secondary Mortgage Market - Primary lenders package portfolio of mortgages sold to government-related agencies and investors.

Primary Market Insurers and Guarantors - Federal Housing Administration (FHA), California Housing Finance Agency (CalFHA), Veterans Administration (VA), Department of Veterans Affairs (DVA)

Secondary Market Insurers and Guarantors - Federal National Mortgage Association (FNMA or Fannie Mae), Government National Mortgage Association (GNMA or Ginnie Mae), Federal Home Loan Mortgage Corporation (FHLMC or Freddie Mac).

Lenders - make or originate and provide funds for mortgage loans.

Mortgage Bankers - privately-owned companies acting as authorized agents and representatives originating and providing funds for mortgage loans.

Mortgage Loan Brokers (MLB) - third parties who find and match borrowers with lenders for a fee.

Mortgage Loan Originators (MLO) - anyone who offers or takes a mortgage loan application or offers to negotiate terms for a fee.

The Safe Mortgage Licensing Act (SAFE Act) - consumer protections setting national minimum standards for the licensing and registration of state-licensed mortgage loan originators (MLOs).

Conventional Fixed-Rate Financing - long term loans (amortized over 30 years) with a fixed rate of interest and no insured backing from FHA or guarantee from VA.

Types of Alternative Financing - Adjustable Rate Mortgages (ARMs), Reverse Mortgages (RMs), Rollover Mortgages (ROMs), Graduated Payment Mortgages (GPMs),

Negotiable instrument - a written, unconditional promise to pay a specific amount of money at a defined time or on demand.

Promissory Note - the evidence of the debt and the contract by which the borrower promises to pay the lender.

Deed of Trust or Mortgage - the instrument making the real property described the security (collateral) for the debt/loan.

Types of Promissory Notes - Installment note, Balloon note, Adjustable rate note, Renegotiable note, Straight note, Demand note.

Security Instrument - document describing both the rights and obligations of the lender and the borrower, such as deeds of trust and mortgages.

Deed of Trust - security instrument drawn between three parties; a trustor (the borrower), a beneficiary (the lender), and a neutral third party (the trustee).

Mortgage - an instrument drawn between two parties; the mortgagor (the borrower) and mortgagee (the lender).

Acceleration Clause - lender can demand immediate full payment of the outstanding balance of principal and interest due.

Alienation Clause (also known as a "due-on-sale" clause) - On sale or any transfer of interest, the lender can demand immediate full payment of the outstanding balance of principal and interest due.

Types of loans - Purchase Loan, Refinance Loan, First Mortgage, Second Mortgage, Junior and Senior Mortgages, Bridge or Swing Loan, Home Equity Mortgage (HELOC), Construction Mortgage, Blanket Mortgage, Seller Financing, Private Financing

Foreclosure - procedure used to terminate the rights, title, and interests of a trustor/mortgagor through sale of the property and use of the proceeds to satisfy the debt/loan.

Deficiency Judgment - a personal judgment against a debtor/borrower for any difference between the unpaid balance of the debt/loan (plus interest, authorized fees, costs, and expenses of sale) and the actual proceeds from the sale.

Judicial Foreclosure - foreclosure usually sought when a beneficiary or mortgagee wants to obtain a deficiency judgment.

Non-Judicial Foreclosure - When the security instrument includes a *power of sale*, the alternative remedy for a creditor/lender to recover the debt requires the lender to direct the Trustee named in the security instrument to hold a public trustee's sale.

Foreclosure Alternatives - Loan modification, Short sale, Deed in lieu of foreclosure, Bankruptcy.

Real Estate Finance Regulations - Equal Credit Opportunity Act (ECOA), Truth In Lending Act (TILA), Real Estate Settlement Procedures Act (RESPA), Seller Financing Disclosure Law.

HUD-1 - standardized document detailing all monies exchanged/paid at settlement and used to compare the estimates given in the GFE to the actual final charges and amounts.

HUD-1A - two-page version used for refinances showing only amounts debited from (paid by) the borrower.

Chapter 8

Quiz & Answers

1) A primary lender:
   a) only sells purchase loans
   b) doesn't sell loans on the secondary market
   c) doesn't use mortgage brokers
   d) sells loans directly to borrowers

2) Which of the following is true of FNMA:
   a) insures loans on the secondary market
   b) only works with certain lenders
   c) only buys FHA and VA backed loans
   d) a and b only

3) A loan originator is:
   a) anyone who arranges a loan
   b) a primary lender only
   c) required to be the employee of a lender
   d) required to be a mortgage broker

4) SAFE Mortgage Act:
   a) sets the approval guidelines for loans
   b) sets the allowable income-to-debt ratios
   c) requires registration and licensing for loan originators
   d) all of the above

5) Real Estate licensees:
   a) can arrange loans in California
   b) can only arrange loans secured by real property
   c) cannot arrange loans without a special license
   d) none of the above

6) Which of the following applies to a residential mortgage:
   a) is used for personal and family use
   b) is available for 1-4 units only
   c) cannot be used for commercial properties
   d) all of the above

7) Conventional fixed-rate financing:
   a) has no FHA or VA backing guarantees
   b) has fixed monthly payments
   c) has a fixed interest rate for the entire term
   d) all of the above

8) A promissory note:
   a) is the security instrument for the mortgage
   b) is the contract governing how the loan will be repaid
   c) cannot include future obligations
   d) is secondary to the mortgage

9) A deed of trust:
   a) must be drawn between 2 parties
   b) contains a power of sale clause
   c) is dissolved when the mortgage is paid
   d) provides the borrower with title, subject to the mortgage

10) A HELOC is:
    a) a type of second mortgage
    b) considered predatory lending
    c) a revolving line of credit
    d) used for purchase money

ANSWERS:

1. d	3. a	5. b	7. d	9. b
2. d	4. c	6. d	8. b	10. c

CHAPTER 9

Chapter 9: The Mortgage Process

9.1 The Path to Homeownership

Most prospective new homebuyers are more than a little overwhelmed at the prospect of embarking on the buying journey. They often take cautious, non-committal steps beginning with casually gazing longingly at properties for sale on the internet and may even venture out to an open house or two. When they get more confident and serious, these are the steps nearly everyone must go through:

- Establishing a realistic price range by getting a loan pre-qualification or pre-approval;
- Property shopping and comparison
- Offer and Acceptance to purchase a specific property
- Property Inspections and Mortgage shopping and comparison
- Formal Mortgage Application
- Mortgage Loan Processing
- Property Appraisal
- Loan Underwriting
- Loan Approval and Commitment
- Insurance comparison and Binder Purchase
- Loan funding, Document signing and Settlement and Recording

In this chapter, we will breakdown the practicalities of obtaining conventional residential financing. Obtaining a loan begins with a homebuyer contacting a mortgage loan broker (MLB) or originator (MLO). The MLO must listen and understand the applicant's needs, gather the appropriate information and respond with accurate loan opportunities best suited to that purchaser/borrower. An MLO must know the details of each loan program as well as the associated underwriting guidelines and processing requirements.

9.2 Preliminary Documentation

Pre-qualification vs. Pre-approval

Generally, the very first questions to be answered are "How much house/mortgage can I afford?" There are two distinct avenues for answering that question: Pre-qualification and Pre-approval.

- **Pre-qualification** - This is a quick, simple estimate generally based on a homebuyer's verbal representation of their income, debts, credit standing and down payment amount. It is generally done verbally and an MLO can nearly instantly provide a "Pre-qualification Letter." This is a preliminary estimate of a loan amount for which the borrower may qualify and when combined with the downpayment amount establishes the price ranges and monthly payments for homes the buyer is likely able to afford. Any MLB/MLO can provide a pre-qualification letter.

- **Pre-approval** - This is also a relatively quick and painless process, however, the pre-approval process involves the MLO verifying the information provided through one of the many electronic underwriting software programs before issuing a "Pre-approval Letter." The type of information provided is the same as pre-qualification, but there may be some fees involved for verification and processing. Only an MLB or an MLO directly representing a lender/creditor may issue a pre-approval letter.

Pre-approvals are clearly the stronger of the two letters. Many agents/homeowners will not enter into negotiations with a prospective buyer who cannot provide an appropriate pre-approval letter to accompany their offer. A pre-approval is NOT a loan commitment, but rather a preliminary approval of the buyer's ability to qualify for a loan. A commitment cannot be issued until the property has also been approved through an appraisal, title examination etc.

Credit History and FICO

Automated approvals rely heavily on credit scores generated from each of three national credit data agencies: Experian, Transunion, and Equifax. Credit scores (also known as "FICO Scores") are complex formulas that evaluate the credit data associated with a borrower. These three-digit scores generally range from 300-850 with the higher score representing the lesser risk. A score of 700 or higher is considered a very good score and will generally qualify a borrower for most loan programs at a competitive interest rate. A credit score of less than 650 will likely result in denial or a higher interest rate.

In addition, credit reports show a potential borrower's history of paying their debts on time. Any revolving credit payments (car loans, credit cards, etc.), utilities and even rent payment histories are shown or can be considered. Delinquencies or charge-offs in the prior 2 years would negatively impact the credit score, jeopardizing approval for a loan.

Debt-to-Income Ratios

Beyond credit histories, another important factor in a buyer's loan approval are two "debt-to-income ratios": monthly housing expenses (principal, interest, taxes and insurance, commonly known as "PITI") to gross monthly income ("front-end" ratios) and total monthly debt (including all monthly payment obligations) to gross monthly income ("back-end" ratios). Different loan programs require more and less strict ratios for qualification. Generally, a front-end ratio of 25% and a back-end ratio between 35% are considered acceptable. FNMA has changed their ratio calculation to reflect a single consideration of maximum debt-to-income ratio (DTI) of 36% in most cases.

9.3 The Mortgage Application

Once a buyer has located the home they wish to purchase, they now know the second component necessary for a formal mortgage application. The application form is a summary of all information required by a lender for both the determination of an applicant's qualification for the loan and whether the collateral (property) is of sufficient quality and value to support the loan amount. A standardized application form has been generally been adopted by most of the major players in the mortgage industry; although the name can differ from agency to agency, it is most often referred to as the FNMA 1003 or simply 1003.

The application process involves filling out 1003 identifying the amount, terms and purpose of the loan and how and when it will be repaid. As previously discussed, the prohibitions under The Federal Equal Credit Opportunity Act (ECOA) and Fair Housing Act all apply.

Advance Fees

MLOs who are MLBs and lenders may collect money in advance to cover the costs arranging or originating the loan. Any money collected up front is considered an "advance fee". As previously discussed, advance fees must be submitted for approval by the CalBRE, held in the broker's trust account and disbursed only after the services have been performed. The exceptions are the fees for obtaining a credit report and/or an appraisal report. The DRE permits MLB/MLOs to collect fees for the anticipated exact amount required by the service providers, which must then be held in the trust account and overages refunded as soon as they are identified.

Loan Guidelines

As previously discussed, there are many different kinds of lenders ranging from institutional lenders such as banks and savings and loans to mortgage bankers (lending their own money) and mortgage brokers (matching borrowers to lenders for a fee). Most lenders offer several different loan products depending on whether they intend to sell the loans on the secondary market or keep them for their own investment portfolio.

As a result, each loan product has a distinct set of guidelines relating to the borrower's financial profile and maximum loan limits on security properties. In 2008, the FHFA (Federal Housing Finance Agency) took over conservatorship of FNMA and Freddie Mac and now oversees much of the secondary market activity and sets guidelines and maximum loan limits for loan products to be sold on the secondary market. Licensees, and certainly MLOs, should familiarize themselves with the various borrower and property guidelines put forth by FHFA for FNMA, FHA, VA, DVA and CALHFA at a minimum. Some terms you should know regarding loan guidelines are:

- **conforming loans** - Loans meeting FHFA guidelines, meaning they are easily sold on the secondary market.

- **non-conforming loans** - Loans not meeting FHFA guidelines, generally more expensive for borrowers.

- **jumbo loans** - Loans exceeding the maximum conforming loan limits, generally more expensive for borrowers. It should be noted in states with higher property values (such as California), a significant number of loans may fall under the jumbo guidelines, rates and terms.
- **portfolio loans** - Loans not intended to be sold on the secondary market, but instead retained in the lender's investment portfolio.

9.4 Loan Processing

Once the application is complete and all supporting documentation provided, the MLB/MLO will usually submit the application to loan processing and provide the applicant with the many disclosures required by RESPA, TILA, ECOA and all other federal and state requirements.

The loan processor assembles and verifies all the necessary information gathered on which the lender will base the decision to extend credit. They are now evaluating both the borrower's ability to repay the debt and the property's value as sufficient collateral for that debt.

Borrower Information

The following information is gathered and verified by the processor to assess the borrower's ability to repay the loan:

- **Purpose of the loan** - This categorizes the type of loan to determine the qualification criteria and what disclosures are required. The three common categories include: purchase, for occupancy or investment; refinance to obtain better rates and terms or receive "cash-out"; or an equity loan to finance home improvements or other disclosed financial needs.

- **Source of Repayment** - For most people, the primary source of repayment is income from employment. Understanding the type of business or employment and how long the applicants have been in that business establishes the stability of the income. Most lenders look for a minimum of 2 years in the same line of work. Sometimes income is derived through self-employment and/or investment income, which requires additional documentation and adds a level of scrutiny, such as future expected trends of the business or profession and the applicant's likelihood of continuing in the same business.

- **Assets** - Every lender looks for an indication of the applicants' ability to save money. The asset breakdown represents the strength of the financial standing of the applicants. Liquidity (easily converted/accessed as cash) is important for down payments, required cash reserves, and the likelihood of weathering unforeseen gaps in income or unexpected expenses.

- **Liabilities** - As mentioned above, these expenses are evaluated as the PITI expense to establish a "front-end" ratio of housing debt to income, and the total monthly obligations to establish a "back-end" ratio of total debt to income. Monthly housing expenses include the monthly loan payment, the payments on any other financing against the property, property taxes, assessments, casualty and hazard insurance premiums, mortgage insurance premiums, and the dues or assessments of homeowners associations. The total monthly obligations include housing expenses and additional monthly debts such as revolving credit debt (credit cards, car payments), alimony and child support, and other liabilities that require monthly payments.

- **Credit History** - Each lender sets general policy guidelines outlining acceptable credit quality. Credit policies are influenced by the lender's intent to keep the loan in their portfolio or to sell the loan in the secondary marketplace. Credit history is a good indication of an applicants' ability to manage their finances. Lenders usually consider repeat borrowers with a tangible record of repayment better risks.

Property Information

The value, condition of title, and overall quality of the property is evaluated to determine if the collateral will be adequate to secure repayment of the loan. Because of the long terms (often 30 years) associated with real estate loans, the lender estimates not only current value and condition, but the economic trends in the neighborhood and community where the property is located. The loan processor orders the following reports for this evaluation:

- **Preliminary "Title" Report** - The borrower acquiring good title to the real property that will secure the loan is of primary concern to every lender. Once the preliminary borrower information is verified and viewed favorably, the loan processor orders a preliminary report be obtained from a title company or title insurer describing the offer to insure title on the property. The preliminary report:

    - identifies the property, including assessor's parcel number, street address, legal description and any issue that may arise by the legal description;
    - identifies the current owner of record; and,
    - reveals proposed title policy exceptions, including property taxes, assessments, encumbrances, liens, easements, claims and conditions of record, etc.

- **Appraisal** - An appraiser is retained to inspect the property and estimate present value and future market trends. The relationship between the amount of the proposed loan and the estimate of fair market value is the "Loan-to-Value" ratio (discussed shortly). Most lenders base their loan amounts on the purchase price or appraised value, whichever is less.

- **Property due diligence** - Any of the following issues may also be uncovered and/or addressed:
    - whether the property is currently occupied, the status of the occupant (do they have a lease; will the property be vacant for the new borrower to occupy) and whether the occupant is asserting any claim affecting title;
    - on purchase money loans, the sales price and proposed terms;
    - on refinance loans, the date, price and terms of the original purchase;
    - are there additional assessments; and
    - has any work been performed within the last 90 days that might result in a mechanics' lien or other title claim.

Once up front disclosures are provided, the applicant has supplied all requested supporting documentation, and the credit, preliminary title and appraisal reports have been received; the loan file is organized to ensure conformity and compliance with the lender's policies and procedures.

9.5 Loan Underwriting Analysis

The underwriter makes the final assessment of the risk of the proposed loan and makes a recommendation whether or not to approve the loan. In addition, the underwriter ensures the loan package is in compliance with the lender's policies and all applicable laws. The underwriter carefully considers the capacity of the borrower to repay the loan along with determining the collateral to be adequate. This analysis is based on:

- Information contained in the loan application and supporting documents;

- Information developed by the loan processer in checking the credit and character of the prospective consumer/borrower;

- Verification of employment, bank deposits, etc.;

- Review of the preliminary title and appraisal reports and from the property due diligence.

Loan-to-Value Ratio (LTV)

Of primary concern in risk assessment for a particular loan is the "loan-to-value" ratio (LTV). The LTV is considered as the amount of the first mortgage (purchase price less down payment) divided by either the purchase price or appraised value, whichever is less. Some lenders require an LTV of 80% or lower. Many lenders will underwrite higher LTVs but require the borrower to buy "private mortgage insurance" (PMI) and/or charge higher rates at less attractive terms.

Private Mortgage Insurance (PMI)

Private Mortgage Insurance Companies (MICs) provide mortgage insurance for residential conventional mortgage loans. PMI enables residential borrowers to obtain loans with higher loan-to-value ratios and to purchase homes with smaller down payments. Private mortgage insurance is typically required when loan-to-value ratios exceed 80%. PMI reduces the monetary risk of loss to lenders and to subsequent investors, making them more saleable in the secondary market. MICs have underwriting standards that conventional lenders must meet in order to qualify for coverage.

Borrowers with a positive payment history can request that PMI be cancelled once the equity/debt ratio in their home reaches the 20/80 benchmark. With some exceptions, the Homeowner's Protection Act (HPA) of 1998 requires lenders to alert borrowers when the date the loan is scheduled to reach 80%. Additionally, PMI must be cancelled at 78% when borrowers are current on their payments.

9.6 Loan Approval and Commitment, Document Signing and Settlement

Once the processing and underwriting processes are complete, the file is then sent for final review and approval. When the loan is approved and a formal commitment generated:

- the lender designates the funds and provides for wiring them to the escrow agent,
- a HUD-1 is prepared and reviewed,
- the closing is scheduled, at which time the documentation necessary to complete the transaction of purchase and security instruments are signed and prepared for recording; and
- the funds are disbursed and the buyer gets the keys.

Study Smart Guide

Pre-qualification - quick, simple preliminary estimate of buyer's loan qualifications based on verbal representation of income, debts, credit standing and down payment amount. Any MLB/MLO can provide a pre-qualification letter.

Pre-approval - uses same information as pre-qualification, but involves an MLO verifying the information through electronic underwriting software programs. There may be some fees and only an MLB or an MLO directly representing a lender/creditor may issue a pre-approval letter.

Credit scores (also known as "FICO Scores") - complex formulas that evaluate the credit data assigning three-digit scores ranging from 300-850; the higher score is best.

Front-end ratio - monthly housing expenses (principal, interest, taxes and insurance, commonly known as "PITI") to gross monthly income.

Back-end ratio - total monthly debt (including all monthly payment obligations) to gross monthly income.

Debt-to-income ratio (DTI) - FNMA single ration calculation.

Loan Guidelines - a distinct set of guidelines relating to the borrower's financial profile and maximum loan limits on security properties.

Conforming loans - Loans meeting FHFA guidelines, easily sold on the secondary market.

Non-conforming loans - Loans not meeting FHFA guidelines, generally more expensive for borrowers.

Jumbo loans - Loans exceeding the maximum conforming loan limits, generally more expensive for borrowers.

Portfolio loans - Loans not intended to be sold on the secondary market.

Loan processing - assembly and verification all information on which the lender will base the decision to extend credit. Evaluates both the borrower's ability to repay and the property's value as sufficient collateral.

Loan Underwriting Analysis - the final assessment of the risk of the proposed loan and the decision whether or not to approve the loan.

Loan-to-Value Ration - amount of the first mortgage (purchase price less down payment) divided by either the purchase price or appraised value, whichever is less.

Chapter 9
Quiz & Answers

1) A pre-approval letter:
    a) is a preliminary loan commitment
    b) can be issued by any MLO or MLB
    c) doesn't verify the borrower's information
    d) none of the above

2) A FICO score:
    a) is the walkability of a location
    b) is the federal income bracket of a borrower
    c) is the future income score of a borrower
    d) is the 3-digit credit score

3) The mortgage application is made:
    a) when a property has been located
    b) after all inspection are completed
    c) after all contingencies have been met
    d) none of the above

4) The debt-to-income ratio measures:
    a) the mortgage amount to property value
    b) the borrower's income amount to debt amounts
    c) b only
    d) both a and b

5) A non-conforming loan:
    a) is designed to be sold on the secondary market
    b) does not meet FHFH guidelines
    c) is considered predatory lending
    d) requires and higher appraisal

239

6) Loan limits:
   a) are based on property value
   b) are based on borrower income
   c) both a or b
   d) neither a and b

7) Loan processing involves:
   a) ordering the preliminary title report
   b) verifying all borrower information
   c) obtaining an appraisal
   d) all of the above

8) The loan underwriter:
   a) orders and reviews the appraisal
   b) reviews borrow information and recommends approval or not
   c) arranges for insurance for the property
   d) arranges for the close of the escrow between the attorneys and the lender

9) Loan-to-value ratios refer to:
   a) loan amount to borrower income
   b) loan amount to property value
   c) loan amount to borrower's future income
   d) loan amount to property's future value

10) Private mortgage insurance is:
    a) required for buyers with low credit scores
    b) required for properties with multiple mortgages
    c) required for mortgages with more than 80% LTV
    d) never required; there's no such thing.

ANSWERS:

1. d	3. a	5. b	7. d	9. b
2. d	4. c	6. d	8. b	10. c

REAL ESTATE MATH

The Real Estate Math section of this guide should not be taken lightly. Most state exams include around 10% math questions, but you don't have to be a mathematician to complete this part effectively. Use this review to refresh your understanding of and learn arithmetic, algebra, geometry, and word problems. You will also have the opportunity to practice with the included sample problems for each math topic.

Some of the math question types you may come across on your exam include:

- Area
- Percents
- Property tax
- Loan-to-Value Ratios
- Points
- Equity
- Qualifying Buyers
- Prorations
- Commissions
- Proceeds from sales
- Transfer Tax/Conveyance Tax/Revenue Stamps
- Competitive Market Analyses
- Income Properties
- Depreciation

Use the following to help you complete the math questions.

Tips for Completing Math Questions

Before taking the exam, and especially while you are completing the math portion of the exam, there are a few things you may want to keep in mind:

Leave No Question Unanswered

Although you may not know the answer to every question right off the top of your head, it is advisable that you answer every question to the best of your ability. You immediately have a one in four chance of getting the answer correct. There are also some instances where an answer choice is clearly not correct, which betters your chance for selecting the right answer.

Use a Calculator

In California, basic calculators are provided for your use, therefore the use of a personal calculator is not allowed. However, you shouldn't rely solely on the calculator as this can slow you down, but using it to work out some mathematical equations can prove to be very helpful.

Utilize Scrap Paper

Let nothing take the place of scrap paper. While using a calculator can help you get the answer quickly, writing down your thought process provides information for you to refer to in case you get stuck.

Review! Review! Review!

Avoiding an incorrect answer can be something as simple as checking your work.

Math Review

Basic math skills in the areas of arithmetic, algebra, geometry, and word problems will be necessary. Here's a review.

Arithmetic

Multiplication

"Factor" is the term used to describe numbers that are being multiplied. The answer is known as the "product."

Example:

2 x 5 = 10   2 and 5 are the factors. 10 is the product.

A multiplication problem can be presented in a variety of ways.

- You may see a dot between two factors, which denotes multiplication:
  $2 \cdot 5 = 10$

- The use of parentheses around one or more factors denotes multiplication:
  (2)5 = 10

  2(5) = 10

  (2)(5) = 10

- A number next to a variable denotes multiplication:

  2a = 10

  Multiply "2" and "a" to arrive at the product of 10.

Division

The "divisor" is the number divided by; while the "dividend" is the number the divisor is going into. The result is the quotient.

Division is similar to multiplication in that there are several ways to indicate the operation.

12÷3 = 4

12/3 = 4

$\frac{12}{3} = 4$

Decimals

The key to understanding decimals is knowing each place value.

Here is a table to help you remember:

4	6	3	2	6	.	5	7	9	1
Ten Thousands	Thousands	Hundreds	Tens	Ones	Decimal	Tenths	Hundredths	Thousandths	Ten Thousandths

Using the above table, this number would be expressed as: 46,326.5791

It is also important to understand how to round decimals. If the number immediately following the number you must round is 5 or greater, you increase the preceding number by 1. If the number immediately following the number you must round is less than 5, drop that number and leave the preceding number as is.

Example:

0.236 would be rounded to 0.24

0.234 would be rounded to 0.23

Adding Fractions

Adding fractions with the same denominators is a simple operation. You add the numerators together and leave the denominator as it appears.

Example:

$$\frac{3}{5} + \frac{1}{5} = \frac{4}{5}$$

Adding fractions with different denominators requires you to find the least common denominator. The least common denominator is the smallest number that each of your denominators can divide into evenly.

Example:

$\frac{4}{6} + \frac{3}{4}$ The least common denominator is 12 because 6 x 2 = 12 and 4 x 3 = 12.

Once you have determined the least common denominator, each fraction should be converted to its new form. This is done by multiplying the numerator and denominator in each fraction by the appropriate number in order to arrive at the least common denominator. Next, you add the new numerators, which gives you the final answer.

Example:

$$\frac{4}{6} + \frac{3}{4} = \frac{2(4)}{2(6)} + \frac{3(3)}{3(4)} = \frac{8}{12} + \frac{9}{12} = \frac{17}{12}$$

Subtracting Fractions

Subtracting fractions with the same denominators is a simple operation. You subtract the numerators and leave the denominator as it appears.

Example:

$$\frac{3}{5} - \frac{1}{5} = \frac{2}{5}$$

Subtracting fractions with different denominators requires you to find the least common denominator. The least common denominator is the smallest number that each of your denominators can divide into evenly.

Example:

$\frac{8}{9} - \frac{3}{6}$ The least-common denominator is 18 because 9 x 2 = 18 and 6 x 3 = 18.

Once you have determined the least common denominator, each fraction should be converted to its new form. This is done by multiplying the numerator and denominator in each fraction by the appropriate number in order to arrive at the least common denominator. Next, you subtract the new numerators, giving you the final answer.

Example:

$\frac{8}{9} - \frac{3}{6} = \frac{2(8)}{2(9)} - \frac{3(3)}{3(6)} = \frac{16}{18} - \frac{9}{18} = \frac{7}{18}$

Multiplying Fractions

When multiplying fractions, the denominators of the fractions can be the same or different. Either way, the operation is performed the same.

Multiply the numerators together and multiply the denominators together.

Example:

$\frac{4}{7} \times \frac{3}{5} = \frac{12}{35}$ (4 x 3) / (7 x 5) = $\frac{12}{35}$

Dividing Fractions

When dividing fractions, you actually multiply the first fraction by the reciprocal of the second fraction.

You find the reciprocal of a number by turning it upside down. For example, the reciprocal of $\frac{3}{8}$ is $\frac{8}{3}$.

Solve the problem.

$\frac{18}{24} \div \frac{2}{4} = \frac{18}{24} \times \frac{4}{2} = \frac{72}{48} = \frac{3}{2}$

Percent

"Percent" is used to describe a portion of a whole, with the whole being 100.

How do I change a decimal to a percentage?

This operation is simple. Move the decimal two places to the right, and add a percentage sign.

Example:

.32 = 32%

.04 = 4%

.1 = 10%

.102 = 10.2%

How do I change a fraction to a percentage?

The first step in converting a fraction to a percentage is to change the fraction to a decimal. Do so by dividing the denominator into the numerator. From here you move the decimal two places to the right of the number, and then add the percentage sign.

Example:

$3/6$ = .5 = 50%

$1/4$ = .25 = 25%

1/8 = .125 = 12.5%

How do I change a percentage to a decimal?

Simply slide the decimal two places to the left and take away the percentage symbol.

Example:

69% = .69

4% = .04

125% = 1.25

How do I change a percentage to a fraction?

Divide the number by 100. Reduce to lowest terms.

Example:

$25\% = {}^{25}/_{100} = {}^{1}/_{4}$

$62\% = {}^{62}/_{100} = {}^{31}/_{50}$

$125\% = {}^{125}/_{50} = 1{}^{1}/_{4}$

How do I change a percentage that is greater than 100 to a decimal or mixed fraction?

To change to a decimal:

Move the decimal point two places to the left and drop the percent sign.

$298\% = 2.98$

$600\% = 6.0$

$980\% = 9.8$

To change to a mixed fraction –

$275\% = {}^{275}/_{100} = {}^{200}/_{100} + {}^{75}/_{100} = 2 + {}^{3}/_{4} = 2{}^{3}/_{4}$

$275\% = 2{}^{3}/_{4}$

$550\% = {}^{550}/_{100} = {}^{500}/_{100} + {}^{50}/_{100} = 5 + {}^{1}/_{2} = 5{}^{1}/_{2}$

$550\% = 5{}^{1}/_{2}$

Conversions Commonly Seen in Real Estate:

Fraction	Decimal	Percentage
½	.5	50%
¼	.25	25%
1/3	.333...	33.3...%
2/3	.666...	66.6...%
1/10	.1	10%
1/8	.125	12.5%
1/6	.1666...	16.6...%
1/5	.2	20%

Algebra

Equations

To solve an equation, you must determine what is equal to the unidentified variable.

Things to remember about equations:

- There are two parts to an equation. They are separated by an equal sign.
- An operation performed on an equation must be done to each part.
- When beginning to solve the equation, priority number one is to get the variables on one side and the known numbers on the other.
- You will sometimes have to divide both parts of the equation using the same divisor. This will enable the variable to equal an exact number.

How do I check an equation to make sure it is correct?

Once you've solved the equation, take the number equal to the variable and input into the original equation.

Example:

x = 5

Original equation: $\frac{1}{x(2)} = \frac{x-4}{10}$

$\frac{1}{5(2)} = \frac{5-4}{10}$

$\frac{1}{10} = \frac{1}{10}$

x = 5

Algebraic Fractions

Example:

How do I subtract two fractions with different denominators?

$\frac{x}{4} - \frac{x}{8}$

$\frac{x}{4} - \frac{x}{8} = \frac{x(2)}{4(2)} - \frac{x}{8}$

$\frac{2x}{8} - \frac{x}{8} = \frac{x}{8}$

Geometry

Terms to remember:

- **Area** – Refers to the space inside a two-dimensional figure.
- **Circumference** – Refers to the distance around the edge of a circle.
- **Perimeter** – Refers to the total distance around a two-dimensional figure.
- **Radius** – Refers to the distance from the center point of a circle to its perimeter.

Area

Area refers to the space inside a two-dimensional figure.

In the triangle below, the area is the part that is shaded green.

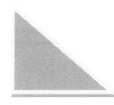   = Area

250

Area Formulas for Various Shapes

Circle: $A = \pi r^2$

Sphere: $A = 4\pi r^2$

Rectangle: $A = lw$

Square: $A = s^2$

Triangle: $A = bh$

Parallelogram: $A = bh$

What do the above letters/symbols mean?

A: Area

π: "pi" 3.14

r: Radius

l: Length

w: Width

s: Side length

b: Base

h: Height

Examples of area:

Area of circle

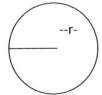

Area of rectangle

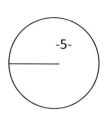

$A = \pi r^2$

$A = \pi \times (5 \times 5)$

$A = \pi \times 25$

$A = 3.14 \times 25$

$A = 78.54$

$A = lw$

$A = 8 \text{ mm} \times 3 \text{ mm} = 24 \text{ mm}^2$

Perimeter

Perimeter refers to the total distance around a two-dimensional figure.

It is calculated simply by adding together all of the sides of the figure.

Example:

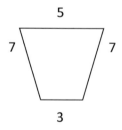

Perimeter = 7 + 7 + 5 + 3 = 22

Circumference is the perimeter of a circle.

Formula for circumference: $C = 2\pi r$

Word Problems

Understanding word problems is crucial to doing well on the math problems of the Real Estate Exam, as these make up a significant portion of the math problems found on the exam.

Before knowing how to solve the problems, you must understand what the problem is asking.

Terms you will commonly see:

- **Increase**
  What operation do you perform?

  Answer: Addition

  Example:

  A number is increased by 7, which means x + 7.

- **Less than**
  What operation do you perform?

  Answer: Subtraction

  Example:

  A number is less than 12 by x, which means 12 − x.

- **Product or times**
  What operation do you perform?

  Answer: Multiplication

  Example:

  A number times 8, which means x (8).

- **Times the sum of**

  What operation do you perform?

  Answer: Multiply a number by a quantity

  Example:

  Six times the sum of nine and a number, which is 6(9 + x).

- **Of**

  What operation do you perform?

  Answer: Multiplication

  Example:

  5% of 100 is 5, which means 5% x 100 = 5.

- **Is**

  What operation do you perform?

  Answer: Equals

  Example:

  10 is 20 minus 10, which means 10 = 20 – 10.

- **The use of two variables**
  What operation do you perform?

  Answer: Whatever the equation states

  Example:

  A number y exceeds 3 times a number x by 8, which means y = 3x + 8.

Creating and Using Variables in Word Problems

In order to solve some word problems, you may be required to create and use variables. The first step in doing so is to determine what you know and don't know regarding the equation.

Examples:

Perry made 5 more dollars than Billy on his paper route.

What do you know? Perry made $5 more

What don't you know? The amount that Billy made

So,

The amount Billy made is x and the amount Perry made is x + 5.

Pam made 3 times as many A's on her report card as Jan.

What do you know? Pam made 3 times as many A's as Jan

What don't you know? The number of A's that Jan made

So,

The number of A's Jan made is x and the number of A's Pam made is 3x.

Greg has 4 more than 2 times the number of marbles that Shelly has.

What do you know? Greg has 4 more than 2 times the number of marbles Shelly has

What don't you know? The number of marbles Shelly has

So,

The number of marbles Shelly has is x and the number of marbles Greg has 2x + 4.

Percentage Word Problems

There are three main types of percentage word problems. All three types follow the same formula for calculating the result.

Formula:

$$\frac{\text{part}}{\text{whole}} = \frac{\#}{100} \; \frac{\%}{}$$

Calculate the problem substituting the appropriate information in the above formula.

Keep this in mind:

- On the percentage side, 100 will always be in the denominator.
- If you are not provided with a percentage amount to use as the numerator, use a variable.
- On the number side, the number always equals the whole (100%). In the word problem, this number follows the term "of."
- On the number side, the numerator is the number that's equal to the percent.

Examples:

How do you find the percentage when you know the number?

What is the number that is equal to 40% of 95?

\#   %

$x/95 = 40/100$

Cross multiply:

100(x) = 40(95)

100x = 3,800

x = 3,800/100

x = 38

Answer: 38 is 40% of 95

How do you find the number when you know the percentage?

40% of what number is 38?

\#   %

$\dfrac{38}{x} = \dfrac{40}{100}$

Cross multiply:

100(38) = 40(x)

3800 = 40x

$\dfrac{3800}{40} = \dfrac{40x}{40}$

95 = x

Answer: 38 is 40% of 95

How do you find what percentage one number is of another?

What percentage of 95 is 38?

   #   %

$38/95 = x/100$

Cross multiply:

100(38) = 95(x)

3800 = 95x

$$\frac{3800}{95} = \frac{95x}{95}$$

40 = x

Answer: 38 is 40% of 95

Calculating Rate

Calculating cost per unit, interest rate, and tax rate are common problems found on the real estate exam. The purpose of rate is to compare two amounts, using various units of measure.

Rate formula:

Calculating cost per unit

Example:

How much do 2 square feet cost if 250 square feet cost $2,500?

Answer:

$$\frac{2,500}{250} = \$10 \text{ / square foot}$$

Therefore, 2 square feet cost $20

Interest rate

The formula for simple interest is:

Interest = principal x rate x time or I = (PRT)

Equivalencies

Here are a few measurement equivalencies that will help you:

- 1 foot (ft.') = 12 inches (in.")
- 1 yard (yd.) = 3 ft. or 36 in.
- 1 mile = 5,280 ft.
- 1 mile = 1,760 yards
- 1 square foot (sq. ft., ft.^{2}) = 144 square inches (sq. in., in.^{2})
- 1 square yard = 9 square feet
- 1 acre = 43,560
- 1 square mile = 640 acres

Basic Percentage

Determining basic percentage.

Example:

How do you calculate 53% of $3,645?

Answer:

Convert 53% to a decimal by moving the decimal two places to the left.

53% = .53

Multiply the result by $3,645.

(.53) ($3,645) = $1,931.85

$1,931.85 is 53% of $3,645.

Percentage: Interest

How do you calculate the rate of interest being charged?

Example:

Paul Billings borrowed $22,000. He is paying $1,200 / year in interest. What is the interest rate he is being charged?

interest = principal x rate x time

The principal amount is $22,000

The interest amount is $1,200

Rate = Let the unknown interest rate be i

Time = 1 year

Using the formula, Interest = principal x rate (i) x time, solve for x.

1,200 = 22,000(i)(1)

1,200 = 22,000i

$$\frac{1,200}{22,000} = \frac{i}{22,000}$$

.055 = i

Convert the decimal to a percent. Do this by moving the decimal two places to the right.

.055 = 5.5%

Area of Various Figures

Rectangles

Keep in mind: The formula for area in a rectangle is: Area = (length) (width)

Example:

Theresa purchased two small lots of land. One is 70 feet by 20 feet and the other, 80 feet by 30 feet. What is the total square feet of land that she has?

Answer:

A = (70) (20) + (80) (30) =

A = 1400 + 2400 = 3,800 square feet

Theresa has a total of 3,800 square feet of land.

How do you find the length of a rectangle if you only know the area and width?

Keep in mind: The formula for area in a rectangle is: Area = (length) (width)

Example:

Theresa has 2,400 square feet of land that is 30 feet in width. What is the length of the land?

Answer:

2,400 = (x) (30)

$2,400/30 = (x)(30)/30$

x = $2400/30$

x = 80 feet

Triangles

Keep in mind: The formula for area in a triangle is: Area = ½ bh

Example:

For their small business, Paul and Sally Green are buying a triangular piece of land. The base of the property is 150 feet. The side that is perpendicular to the base is also 150 feet. What is the total number of square feet for the property?

Area = x

Base = 150

Height = 150

x = (½ or .5) (150) (150)

x = (½ or .5) (22,500)

x = 11,250 square feet

Circles

Keep in mind: The formula for area in a circle is: $A = \pi r^2$

Example:

Gill is using a circular cover over a circular piece of land for a special project. The radius of the circular land area is 23 feet. What is the area of the cover over it?

For "π," use 3.14.

What do you know?

Radius = 23

π = 3.14

Area = x

Solve.

$A = \pi r^2$

A = (3.14) (23)(23) = 1,661.06 square feet

The area of the cover is 1,661.06 square feet.

Property Tax

Property tax questions are solved using percentages and rates.

Example:

Laurie Collins lives in Purple County. The tax rate for Purple County is $5.89 per one hundred of assessed valuation. Ms. Collins shares that she pays $2,550 in taxes. What is her property assessment? Round answer to nearest 10 cents.

What do you know?

Taxes = $2,550

Tax rate = $5.89 per hundred (%)

Assessment = x

$5.89 is 5.89%. Convert the percentage to a decimal: .0589

.0589 of the assessed value of the house is $2,550, which means:

(.0589) (x) = 2,550

Solve.

$(.0589)(x) / .0589 = (2,550) / .0589$

x = $43,293.718

Rounded to the nearest 10 cents, the answer is $43,293.70.

How do you determine the tax rate if you know the amount of taxes paid and assessment amount?

Example:

Mrs. Ferguson said her taxes are $1,300 and property assessment $40,000. What is the tax rate percentage?

What do you know?

Taxes = $1,300

Assessment = $40,000

Rate (%) = x

In equation form, this means:

($40,000) (x) = 1,300

Solve.

$40,000x / 40,000 = 1,300 / 40,000$

x = .0325

Convert to a percentage.

The rate is 3.25%

Loan-to-Value Ratios (LTV)

Problems regarding Loan-to-Value ratios typically involve percentages.

A mortgage loan that bears interest at 25% per annum is at an 85% LTV. The interest on the original balance for year one is $21,474. When securing the loan, what was the value of the property? Round to the nearest dollar.

Step #1: Determine the loan amount.

What do you know?

25% of the loan amount is $21,474.

Loan amount = x

In equation form this means:

($21,474) = (25%) (x) or ($21,474) = (.25) (x)

21,474/ .25 =

x = $85,896

The loan amount is $85,896

Step #2: Determine the value of the property.

What do you know?

Loan amount = $85,896

Loan-to-value ratio = 85%

Value = x

$85,896 is 85% of the value

In equation form this means:

(85% or .85) (x) = $85,896

$.85x/.85 = 85,896/.85$

x = $101,054.118

The value amount is $101,054

Points

"Point" is the term used to describe loan discounts. Each point represents one percent of the face amount of the loan. For example, 3 points means 3% of the face amount of the loan.

Example:

Burt is attempting to obtain an $80,000 FHA mortgage loan. In order to do so, he must pay a 2-point discount (2%). What is the discount amount?

Answer:

Before solving the problem, convert the percentage to a decimal.

2% = .02

What do you know?

Amount of the loan = $80,000

Points = .02

Amount of the discount = x

x = (.02) (80,000)

x = $1,600

Equity

How do you calculate the value of a home?

Example:

John owns a home on which he has three mortgages. The first mortgage balance is $190,000. The second mortgage balance is $20,000 and third mortgage balance, $10,000. The equity in John's home is $50,000. What is the value of John's home?

In this problem, the value of the home is the total of all three mortgages plus the equity.

Answer:

$190,000 + $20,000 + $10,000 + $50,000 = $270,000

The value of the home is $270,000.

Qualifying Buyers

Megan is attempting to qualify for an FHA loan to buy a home. Her ratio requirement is 34/41. She makes $75,000/year and has a $900 monthly car payment. What is her maximum PITI payment?

Answer:

First, divide Megan's annual income by the number of months in a year (12).

$75,000/12 = $6,250

Megan's monthly income is $6,250

Next, determine the front-end qualifier by multiplying Megan's monthly income by the front-end portion (in decimal form) of the ratio.

$6,250 (.34) = $2,125

$2,125 is the front-end qualifier

Lastly, determine the back-end qualifier by multiplying Megan's monthly income by the back-end portion (in decimal form) of the ratio. Then subtract Megan's debt amount from this number.

$6,250 (.41) = $2,562.50 - $900 = $1,662.50

$1,662.50 is the back-end qualifier

The maximum PITI is $1,662.50. The maximum PITI is the lower of the two qualifiers.

Prorations

During settlement, there is typically a reconciliation that needs to take place regarding money that is owed as of the settlement date. The best way to remember who owes what is by remembering the simple fact that he who uses the service is the one who has to pay for it. When calculating these figures, unless otherwise noted, you may always use a 30-day month and 360-day calendar year.

Example:

Mr. Perkins paid his 2012 calendar year property taxes in the amount of $2,400 one year in advance. He sells his house to Mr. Dickinson in April 2012 and settles in May of that same year. With regard to the amount paid in taxes for 2012, how much do the two parties owe each other?

What do you know?

	Mr. Perkins	Mr. Dickinson
How many months paid for?	12 ($2,400)	0 ($0)
How many months used/will use?	4 ($800)	8 ($1,600)
How many months should he be reimbursed for?	8 ($1,600)	0 ($0)
How many months should he reimbursed for?	0 ($0)	8 ($1,600)

Mr. Dickinson should be debited $1,600. Mr. Perkins should be credited $1,600.

Commissions

Commission calculation problems are common. They usually seek to determine a percentage, but they may also ask for a dollar amount.

Example:

The broker made her first home sale for $127,000. The total amount of commission is $7,700. What is the broker's commission rate?

Answer:

What do you know?

Home price: $127,000

Commission: $7,700

Commission rate: x

In equation form, this means:

127,000 x = 7,700

Solve.

x = 7,700/127,000

x = 0.060

Change to a decimal and round to the nearest whole percent.

0.060 = 6%

Example:

An agent made a 6% commission on the sale of a home. The sale price was $345,867. The agent made another 6% commission on the sale of a $243,542 home. What is the total dollar amount the agent received in commission on the two homes?

Determine the commission amount on the first home sale.

$345,867 (.06) = $20,752.02

Determine the commission amount on the second home sale.

$243,542 (.06) = $14,612.52

Add together the two commission amounts.

$20,752.02 + $14,612.52 = $35,364.54

Total commission = $35,364.54

Sale Proceeds

Example:

The agent is working with the homeowner to determine the list price for the homeowner's home in order to meet the homeowner's desire to net at least $30,000. The current mortgage balance is $235,000 and commission to take into consideration is 7%. If they list and sell the property at $300,000, would the homeowner net at least $30,000?

What do you know?

Expenses: Total - $256,000

        Mortgage balance: $235,000

        Commission: $21,000

Sale price: $300,000

$235,000 + $21,000 = $256,000

$300,000 - $256,000 = $44,000

The homeowner would net $44,000. Therefore, he would net at least $30,000.

Transfer Tax

The California Transfer Tax in most counties is $0.55/$500 of the home's sale price.

Transfer Tax (California) Example:

A homeowner sells her house for $450,000. How much does she owe the state in transfer tax?

There are 900 ($500s) in $450,000. Therefore, you multiply the tax amount which is $0.55 per $500 by 900.

$0.55 x 900 = $495

The transfer tax amount for the sale of a $450,000 home is $495.

Transfer Tax (California Tax) Example:

A homeowner sells his property for $297,765. The transfer tax is $1,357.81. If the transfer tax is calculated per $500 of the sale price, what is the rate (per $500) of the transfer tax?

Answer:

What do you know?

Sale price: $297,765

Transfer tax: x per $500

Transfer tax amount: $327.54

Solve.

$297,765/500 = $595.54

$327.54 = (x)($595.54)

x = $327.54/$595.54

0.55 = x

The transfer tax rate is $0.55 per $500.

Competitive Market Analyses (CMA)

CMAs help sellers get a better understanding of the market value of their property, which could in turn help them decide on the sale price. Although very useful, it is important to note that CMAs are not appraisals.

CMA problems are solved by using measurable aspects of comparable properties to come to a specific value.

Example:

Mr. Stone has the blueprint for two homes he would like to build. Home A is 62' x 94' in size and will cost $234,985 to build. Home B is 90' x 112' in size. If each house costs the same per square foot to build, how much will it cost to build Home B?

Answer:

Remember, the formula to find area for a rectangle is: A = lw.

Area of Home A: 62(94) = 5,828 square feet

Area of Home B: 90(112) = 10,080 square feet

Cost to build Home A/square foot: = $40.32

Cost to build Home B = 10,080($40.32) = $406,425.60

Income Properties

Example:

Bob, a local real estate investor is interested in buying an income property that creates gross income in the amount of $270,500. He discovers that the operating costs of this property will equal 65% of the gross income. Ideally, he would like to acquire a 15% return. With his desire to have a 15% return, what is the most he can pay for the property?

Answer:

What do you know?

Gross income = $270,500

Operating costs = 65% of $270,500

Net income = Gross income – operating costs

Desired return = 15%

Most the investor can pay = x

Step #1:

Determine the dollar amount of the operating costs. Start off by converting the percentage to a decimal.

65% = .65

Operating costs = (.65)(270,500) = $175,825

Step #2:

Gross income – Operating costs = Net income

$270,500 - $175,825 = $94,675

Step #3:

The investor wants his net income to be 15% of what he pays for the property. Convert the percent to a decimal, and then determine the most he can pay.

15% = .15

$94,675 = (.15)(x)

$$\frac{\$94{,}675}{.15} = \frac{(.15)(x)}{.15}$$

$$\frac{\$94{,}675}{.15} = x$$

$631,167 (Rounded to the nearest dollar)

Depreciation

You may encounter "depreciation" problems on the exam, but those representing the straight-line method are the only ones you will probably see.

The formula for the straight-line method of depreciation:

$$\frac{replacement\ cost}{years\ of\ useful\ life} = \text{annual depreciation}$$

If the depreciation rate is not given, you can calculate it by dividing the total depreciation, which is 100%, by the useful life of the building.

For example, if a building has 25 years of useful life, then you will use this calculation:

$$\frac{100\%}{25} = 4\%$$

This means that the building has an annual depreciation rate of 4%.

Example:

It has been determined that the replacement cost of a 15-year-old building is $90,000. Since it has 35 years of useful life left, how much can be charged to annual depreciation?

What do you know?

Replacement cost = $90,000

Useful life = 35 years

Using the formula $\frac{replacement\ cost}{years\ of\ useful\ life}$ = annual depreciation, calculate annual depreciation.

$$\frac{\$90,000}{35} = \$2,571\ \text{(Rounded to the nearest dollar)}$$

Example:

The annual depreciation of a building is $3,245. What is the total depreciation of a 19 year-old building?

annual depreciation x age of building = total depreciation

$3,245 x 19 = $61,655

Total depreciation = $61,655

Example:

The replacement cost of a building is $62,000. The total depreciation of said building is $19,354. What is the current value of the building?

replacement cost – depreciation = current value

$62,000 - $19,354 = $42,646

Current value of the building = $42,646

Summary

It is our hope that this Real Estate Math review has helped reinforce your knowledge of the topics you will most likely see on the math section of the Real Estate Exam. For those of you who think you could use a bit more of a refresher, feel free to take the included practice exams over and over until you are confident that you can triumphantly complete the Real Estate Exam. Good luck!

Real Estate Glossary

>A

abandonment giving up the right to possess a property, building or real estate area through non-use and intention.

abstract of title the background of a property listing legal transactions and information.

abutting sitting next to another property.

acceleration clause a clause that forces the borrower to repay the entire loan upon the lender's demand for specific reasons.

acceptance agreement to an offer essential to a valid contract.

accretion increase of the amount of land by natural deposits of soil on onto the property.

accrued depreciation the total loss of value on the property.

accrued items the additional costs still outstanding at the close of the real estate deal, such as interest, insurance, HOA fees or taxes.

acknowledgement statement before a notary public when executing legal documents.

acre a measurement of land that is 4,840 square yards or 43,560 square feet in area.

actual eviction a step-by-step procedure to remove renters from property.

actual notice specific information given to a party, such as a tenant, landlord, buyer or seller.

addendum a clause that provides more specific information to clarify a contract.

adjacent property or buildings next to each other but might not touch each other.

adjoining property or buildings next to each other that do touch each other.

adjustable rate mortgage (ARM) a loan rate that changes throughout the period of the loan. Sometimes called a variable rate or flexible rate.

adjusted basis the final cost of a property after improvements are added and deductions or reduced value are subtracted.

adjustment date the date agreed upon by the buyer and seller for financial changes.

administrator a court-appointed individual who executes a person's estate if there is not a will.

ad valorem **tax** property tax on the current value of the land.

adverse possession the acquisition of property through open and continuous use over time.

adverse selection principal is not able to determine if an agent has accurately represented his or her ability.

affidavit a sworn statement before a person in authority.

agency the relationship or agreement created when one persons acts on behalf of another.

agency theory addresses conflicts of interest between agents and principals.

agent the individual (or company) authorized to act on behalf of another.

agreement of sale a contract between two parties to buy/sell.

air rights the right to air space above a property, separate from the property land itself.

alienation the termination of rights or benefits.

alienation clause the "due on sale" clause requiring the borrower to repay the mortgage in full upon the transfer of title.

amenities "extras" on a property that make it more valuable or more attractive to buyers, i.e., kitchen upgrades.

amortization paying off the principal amount of a debt over the term of the loan.

amortization schedule the timeline showing the reductions of principal with each payment over the life of a loan.

amortize the distribution of payments on principal over the term on a loan.

annual percentage rate (APR) the numerical representation of the actual cost of borrowed money over 12 months. It includes additional costs, such as closing costs and fees, and not just interest rates.

anti-deficiency law a statute that stops the lender from pursuing the buyer for a loss on a property after a foreclosure sale.

antitrust laws national laws that encourage free market trade and practices and prohibit the restriction of such.

apportionments the division of costs, such as fees and HOA responsibilities, between the seller and purchaser.

appraisal assessing the worth of land or property by a professional, qualified person who is usually licensed.

appraised value the worth of the land or property as determined by the licensed professional.

appraiser a professional, qualified person so licensed by the state to determine the value of land or property.

appreciation increase in the value of an asset, such as real estate.

appurtenance an object, right or benefit of ownership that transfers with the sale of real property.

arbitration dispute resolution through the use of a third party.

ARELLO an online company that encourages the cooperation of decision makers in the real estate business.

assessed value the tax-related value put on a property.

assessment the placement of tax-related value on a property.

assessor a professional who determines the tax-related value of a property.

asset something of value that belongs to a person, such as cash, property, bonds, etc.

assignment the transfer of a mortgage from one agency to another.

assumption of mortgage the process of the buyer taking over the seller's mortgage.

attachment placing a legal hold on a property to pay for a judgment.

attest to agree to the truth of a document by signing it.

attorney-in-fact a person who acts as a legal representative for another; does not need to be a professional lawyer.

avulsion transfer of land because water, such as a stream or brook, changes course.

>B

balloon mortgage a mortgage with small payments due for a specified period, such as three to five years, with a lump sum or balloon due at the end of the mortgage.

balloon payment the lump payment at the end of a balloon mortgage.

bankruptcy the legal discharge of most debts through the courts.

bargain and sale deed a document transferring property from seller to buyer without guaranteeing the validity of the transfer.

baseline a line in surveying that runs east to west and acts a point of reference for corresponding lines that run north to south.

benchmark a fixed point of reference by which elevation is marked.

beneficiary the recipient of the profits that occur as a result of someone else's actions.

bequest similar to an inheritance, a transfer of personal property through a will.

betterment an community improvement that benefits a property.

bilateral contract a contract requiring both parties to act or not act in order to fulfill the agreement.

bill of sale transfers ownership of personal property.

binder money paid to hold a property for set terms.

biweekly mortgage payments made on real estate every two weeks as opposed to once a month. In some cases, this reduces the time needed to pay off the loan.

blanket mortgage a mortgage with at least two properties as collateral.

blockbusting an illegal process that involves scaring residents of an area into selling their property at reduced prices so that an agent can take advantage of them.

bona fide legal adjective that describes faithful, trustworthy actions or people.

bond a type of insurance money that protects a professional against loss.

boot a sum of cash included in a buyer/seller agreement to even out exchange.

branch office a satellite or another office that is at a separate place from headquarters.

breach of contract not fulfilling the terms or breaking a binding contract.

bribery giving, receiving, or soliciting something of value to influence an action, such as an illegal gratuity.

broker professional or entity that is qualified through classes and licensed to buy or sell property.

brokerage a firm that employs one or more real estate professionals; real estate company.

broker's price opinion (BPO) an estimate on the worth of real estate by a professional in the industry.

building code state and local legislation that regulates new edifices or structural changes or existing ones.

building line an invisible boundary line around the property. The building must stay within this boundary.

building restrictions state, local and neighborhood guidelines or constraints that guide how something is built or to determine property use.

bundle of rights privileges associated with property ownership, such as residency or use.

buy down payment by the buyer of added fees or points to the seller or lender for a lower interest rate.

buyer's broker a real estate professional who searches for a property and conducts negotiations in order to purchase the property.

bylaws procedural guidelines used to conduct business or meetings at an organization like a homeowners association.

>C

cancellation clause a section in a contract that permits parties to nullify the obligations of the contract.

canvassing surveying or soliciting an area to see if people are interested in selling their homes.

cap the maximum increase in interest for a mortgage with changing rates.

capital funds used to generate more money.

capital expenditure money spent to improve the value of real estate.

capital gains tax taxation on profit from the sale of an investment.

capitalization the total yearly potential earnings on a property, such as a rental.

capitalization rate a percentage that can be used to compare investment opportunities. This is determined by dividing the yearly capitalization by the cost of the property.

cash flow the total amount of money being transferred in or out during the normal course of doing business.

caveat emptor Latin expression meaning "let the buyer beware." Serves as a warning to the buyer.

CC&R covenants, conditions and restrictions – the bylaws for a group of homeowners.

certificate of discharge a document acknowledging the repayment or forgiveness of a debt.

certificate of eligibility formal document from the Veterans Administration that proves the person qualifies for a VA loan.

certificate of reasonable value (CRV) the maximum value permitted for a VA mortgage.

certificate of title an official decision on the ownership, status or availability of a piece of real estate through public documents.

chain of title a document showing the history of ownership of a piece of real property.

chattel any personal property someone owns.

chattel mortgage the use of personal property as security for debt repayment.

city an incorporated group of residences larger than a town or village.

clear title a document showing that a property is free and clear of any liens or encumbrances.

closing the legal transfer of ownership through the exchange of money and the deed.

closing costs the additional monies associated with the transfer of property, such as appraisal fees.

closing date the actual date the property will transfer from the buyer to the seller.

closing statement a final summary of all costs involved in the transfer of real estate.

cloud on the title an unresolved lien or encumbrance on the title to property.

clustering a group of residential buildings used to maximize land use.

codicil an addendum to a will that explains additions or deletions to the document.

coinsurance clause a clause in an insurance policy that divides financial responsibility for a loss between at least two parties.

collateral something of value that promises the repayment of a loan.

collection efforts to acquire delinquent rent or mortgage payments.

color of title a title that is invalid although initially it seemed to be valid.

commercial property real estate restricted to business use.

commingling combining the funds of two parties in a trust account

commission the payment that a broker or real estate agent receives for the sale of a property, usually a percentage of the sale price.

commitment letter a document from lender that commits the funds to a borrower and sets out the basic terms of the promissory note.

common areas sections of a neighborhood or condominium/apartment complex that that are available for resident's use, such as a pool, playground or parking lot.

common law originating in England, law based in part on traditions and in part on the courts.

community property real estate and chattel in which spouses have an equal interest.

comparable sales the most recent sales of similar property in a specific area used to determine current market value through the Comparative Market Approach.

comparative market analysis (CMA) assessing the market value of real estate through a comparison of the recent activity of similar pieces of real estate in an area. See comparable sales.

competent parties those who can legally enter into a contract.

condemnation the procedure used by the government to take property by eminent domain.

condominium ownership of an individual residence, along with a percentage ownership of all common areas shared jointly.

condominium conversion the act of creating a condominium and the initial transfer of the ownership from a single entity to individual condominium owners.

conflict of interest occurs when there is a bias or self interest against a represented individual or organization.

conformity the belief that similar pieces of real estate will retain their worth.

consideration a legal enticement required for a valid contract.

construction mortgage a two-part loan – first, to pay for construction costs and next for permanent financing of the finished product.

constructive eviction a landlord's breach of the lease through a lack of maintenance or disturbance of quiet enjoyment that renders the property uninhabitable as defined by law.

constructive notice public record and therefore common information to all.

contingency future requirements that must be met or waived in order to fulfill a contract.

contract the agreement that two parties will do or not do a specified thing.

contract for deed the buyer takes possession of the property and makes installment payments over a set period time that will result in ownership. The seller retains title until the full purchase price is made.

conventional loan any loan that is not insured by the government (not FHA or VA, etc.).

conversion option an agreement that the buyer can change an adjustable interest rate to a fixed rate. There is a cost-associated with this option.

convertible ARM an agreement that the buyer can change an adjustable interest rate to a fixed rate. There is a cost associated with this option.

conveyance the legal transfer of property from one party to another.

cooperative a corporation that holds title to the real estate. On sale, shares of the corporation are transferred, rather than any real property.

corporation a company acts as its own business with liability and management.

cost approach valuation by estimating the value of the land as if vacant + the cost of the current improvements - the depreciation of the improvements.

counteroffer saying no to a real estate offer and then suggesting a different offer.

covenant the contractual agreement between parties.

covenant of seizing a legal verification that the owner has the right to the property.

credit available money that must be repaid in the future.

credit history a list of creditors or lenders who have extended credit to an individual money and the history of the individual's timely performance in fulfilling the obligations.

cul-de-sac a dead-end street with a circular turn around at the closed end.

curtesy a man's ownership of some or all of his spouse's property even if she will deny him such ownership.

curtilage the area in close proximity to a residence, including other buildings, but not including open lands away from the home.

>D

damages financial or other compensation to the insured party for tangible or intangible losses.

datum a horizontal reference point used to make vertical measurements.

DBA "doing business as" – a sole proprietorship doing business under a company name.

debt money or property that is owed to another and must be repaid.

debt service the cash required for the repayment of principal and interest over a specific time frame.

decedent a person who passed away, often used in discussions of their estate, will, inheritance or other financial matters.

dedication a gift and acceptance of property for the benefit of the public.

deed the official document signed by the grantor and delivered to the grantee that transfers legal title to real property.

deed-in-lieu a defaulting borrower signs their deed over the lender in exchange for forgiveness of the debt, allowing both parties to avoid the foreclosure process.

deed of trust a three-party security involving a trustor (the borrower), a beneficiary (the lender) and a trustee, who holds legal title until the debt is repaid).

deed restriction covenant in a deed that requires or prevents future actions or use of property.

default failure to abide by the terms of a loan.

defeasance clause the clause that requires the lender to release the encumbrance on the title of a property upon repayment of the debt.

deficiency judgment a court document ordering the collection of the difference between the sale price and lien amounts after a foreclosure sale.

delinquency late payment on a loan.

density zoning regulations involving the sizes, numbers and/or lots sizes etc. in a particular area.

depreciation the loss of value of an asset due to age or use.

descent the passing down of property to an heir if the deceased person has not left specific provisions.

devise a gift of real estate to an heir through a will.

devisee the person who receives a gift of property from a will.

devisor the person who gives a gift of property to another through a will.

directional growth the direction in which a city is expanding.

discount point charges levied by a lender in exchange for a lower interest rate.

discount rate the interest rate that a bank will pay to the Federal Reserve to borrow cash for short-term loans.

dispossess to deprive someone of possession; the legal process of eviction.

divisible contract called a severable contract; has two or more components that act as independent contracts when breached.

dominant estate (tenement) property that benefits from an easement or the shared use of land.

dower a woman's ownership right to some or all of her spouse's property even if his will denies her such ownership.

down payment the initial up-front portion of the purchase price of a property; usually paid in cash and is the amount NOT being financed.

dual agency a real estate agent or broker who acts on behalf of two or more parties in a sale.

due-on-sale clause requires the loan to be repaid in full when the real estate is sold.

duress unlawful force to compel a person feels into entering into a contract.

>E

earnest money the legal consideration required for a valid contract.

easement the privilege of use of another's land for a specific purpose.

easement by necessity a court ordered easement arising from the discovery of a lack of access after a property has been purchased.

easement by prescription accepted use of property by another person that is unnecessary. This becomes legal when it occurs over a certain number of years, such as a shortcut through a neighbor's yard - similar to adverse possession, but does not grant title, only use.

easement in gross an easement that benefits a person or business entity, rather than another piece of land (i.e., a utility's right to erect and maintain power lines across property lines)

economic life the length of time when an asset is useful or profitable.

effective age the age of the building based on the condition; most used in valuation.

emblements farming crops considered part of personal property.

embezzlement the fraudulent conversion of property when the possession was given through a trust relationship.

eminent domain the government's purchase of private property for public purposes through the process of condemnation.

encroachment an object or improvement that crosses property boundaries onto another's property.

encumbrance liens and obligations against a property, such as delinquent HOA fees, any mortgages or easements that impact the title.

equitable title the right use and possess a property during the time you are paying for it.

equity the value of the property above the mortgage or other debts on the property.

equity of redemption the reclaiming of real estate by the mortgage holder because of foreclosure.

erosion slow wearing away of land by natural elements, such as wave action.

escalation clause passing on increased expenses to tenants, such as increases in taxes or HOA fees.

escheat the government claims on real estate when a person dies without any heirs.

escrow money or something of value held in trust by a third party until the completion of a specified transaction.

escrow account an account or neutral depository maintained by a third party (escrow agent) for the specific purpose of holding client's funds or valuables until all conditions of the escrow instructions have been met and the contract is fully executed.

escrow agent an impartial third party who maintains the escrow instruction and responsible for managing the activities required under the instructions until the transaction is complete.

escrow analysis or activity report a review that details the disposition of escrow..

escrow disbursements the lawful distribution of escrow funds according to the instructions.

escrow holder see escrow agent

escrow instructions a set of written instructions signed by all principals (buyer, seller, lender) detailing the conditions that must be met to fully perform the transaction.

estate the extent, nature and degree of the ownership interest in real property.

estate at will a lease that has no specified termination, but requires specified notice of termination.

estate for years a lease that has a fixed beginning and end date; can be hours, days, months or years.

estate from period to period a lease that continues from period to period until one party terminates with property notice; generally days, weeks, months or years.

estate tax the tax on the value of the assets when a person dies. A certain portion of the estate is exempt.

estoppel a legal term related to preventing a party from claiming or denying a fact based on their previous actions or claims otherwise.

et al. Latin for "and others," used to refer to property ownership by several people, "Jane Doe, et. al."

et ux. Latin for "and wife."

et vir Latin for "and husband."

eviction the process by which a defaulting party is legally removed from a property.

evidence of title official paperwork that proves that someone owns the property.

examination of title the act of performing a title search.

exchange simultaneously buying/selling "like kind" investment properties under IRS Code 1031 for the purpose of deferring taxes to a future date.

exclusive agency listing a binding legal agreement that engages an agent/broker to sell a piece of property for a certain time frame; however, the owner retains the right to sell.

exclusive right to sell a binding legal agreement that engages a real estate agent/broker the right to sell a piece property for a certain time frame; the owner is responsible for compensating the broker regardless of who sells the property.

execution a legal writ to perform a court ordered action.

executor/executrix the male/female designated by the deceased to direct the disposition of an estate under the terms of the will after death.

executory contract a contract that is not fully performed by at least one party.

executed contract a completed/fully performed contract.

express contract a contract specifically detailed by words, whether written or oral.

extension agreement a mutual decision to lengthen the time frame for performance of a contract.

external obsolescence depreciation of property because of something in the surroundings such as being on a busy street, in the flight path of an airport, zoning etc.

>F

fair market value the value of property when offered on the open market in an arm's length transaction.

Federal Housing Administration (FHA) a government agency that guarantees loans to make mortgages more affordable.

Federal National Mortgage Association (FNMA or Fannie Mae) a federal conservatorship that purchases mortgages from primary lenders.

Federal Reserve System the government banking system that oversees banks, offers services and sets national economic policy.

fee simple a full and complete ownership of real property.

fee simple defeasible a fee simple estate with a provision or restriction that, if violated, would cause the ownership to revert to the grantor.

FHA-insured loan a mortgage that is insured by FHA. VA loans are also backed by the government.

fiduciary relationship the relationship between parties when one person acts on another's behalf in business or general matters and the duties of lawful obedience, utmost care, loyalty, confidentiality and honesty associated therewith.

finder a person who introduces a buyer and seller, but does not perform any acts requiring a real estate license and cannot participate in any commission compensation.

first mortgage the loan in the first position for repayment.

fixed-rate loan a loan where the interest rate remains the same throughout the loan term.

fixture something affixed to real property that conveys with sale.

foreclosure the process the lender seeks to recover the debt from a buyer in default.

forfeiture court ordered seizure of property due of criminal actions or breach of a contract or obligation.

franchise a business owner buying a license to use a company name, marketing and methods. company backing, such as member brokerages.

fraud deceptive actions mislead another person whether by intention or mistake

freehold estate indefinite ownership of property (vs. a lease that has can be terminated or expire).

functional obsolescence the decrease in value of property due to changing style preferences, lack or deferral of maintenance.

future interest a right to real estate that will occur in the future.

>G

general agent an agent authorized to act on behalf of a principal on an on-going basis, rather than a single transaction.

general lien a lien against all of a person's property rather than a single piece of real property.

general warranty deed a deed including a warranty from the grantor that the title is free and clear of other claims and obliges the grantor to defend against any future claims.

government-backed mortgage a loan that is backed by the federal government (FHA, VA) as contrasted with a conventional loan.

Government National Mortgage Association (GNMA or Ginnie Mae) a government agency that guarantees pools of loans that may be sold as GNMA-backed securities.

government survey system a process of dividing land into rectangular sections in order to set area boundaries.

graduated lease a rental agreement that permits periodic increases in rental price.

grant the transfer of title from one party to another party as through a deed.

grant deed the legal document used to transfer title from one to another with the implied warranties of: the title has not been transferred to another party; and the title is free and clear of encumbrances made by the grantor.

grantee the person who receives the title; buyer.

grantor the person who grants the title.

gross income all income generated from an investment property before any losses or expenses are applied.

gross income multiplier a way to assess the profitability of property arrived at by dividing the value of the property by the annual gross income.

gross lease a rental agreement wherein the landlord pays all costs associated with the property, including HOA fees, repairs, taxes, and more.

ground lease a lease whereby the tenant agrees to improve a piece of land. The improvements become the property of the landlord upon termination/expiration of the lease.

guardian a person whom the court appoints to be legally responsible for someone who is incapable of managing his affairs.

>H

hamlet a small, populated area; municipality.

heir someone who receives property through a will after a death.

hereditament anything tangible or intangible that can be given through a will.

highest and best use the most productive use of real estate that will provide the greatest financial return over a specified period of time.

holdover tenancy a renter who stays on the property after the lease ends.

holographic will a handwritten will signed by the person who makes the will; does not need a notary or witness.

home equity conversion mortgage (HECM) reverse mortgage wherein a lender makes payments, to a homeowner who is 62 or older with a large amount of equity in their home.

home equity line of credit (HELOC) a revolving line of credit available to homeowners based on the equity in the home.

home inspection a professional assessment of the condition and structure of real estate that closely examines the property.

homeowners association (HOA) a corporation or association formed by a real estate developer and designed to market, manage or sell homes in a subdivision area.

homeowner's insurance an insurance policy that covers the property and contents against all types of natural and other damages, includes liability.

homeowner's warranty insurance coverage that protects the buyer against any defects in the residence.

homestead protection of a portion of assets against lawsuits or judgments up to certain limits.

Housing Urban and Development Department (HUD) federal agency that regulates many aspects of the housing industry.

hypothecate a promise of something as pledge for a loan without physically relinquishing that item. Most homeowners live in their primary residence through this method unless they own the residence free and clear.

>I

implied contract a contract no expressed in words, but through actions and understanding.

improvement any structure or work done on land or property that increases value.

income capitalization approach a specific formula used to assess the income-producing worth of a property.

income property real estate that generates cash flow for the owner.

incorporeal right intangible rights associated with real estate, such as easements and future income.

indemnify to insure against loss.

independent contractor the relationship between real estate agents and their managing broker; those who work independently and paid for end results; do not have an employer/employee relationship and special income tax structures.

index an assessment of the current financial atmosphere by the government; used to adjust prices and often a measurement used to adjust interest rates on an adjustable rate mortgage.

industrial property real estate restricted to specific, non-residential uses, such as a warehouse or manufacturing property.

inflation an increase in overall costs and expenses that results in a decrease in what money will buy.

initial interest rate the first or starting rate for an adjustable mortgage.

installment a scheduled payment toward the reduction of debt, such as a mortgage.

installment note a loan that is repaid in periodic payments at a set schedule; payments usually consist of interest and only some reduction in principal.

installment sale payments made to a seller over a longer period of time in order to defer taxes.

insurance money paid to an indemnity holder to reduce the expenses associated with the specific emergencies being insured, such as flooding or earthquakes.

insurance binder temporary proof of insurance until the permanent paperwork is completed.

interest 1- the legal compensation for lending money and 2 - the legal right to real estate or other property.

interest accrual rate how often the interest accrues, such as daily, weekly or monthly, until it is paid to the lender.

interest rate the rate used to calculate the compensation to a lender, usually specified as a percentage.

interest rate cap or ceiling the highest percentage rate allowed on an adjustable rate mortgage.

interest rate floor the lowest percentage rate on an adjustable rate mortgage.

interim financing a transitional loan until the buyer can obtain permanent financing, for example a construction loan.

intestate death without a legal will or without any will at all.

invalid not legally enforceable, such as a will or a contract.

investment property real estate purchased for the purpose of generating income and/or profit.

>J

joint tenancy a form of co-ownership with a right of survivorship.

joint venture more than one entity who works toward the same professional goal, usually for a specific purpose.

judgment the court order that makes the final determination of the rights and obligations between the parties in a lawsuit.

judgment lien the lien against an asset as the result of a court order.

judicial foreclosure a foreclosure process monitored by a court order, generally used when the lender seeks a deficiency judgment.

jumbo loan a mortgage loan amount above the prevailing conforming FNMA loan limits.

junior mortgage a loan in a junior position that will only be satisfied after the liens in a senior position.

>L

laches the delay of the time during which a legal claim can be enforced.

land the ground, plant life and minerals beneath it, separate from water or air.

land cover the physical cover on the earth.

landlocked property that is not accessible by public roads.

land use the uses and activities of people on the land.

land use analysis studies land use to find efficient patterns and necessary protections.

lease the contract by which a tenant pays for the right to possess and enjoy a piece of property.

lease option a contract under which the lessee is granted the right to purchase for a period of time under agreed upon conditions.

leasehold a non-freehold estate granting the exclusive right to possess and enjoy a piece of property for a period of time that reverts to the owner upon termination or expiration.

legal description authoritative definition of a specific property through written and/or technical means.

lessee tenant/the holder of a lease.

lessor the grantor of a lease.

leverage the use of credit/debt rather than depleting available cash or liquidating assets.

levy a legal obligation to pay charges or fees, such as taxes or homeowner association fees.

license legal permission or authority granted for a particular purpose as in a franchise.

lien an encumbrance against the title on a piece of real property.

life estate an estate granted only for the life of the holder, ending when they die.

life tenant a leasehold estate granted for the entire life of the holder, ending upon their death.

liquidity the availability of assets that can be easily converted to cash.

lis pendens Latin for "suit pending." A public notice of possible restrictions on title as the result of a pending lawsuit.

listing agreement the contract between a real estate agent and client which details the rights, obligations, duties and compensation between the parties for representation in the sale of real property.

listing broker the real estate agent engaged as the primary agent representing the seller in a real estate transaction.

littoral rights the water rights afforded to an owner of property abutting a large body of non-flowing water, such as the ocean or lake.

loan money received from another party in exchange for a promise of repayment according to certain terms and conditions.

loan officer a representative of a primary lender.

lock-in the borrower pays a fee to guarantee an interest rate for a specific time period.

lock-in period the time frame of the lock-in, generally between 30-120 days.

lot and block description a legal process of finding real estate based on its lot and block identification within the housing area.

>M

management agreement the agreement between a property owner and a property manager for performance of the duties to rent, maintain and otherwise manage the operations of a property; compensation is often a percentage of the rental income.

margin a predetermined amount added to the index pricing used in calculate the amount of the adjustment in rate on ARMs.

market data approach an appraisal approach using the comparison of recent, similar property sales in a particular area to valuate property.

market value the likely price a piece of property will bring when offered on the open market in an arm's length transaction. **marketable title** a free-and-clear title.

mechanic's lien a lien on the title of real property as a result of non-payment of work performed by a tradesperson.

metes and bounds specific description of the land that identifies all boundaries of the real estate.

mill one-tenth of a penny; used for taxation.

minor a person who has not reached the majority age of 18 required to enter into contracts.

misrepresentation mistaken or misleading information, regardless of intention.

modification a legal alteration to a contract or promissory note.

money judgment the court ordered payment awarded to the prevailing party in a lawsuit.

month-to-month tenancy a rental agreement that automatically extends each month until either party gives lawful notice of termination - also known as an estate from period to period and tenancy at will.

monument a landmark or immovable object used to mark property boundaries.

mortgage a security instrument pledging the property as collateral to secure the repayment a loan.

mortgage banker a primary lender that uses their funds to finances loans for others.

mortgage broker an individual that arranges financing between lenders and borrowers, but does not lend money.

mortgage loan originator (MLO) anyone who takes or offers to take a mortgage loan application or offers to negotiate the terms of a mortgage loan for a fee.

mortgage lien an encumbrance on the title of real property evidencing the property is collateral to satisfy a debt.

mortgagee the person/agency who holds the promissory note and mortgage in exchange for providing funds in a real estate transaction.

mortgagor the person/agency who pledges the property and gives the not in exchange for money in a real estate transaction.

multi-dwelling units a property that houses multiple separate living units on a single deed.

multiple-listing service (MLS) an association of real estate agents that share the pertinent details of available properties for sale among member agents.

mutual rescission an agreement among the parties to cancel a contract returning each party to their position prior to the contract.

>N

negative amortization the deferment of a unpaid portion of interest due on a loan, which is then added to the original principal amount.

net income the profit remaining when all expenses and losses are deducted from the gross income of a property.

net lease the tenant pays rent and some portion of the operating expenses of the property.

net listing an agreement between an agent and owner that designates any amount above the offering price of the property paid the agent's compensation. If the property sells for less than the offering price, the agent receives nothing. Not legal in every state.

net worth the positive, monetary difference between the value of assets and liabilities.

no cash-out refinance sometimes called a "rate and term refinance," the borrower discharges a debt and replaces it a new loan on more favorable rates and terms., but receives no cash.

non-conforming use a permitted use of a property that does not meet the current building codes, usually "grandfathered" as a result of the zoning regulations changing after the building was already in use.

non-liquid asset something of value that is difficult to convert to cash.

notarize to hear the declarations and acknowledgements and witness the veracity of a signature under a seal.

notary public a person with the legal and official authority to notarize and affix their seal to documents.

note the security instrument that sets forth the rights, obligations and terms detailing the extension of loan and the promise to repay.

note rate the interest rate on a loan or mortgage.

notice of default official notification that the borrower is in breach of the promissory note and that then allows lender to pursue additional legal remedies.

novation the substitution of one party for another party or substitution of one obligation for another obligation in a contract.

>O

obligee a person receiving the promise of performance of an obligation in their favor (i.e., lender).

obligor a person obligated to perform under a contract (i.e., repay the debt).

obsolescence a decrease in value of property due to economic or functional influences.

offer a suggestion or expression of desire to buy or sell real estate.

offer and acceptance the suggestion or expression of desire to buy or sell real estate and the acceptance of the offer by the other party.

open listing a non-exclusive contract engaging an agent to offer real estate for sale. The owner retains the right to sell privately and it can be offered to more than one agent or agency. Only the agent who fulfills the actual contract for sale is compensated.

opinion of title legal authentication that the title is clear.

option an binding agreement from a property owner granting an option to buy to another party under specific terms for a specific amount of time.

optionee the holder of an option.

optionor the grantor of an option.

original principal balance the loan amount before the first payment is made.

origination fee fees charged by a lender to the borrower that cover expenses of lending related to the application fees, title, appraisal and credit checks.

owner financing the seller accepts a note and mortgage for some portion of the purchase in lieu of the full cash amount.

ownership the exclusive rights to use, control, possess and transfer real property.

>P

parcel a plot of land, usually referred to by parcel number for identification purposes.

participation mortgage a loan that permits the lien holder to receive a portion of the profits from the property.

partition legal division of each owner's interests in a property.

partnership business relationship between two or more parties subject to debt and tax laws.

party wall a partitioning wall dividing two dwellings with separate ownership rights.

payee the party who receives money or something of value.

payor the party who gives the payee money or something of value.

percentage lease a commercial lease whose payments includes a percentage sales volume, often used in retail leases.

periodic estate see estate from period to period.

personal property objects that are moveable and not affixed and do not transfer under a deed, but rather a bill of sale.

physical deterioration decrease in value because of normal wear or deferred maintenance.

PITI stands for: principal, interest, taxes and insurance payment; usually the total housing payments used for front end qualifying ratio.

planned unit development (PUD) development project that includes a mix of housing, recreation and commercial enterprises.

plat description of a section of land that provides detailed information about the area.

plat book public information with the description of a section of land that provides detailed information about the area.

plat number the number associated with each lot in a plat.

plottage combining small sections of real estate into a larger parcel.

PMI private mortgage insurance; generally required when loan-to-value ratios are greater than 80%.

point one percent of the loan amount; a lender's fee included in closing costs; sometimes charge in exchange for a lower interest.

point of beginning the same starting and ending point on a land survey as the survey borders and encloses the property.

police power the government's authority to address public safety and community development.

power of attorney the legal authority granted for one person to act on another's behalf.

preapproval a preliminary mortgage approval.

prepayment monies generally collected at closing for loan interest due through the end of the current month or to fund mortgage escrows. For instance, if your monthly payment includes property taxes, depending on the date of closing, they may not yet have collected enough money to pay the upcoming tax bill.

prepayment penalty the expenses associated with early payoff of a loan.

prequalification similar to preapproval but without any verifications.

prescription a form of property rights through common use.

primary mortgage market the marketplace where mortgage loans are initiated directly between borrowers and lender, before they are pooled and resold as securities on the secondary market.

prime rate the lowest available interest rate a lending institution charges on short-term loans to businesses.

principal the loan amount received in cash before interest, taxes, insurance etc are applied.

principal meridian an imaginary north/south line used as a reference point in surveying to describe land.

probate the legal process for the disposition of a will.

procuring cause the method of an agent the commission in the event of a dispute among agents; legal expression that means the goal was realized through the actions.

promissory note the security agreement that lays out the terms of the loan and the promise to repay.

property management oversight of the business aspects of owning income property, including leasing, maintenance, record keeping etc.

property tax taxes on real property collected by the government.

prorate anything that is allocated or distributed; for instance, if you lease on apartment on the 10th of the month, the first month's rent would be divided into a per/day amount and then prorated to reflect the 20 days of rent due.

pur autre vie "For the life of another," a form of life estate; granted to the holder for as long as a third person is alive.

purchase agreement also called purchase and sale or deposit receipt; the governing contract between a buyer and seller detailing the final terms of the transaction through the closing.

purchase money mortgage a mortgage specifically for the purchase of property, rather than refinance or home equity.

>Q

qualifying ratios the ratio of the buyer's debt when compared to the buyer's income and buyer's income compared to housing expenses. Lenders have set maximums used in the decisions to approval or decline loans and borrowers.

quitclaim deed a transfer of title to property with no warranties of past title.

>R

range a six-mile-wide area of land. Using the rectangular survey system, it is labeled east or west.

ready, willing, and able refers to the buyer's ability to complete the purchase. Used as a test of when a commission has been earned.

real estate real property including the land, improvements and anything affixed to the land; and air, water and mineral rights.

real estate agent a duly licensed salesperson or broker representing another in the transfer of real property for compensation.

real estate broker a duly licensed broker representing another in the transfer of real property for compensation; authorized to work as a sole proprietor and supervise salespeople.

real estate salesperson a duly licensed salesperson representing another in the transfer of real property for compensation; must work under the supervision of a duly licensed real estate broker.

Real Estate Settlement Procedures Act (RESPA) federal law preventing the professionals servicing the real estate industry from paying kickbacks to one another and eliminating "bait and switch" tactics.

real property real estate; land, improvements and anything affixed to the land; and air, water and mineral rights.

realtor a trademarked member of the National Association of Realtors.

recording the legal filing of documents related to changes in property title, such as by a sale, transfer and encumbrance; generally located in the county clerk's office.

rectangular survey system a survey method of dividing land into squares and grids.

redemption period the time frame during which a borrower can clear their default and redeem the property during a foreclosure proceeding.

redlining illegal action lenders using different guidelines and restrictions when lending in a particular area or to particular classes of people. **refinance transaction** obtaining a new loan on real estate and paying off an earlier loan using the same real estate as collateral.

Regulation Z federal regulations that implement the Truth in Lending Act.

release clause the mortgage clause authorizing a partial release of the lien without re-writing the entire loan document. Primarily used for mortgages associated with developments and subdivisions. As each lot or home closes, the proceeds are applied to the mortgage reducing the loan amount.

remainder estate the title interest that passes to another when the first individual's rights in the real estate end.

remainderman the individual to whom title passes when a life estate is terminated.

remaining balance the amount still left to pay on a loan.

remaining term the length of time still left to pay on a loan.

rent the consideration paid under the terms of a lease.

replacement cost the cost to replace an improvement on a piece of property; used in the appraisal cost approach.

reproduction cost the cost to duplicate an exact replica of an improvement; used in the appraisal cost approach.

rescission voiding a contract so that it is no longer in effect and returning each party to their position prior to the agreement.

restriction (restrictive covenant) prohibitions on the use of real estate; by deed or property or local by-laws.

reversion upon the termination of a freehold estate, title reverts to the grantor.

reversionary interest the interest in the title that reverts to the grantor in a reversion.

reverse annuity mortgage see reverse mortgage.

revision alteration or change (e.g. of a contract).

right of first refusal the option an individual or entity has to fulfill a contract before another person or entity may enter into a contract.

right of redemption the borrower's right to clear the default under the mortgage and redeem the property during a foreclosure proceeding.

right of survivorship the remaining spouse's right to the interest of a deceased co-owner.

riparian rights rights to the use of flowing water in proximity to a person's property.

>S

safety clause an extender clause or protection clause that entitles the broker to a commission if a buyer was escorted through the property during their listing term and later returns to close the sale.

sale-leaseback upon sale, the new owner rents back to the original owner.

sales contract a legal agreement between a buyer and seller to finalize a sale.

salesperson see real estate salesperson.

salvage value used to determine depreciation; the worth of a property or asset when its service is over.

second mortgage the mortgage in a second position for repayment; junior mortgage

section a unit of measurement in the government rectangular system, one-square mile.

secured loan a loan secured by collateral in the case of default.

security the property used as collateral in for a secured loan.

seisin the owner who holds the title to the property free and clear.

selling broker the real estate agent brings the buyer who purchases a property.

separate property relates to community property laws; property that belongs to one spouse, generally acquired before marriage.

servient tenement the property encumbered by granting an easement.

setback a measurement inward from the boundary of a property that must remain free of buildings.

settlement statement (HUD-1) the detailed accounting of all the money exchanged between the parties at a real estate closing.

severalty title to real property held by one person.

special assessment a financial levy against real estate to pay for something of benefit.

special warranty deed a deed including a warranty from the grantor that the title is free and clear and the grantor will defend against all future suits.

specific lien a lien attached to a specific asset/property as opposed to general liens which attach to all assets.

specific performance mandate by the court that the party in a contract fulfill their obligations.

standard payment calculation a process of calculating equal monthly payments needed to pay the balance owed on a mortgage at the present interest rate.

statute of frauds the law requiring certain contract to be in writing in order to be enforceable; nearly all real estate contracts are governed by this statute.

statute of limitations the time period during which someone can file a lawsuit.

statutory lien a legal obligation on the property, such as taxes.

steering illegal action of agents showing a property or locations to certain racial or cultural groups only.

straight-line depreciation the total depreciation divided by the number of years of depreciation.

subdivision a division of land into lots upon which homes are built.

sublet a tenant enters into a lease with another tenant for the whole or a portion of the leased unit; subject to their original lease with the landlord.

subordinate a lesser priority or subject to another agreement, as in a subordinate or junior mortgage will only be paid after the senior mortgage has been satisfied.

substitution appraising principal that property is only worth what a buyer is willing to pay for a reasonable substitute.

subrogation the legal substitution of one individual for another individual, with all rights passing onto the new party.

suit for possession eviction lawsuit required for landlord to regain possession of the leased unit.

suit for specific performance the lawsuit requesting the court compel one party to fulfill their obligations under a contract.

survey the legal measurement of the boundaries of a parcel of land; a map of the property surveyed.

syndicate a group of people or entities who join resources to invest in real estate.

>T

tax deed the title to real property after the government has performed a "tax taking" for unpaid taxes.

tax lien an encumbrance against real estate for unpaid taxes.

tax rate the rate by which property taxes are calculated.

tax sale the public sale of real estate to satisfy unpaid taxes.

tenancy at sufferance a tenant who does not surrender the premises after the termination of a lease.

tenancy at will a tenancy that has no specific duration and continues until one party give proper notice to the other.

tenancy by the entirety equal rights to property shared between spouses, with the right of survivorship.

tenancy in common equal rights to property shared between individuals without surviving rights.

tenant renter who pays the landlord a fee for exclusive possession and use.

tenement a fixture that remains as part of the land.

testate an estate with a legal will in place.

"time is of the essence" the principal that obligations under a contract must be fulfilled promptly and if no time is given, performance is required in a "reasonable" time.

time sharing a piece of real estate owned by more than one person; each owner purchases exclusive time at the property, rather than an exclusive unit.

title the evidence of ownership of real property.

title insurance to defend any future claims against the title or ownership of property.

title search scrutiny of legal records to review the rights to and encumbrances against real estate.

Torrens system a shortcut type of title registration available in some jurisdictions.

township a section of land in the government rectangular survey system; six square miles.

trade fixtures fixtures used in a specific business, such as a pizza oven; considered personal property, but may convey with the property upon the expiration of the lease.

transfer tax an tax levied by state and/or local authority when title to real property transfers.

trust a property interest held by one for the benefit of another.

trustee the person/entity who performs the business of and is the holder of the trust on behalf of a beneficiary.

Truth-in-Lending Law (TILA) federal law requiring lenders to disclose all costs associated with borrowing, specifically APR.

>U

underwriting the process of the final review of a mortgage application package and the recommendation to approve or deny a loan.

undivided interest shared rights and ownership of property among owners that cannot be separated.

unilateral contract only one party must act to create the contract.

unsecured loan a loan that has no collateral asset, based on the borrower's credit worthiness.

useful life the period of time during which improvements have value.

usury charging a higher than maximum interest rate; illegal.

>V

VA-guaranteed loan a government-backed mortgage guaranteed by the Veterans Administration; available to veterans only.

valid contract a legally binding and enforceable contract.

valuation the option or act of establishing the value of real estate.

variance a special permission granted from the local zoning authority for a non-conforming structure or use of property.

vendee buyer of real or personal property.

vendor seller of real or personal property.

village a small grouping of residential properties and other buildings.

void contract an agreement that cannot be enforced.

voidable contract a contract that can be terminated by one of the parties.

>W

waiver the abdication of certain rights.

warranty deed a deed including the warranty that title is free and clear and the grantor will defend against any claims in the future.

waste specified abuse of mortgage or rental property that causes damages.

will legal document that details the disposition of property to upon death of the author.

wraparound mortgage a property loan that combines a first mortgage with a second mortgage at a higher loan amount and higher payment.

writ of execution a court order for a public official to seize and sell property to satisfy a debt, such as during a foreclosure proceeding.

>Z

zone a specified area regulated by local rules and conditions, such as a business zone that is prohibited from residential housing.

zoning ordinance the regulation governing the type and use of property in a particular zone.

Real Estate Sales Exam I

1. A couple executes a sales contract on their home after several counteroffers with the buyer. On the deed, the seller is:

a) the mortgagee

b) the grantor

c) the grantee

d) the mortgagor

2. The Cambridge family bought a house with a lot size of a quarter of an acre. This is equivalent to:

a) 10,890 square feet

b) 43,560 square feet

c) 11,000 square feet

d) 5,250 square feet

3. A primary residence is sold for $527,000 by a couple in the 28% tax bracket. The home was originally purchased eight years ago for $313,000 and the family lived there the entire eight years. How much will be paid in capital gains tax?

a) $59,920

b) $32,100

c) $214,000

d) none of the above

4. An owner-occupied, four-unit dwelling worth $525,000 generates $4,500 in monthly income from three units and $150/month from the onsite laundry. If the current owner typically yields roughly 9% annually on his investment, what is the monthly effective gross amount?

a) $4,350

b) $6,000

c) $4,905

d) $4,650

5. A brother is moving out of the country and decides to sell his home to his sister for $275,000, making this the latest sale in that area. The sister decides to pay cash, as she says she will later get a home equity loan for $200,000. Recent sales comps of very similar homes had values of $325,000. Based on the information provided, what is best estimate of the market value of the subject property?

a) $325,000

b) $200,000

c) $275,000

d) not enough information provided

6. When can a landlord choose not to rent to someone with children?

a) Never, children are protected under the Fair Housing Act

b) If the unit has evidence of lead paint

c) A lease of an owner-occupied three-family home

d) Someone on a temporary lease

7. A seller provides written permission allowing his listing broker to also represent the buyer. This relationship is known as:

a) Dual agency

b) Sub agency

c) Special agency

d) Implied agency

8. Bob, the builder applies for a mortgage to buy a new piece of land, offering three other lots he owns as collateral. What type of mortgage is he trying to secure?

a) a blanket mortgage

b) a reverse mortgage

c) an equity line of credit mortgage

d) a bridge loan mortgage

9. Which of these is considered be a valid contract?

a) a verbal agreement between neighbors for Neighbor A to mow Neighbor B's lawn in exchange for Neighbor B setting out the trash for pickup and bringing in the barrels.

b) a written lease for 23-year old Kathy to rent Sam's apartment for $1200 over the next 6 months.

c) both A and B

d) B only

10. A homeowner originally purchased a home for $300,000 on a FHA loan with an interest rate of 4.25%. Home values have remained the same, so he wants to do a cash-out, refinance, change to a conventional mortgage and eliminate his private mortgage insurance premiums, what is the highest amount he can mortgage?

a) $276,500

b) $310,000

c) $300,000

d) $240,000

11. Which best describes an example of emblements?

a) cherry tree, apple tree and tomato plants

b) cherry tree, apple tree and peach tree

c) tomato, lettuce and onion crops

d) none of these

12. What type of ownership includes married couples having an equal interest in property acquired during marriage?

a) common-law

b) community property

c) commingling

d) common title

13. A dad who owns his house free and clear decides to take out a HELOC and let his son make the payments. He also signs a quitclaim deed to transfer the home into his son's name. What clause might the lender enforce?

a) co-insurance clause

b) acceleration clause

c) due-on-sale clause

d) cancellation clause

14. A couple in California requests the name of an excellent home inspector from their agent. All are things the realtor should do EXCEPT which of the following:

a) provide them with a brochure

b) tell them that it is a conflict for her to recommend an inspector

c) give them a list of at least five home inspectors

d) direct them to the state home inspection website

15. The Federal Home Loan Mortgage Corporation primarily purchases which loan types:

a) FHA

b) owner-financed notes

c) VA

d) conventional

16. Sally works for ABC Bank. Her job duties are to gather documents, review applications for accuracy, package the loan and take each file from pre-approval to closing. What is most likely her job title?

a) underwriter

b) processor

c) loan officer

d) appraiser

17. Which of the following does not lend money directly to borrowers?

a) insurance company

b) mortgage broker

c) cooperative bank

d) private lender

18. Jay decides that he's ready to move out of his parents' home and purchase his own home. He has a roommate who will be moving in so he would like at least a three-bedroom house. What should his first step be?

a) get preapproved by submitting a mortgage application

b) purchase new furniture

c) pick out a house

d) purchase a new car to go with the new house

19. Which of the following actions would constitute the unlawful practice of law?

a) the agent informing the buyer of the legal ramifications of signing the purchase contract.

b) the agent filling out the purchase contract form and arranging for their client sign it.

c) the agent advising their client that they don't need an attorney if they use the standard purchase contract form.

d) the agent advising the seller that they must maintain property insurance until closing.

20. A lender offers you a very low interest of 2.75% in exchange for part of your equity. What type of mortgage is this?

a) balloon

b) shared equity

c) wraparound mortgage

d) equity loan

21. Sellers Keith and Rita execute a purchase agreement on November 1st. The contract also states that by November 15th their agent should receive a mortgage commitment letter. On November 14th, the buyer's agent sends over a letter that the buyer has been unable to secure financing. The purchaser should expect:

a) their earnest money deposit back

b) to withdraw from the transaction

c) both a and b

d) neither a nor b

22. House and Home Realty Brokerage leased a two-family residence for $1,500/month for each unit. Tenant 1 wrote a check to cover the first month's rent and deposit and Tenant 2 paid by money order. Which is the best representation of what the brokerage must do?

a) Make and keep a copy of all funds collected from each tenant

b) Nothing as long as the broker received the money that is sufficient

c) Only copy the money order because a check is a legal record

d) Tell the tenant to pay the owner directly

23. Kimberly finds the home of her dreams, a cozy bungalow built in 1932. Her agent suspects that the home may have lead-based paint. Kimberly has how many days to test for lead-based paint?

a) 5

b) 3

c) 7

d) 10

24. Who appoints the Commissioner of the Bureau of Real Estate in California?

a) The Governor

b) The people, by popular election

c) A committee of 10 licensed realtors

d) The State Legislature

25. An appraisal is done on a unique property that sits on 42.5 acres. The approach the appraiser will more than likely use is _____.

a) assumption

b) cost

c) income

d) market data

26. Jill secures a 15-year-fixed conventional home loan. This loan was more than likely purchased by which investor?

a) FNMA

b) insurance company

c) an orb

d) GNMA

27. Under the Equal Credit Opportunity Act, which of the following is prohibited when qualifying an potential borrower?

a) ask the borrower if they are buying a house because they are planning a family

b) ask the borrower what country their family is originally from

c) ask the borrower if the additional income they are claiming is from alimony

d) none of these

28. When determining whether a buyer is a good credit risk, the lender needs to evaluate:

a) borrower's credit, the borrower's ability to pay, and homeowner's age

b) ability to pay, property, borrower's 401(k)

c) borrower's credit, future expected value of the property, job stability

d) property, ability to pay, credit

29. When a buyer chooses to pay discount points, her goal is to receive_____.

a) cash back at closing

b) a lower interest rate

c) principal reduction

d) none of these

30. Kevin's sister Kim decides she wants to purchase a home and needs to get prequalified. Kevin's sister's best friend James is a loan officer at the bank and tells him once the loan closes he will give him a referral fee. Which statement is true?

a) As long as James gives Kim the HUD information booklet within three days, he can pay a referral fee

b) James is protected under RESPA

c) James must disclose the referral amount on the GFE

d) Fees and kickbacks to individuals who do not provide a loan are prohibited

31. Which of the following governs the activities of licensees in California.

a) USPAP

b) GNMA

c) CalFHA

d) CalBRE

32. The purpose of which of the following laws is to prohibit discrimination on the basis of only race in the sale of real property?

a) The Federal Fair Housing Act

b) Regulation Z

c) Federal Civil Rights Act of 1866

d) Federal Fair Housing Act of 1868

33. Another name for a HUD-1 is _____,

a) Good Faith Estimate

b) Uniform Settlement Statement

c) Truth in Lending document

d) Housing Uniform document

34. A homeowner attempts a refinance on his home only to find out that the home has two liens from the previous owner that were never paid off. Whom should he contact?

a) the title insurance company

b) the escrow office

c) the loan officer

d) a real estate attorney

35. All listing types below allow the seller the right to sell their property on their own without paying a commission, EXCEPT_____.

a) an exclusive agency

b) open

c) exclusive right to sell

d) none of the above

36. Kurt receives a letter that an expressway is being built where his property sits. The state offers to purchase his home. What right is the state exercising?

a) escheatment

b) foreclosure

c) adverse passion

d) eminent domain

37. A family leases a home with a pool. The contract states that the owner will pay property taxes and insurance, but the tenant must pay the pool and yard expenses. This is known as a _____ lease.

a) percentage

b) gross

c) net

d) month-to-month

38. Mr. Green has purchased new energy-efficient windows, put weather stripping around the doors and replaced his old wall heater with a new central air and heat system. Mr. Green has _____ his home.

a) weatherized

b) energized

c) overhauled

d) redlined

39. Tenant James is renting a one-bedroom apartment and his rent will be $923 per month. If the cost to replace the lock and key is $150 and the security deposit is the same as the rent, what is the maximum amount James may be asked to give to the owner at the beginning of the lease?

a) $923

b) $2,919

c) $1,073

d) $1,996

40. The total commission for the sale of a $449,000 property is 6%. The listing states that they will offer 3.5% to a co-broker who brings a buyer which ends in a successfully closed transaction. How much will the listing broker net after his sales agent, who is on a 45/55 (listing broker gets 55%) split, is paid?

a) $26,940

b) $15,715

c) $6,174

d) $11,225

41. Several first-time home buyers purchasing in a community redevelopment area noticed that they were not offered a fixed-rate loan by the developer's lender. They were only offered adjustable rate mortgages. This is most likely an example of _____.

a) economic adjustments

b) redlining

c) conforming

d) steering

42. Susie has been a licensed sales agent for several years and would like to pursue her broker's license. What must she do?

a) pass the test

b) complete additional hours of classroom instruction

c) be a legal resident of the United States

d) all of the above

43. All are true except:

a) real estate licenses are valid for four years

b) an inactive sales agent cannot collect referral fees

c) a salesperson must take and pass the renewal exam

d) a salesperson must take continuing education in order to remain in active status

44. FHA insured loans protect the:

a) lender

b) realtor

c) seller

d) buyer

45. Which category is protected by the Unruh Civil Rights Act?

a) sexual orientation

b) race

c) medical condition

d) all of the above

46. A tenant signs a one-year lease where the owner allows him to occupy the property during this time. This is an example of _____.

a) fee simple

b) freehold estate

c) time share

d) non-freehold estate

47. After being asked several times, Carolyn has not removed her personal belongings blocking the fire exit in her building. What type of Notice does her landlord serve?

a) Notice to Vacate

b) 3-day Notice to Quit

c) 3-day Notice to Perform Covenants or Quit

d) Notice of Eviction

48. When someone who is upside down with their mortgage gets permission to sell their house for less than they owe, this process is known as:

a) short sale

b) foreclosure

c) deed restructure

d) deed-in-lieu of foreclosure

49. When an owner enters into a lease with a tenant, what ownership right or obligation do they temporarily relinquish?

a) the right to sell the property

b) the right to further encumber the property

c) the responsibility to maintain insurance

d) the right to possession

50. A couple's agent takes them to see a for-sale-by-owner listing. The couple decides they really like the house and make an offer. The seller, impressed by the agent's professionalism, asks if she can represent him also. What should she do now?

a) say thank you, but say no explaining that would breach her duty to her clients

b) say thank you and explain this is illegal

c) say thank you and ask both parties to sign a consent form

d) say thank you and negotiate fairly for both parties

51. A broker's license can be revoked if he:

a) fails to return deposit funds to a client when instructed

b) commingles business and personal funds

c) fails to pay the agent his commission split

d) any of the above

52. A person dies leaving no will and no heirs. The decedent's property would transfer by:

a) adverse possession

b) state

c) escheat

d) laws of descent

53. Describe the ownership of a property if four cousins, Keenan, Kelly, Shon and Marcia are tenants in common and Marcia sells her interest to cousin Michael. The new deed will read:

a) tenants in common with Keenan, Kelly and Shon

b) tenants in will

c) joint tenants Keenan, Kelly and Shon

d) Marcia is not allowed to sell her interest

54. If the seller received some cash, a promissory note and a mortgage at the closing, what kind of loan did the Buyer get?

a) a carry back mortgage

b) blanket mortgage

c) non-conforming loan

d) purchase money mortgage

55. A 2,980 square foot home sells for $328,000. If it sits on an acre lot, what is the price per square foot the home sold for?

a) $94

b) $110

c) $116

d) $154

56. A lot recently sold for $198,000. It is 378' x 296'. What was the cost per acre?

a) $67,074

b) $70,774

c) $77,774

d) $77,042

57. If Michelle sells her home but remains in the property by becoming a tenant of the new landlord, this is known as:

a) testate

b) wraparound mortgage

c) leaseback

d) freehold

58. A homeowner puts a $104,250 down payment on a $417,000 home. What percentage is the down payment?

a) 25%

b) 18%

c) 20%

d) 30%

59. Matthew sells his home to Sam. Who pays the transfer tax?

a) Matthew

b) Sam

c) a and b

d) neither

60. An investor gets a loan with payments amortized over 30 year that must be paid in full on year 15. What kind of loan did she get?

a) VA loan

b) package mortgage

c) balloon mortgage

d) open-end mortgage

61. Farrah has been a licensed Broker for 7 years and needs to renew her license next year. What must she do in the coming year to renew her license?:

a) complete 15 hours of continuing education

b) complete 12 hours of continuing education

c) complete 45 hours of his continuing education

d) complete 12 hours of continuing education and pass the renewal exam

62. The most probable price that an informed purchaser would pay is the:

a) sales price

b) broker price opinion

c) market value

d) assessed value

63. A lender prequalifies a couple for a loan amount up to $375,000 with a 3.5% down payment. What booklet must he give them within three days of application?

a) an information booklet prepared by HUD

b) a booklet on the explanation of closing costs

c) Regulation Z booklet

d) HUD-1 booklet

64. When a borrower makes a down payment less than 20% and gets an FHA loan, what monthly charge should he expect to be added to his mortgage payment?

a) property taxes

b) funding fee

c) private mortgage insurance

d) equity loan payment

65. The "four unities" required to create a joint tenancy include which of the following?

a) they must be residents of the same state when they acquired the property

b) they must be related to one another

c) they must have joint financial responsibility for the property

d) they must acquire ownership rights at the same time

66. The sales comparison approach is also known as the:

a) appraisal process

b) market data approach

c) replacement cost approach

d) cost approach

67. "DUST" is a term associated with:

a) licensing

b) title

c) appraisals

d) conformity

68. When there are more homes on the market than buyers looking for property, there is:

a) regression

b) more supply than demand

c) substitution

d) law of decreasing return

69. If a three-family home is valued at $769,000 and the cap rate is 9%, what is the annual net operating income?

a) $69,210

b) $85,444

c) $100,000

d) $71,000

70. Tim inherits his family's farm which has suffered years of neglect. He decides to take an equity loan on the property, so his realtor orders an appraisal. The appraiser sees obvious physical deterioration and also notices that a bathroom was never added to the home, it still has an outhouse. The lack of an inside bathroom is a _____.

a) functional obsolescence

b) physical deterioration

c) economic obsolescence

d) accrued depreciation

71. Another name for the Federal Fair Housing Act is _____.

a) Fair Housing

b) Title VIII of the Civil Rights Act of 1968

c) Federal Civil Rights Act of 1866

d) Consumer Protection Law

72. California allows nonresidents to hold a real estate license if they:

a) move to California

b) sign a notarized letter appointing a family member as their attorney-in-fact

c) purchase a two-family home and keep the unit as their second residence

d) file a power of attorney appointing the chairman of the board as their attorney-in-fact

73. All of these are grounds for license suspension or revocation EXCEPT:

a) commingling personal and business funds

b) acting as an undisclosed dual agent

c) telling the buyer agent the air conditioning isn't working

d) receiving a referral fee from the title company after the closing

74. All have right of survivorship EXCEPT:

a) tenancy in common

b) tenancy by entirety

c) joint tenancy

d) none of the above

75. The best form of ownership is:

a) *pur autre vie*

b) leasehold

c) fee simple

d) freehold

76. Mary and John owned their home as joint tenants until Mary died. Which statement is true?

a) John now has to sell his home.

b) If there is a loan on the property, the lender will call the loan due.

c) John has become the sole owner

d) John will have to move

77. Which of the following violates the anti-trust laws?

a) Agreeing everyone should charge 6% commissions at the monthly brokers' breakfast

b) Agreeing with your supervising broker that you want to always charge 6% commissions

c) Charging a 6% commission after seeing another broker charge that amount

d) Discussing the different rates of commissions broker get at the monthly brokers' breakfast

78. A licensed agent who is associated with a brokerage is a(n):

a) broker

b) salesperson

c) escrow agent

d) either a or b

79. Which of these is NOT a cost of owning a home?

a) repairs

b) interest paid on the mortgage loan

c) personal property taxes

d) maintenance

80. Which commonly influences a person's decision to purchase a home in a certain location?

a) street signage

b) school ratings

c) high number of planned unit developments

d) loan types

81. The only time a broker can add personal funds to the escrow account is:

a) never

b) to maintain a minimum balance in the escrow account

c) to purchase investment property using the escrow account

d) if a purchaser asks the broker to hold funds

82. California is a _____ contract state.

a) 2

b) 1

c) 4

d) 3

83. Mr. and Mrs. Sellers signed the purchase and sale agreement in which they are selling their home to the Buyer family. The Buyers have moved forward in getting all inspections, appraisals, etc., ordered on the property. However, the Sellers are now feeling sad and desire to terminate the contract. Which statement is true?

a) they are the owners and maintain the right to terminate the contract at any time

b) they may be forced to sell their home as the contract is legal and binding

c) if they offer to return the Buyers' deposit and pay other incurred expenses the Buyers must accept this and allow them to terminate the contract

d) none of the above is true

84. Which of the following ads will require more disclosures?

a) We have no-money-down loans

b) VA, FHA and conventional loans offered here

c) The interest rate is 4.375% per year

d) both a and c

85. Why do lenders scrutinize the income-to-debt ratios?

a) they are prohibited from lending more money than is necessary

b) the lower the ratio, the more profitable the loan

c) they must demonstrate the buyer's ability to repay the loan

d) they must ensure the property value covers the loan amount in the event of a default

86. Larry is purchasing a home that has $20,000 in needed repairs but he doesn't have $20,000. What loan is a good option for him?

a) FHA 203(b)

b) FHA 203(k)

c) FHA 203(c)

d) FHA

87. The minimum age in California to receive a salesperson's license is:

a) 21

b) 25

c) 16

d) 18

88. When an agent shares the property listing details and offers compensation to another agent, this is known as:

a) an offer to cooperate

b) an equity share

c) an offer to co-broke

d) both a and c

89. In California, a salesperson can work as a(n):

a) employee of the broker

b) independent contractor under the broker

c) a or b

d) neither

90. A California law that protects consumers is:

a) Civil Rights Act of 1966

b) Fair Housing Act

c) Fair Employment and Housing Act

d) Title VIII

91. Jim does a lot of home improvement projects, so he built a shed on his neighbor Jerry's land. Jim has used this shed continuously for over 20 years. Jim can pursue a claim of _____ in order to gain title the property.

a) adverse possession

b) eminent domain

c) servient tenement

d) concurrent ownership

92. An ad reads "2 story traditional 1,500 square foot home in San Clemente, California, for sale. Asking $423,000. Please call Rhonda at 857-455-8234." From a legal perspective, the ad is missing:

a) Rhonda's last name

b) Rhonda disclosing that she is a broker

c) Number of bedrooms and bathrooms

d) Rhonda disclosing her brokerage's name and that she is a licensed broker

93. What is a broker's commission fee percent if she sells a building for $673,225 and her fee earned is $16,830.62?

a) 2.5%

b) 6.5%

c) 3.5%

d) 4.0%

94. Another name for some loan closing costs is:

a) application fee

b) credit report fee

c) discount points

d) all of the above

95. The Federal Civil Rights Act was passed in:

a) 1968

b) 1866

c) 1868

d) 1986

96. The _____ sets the minimum requirements for appraisals.

a) RESPA

b) MLS

c) TILA

d) USPAP

97. A section is:

a) two square miles

b) a city block

c) 27,878,400 square feet

d) 43,560 acres

98. After what year did California mandate that all new or rehabbed four-family homes or larger first-floor units be handicap accessible?

a) 1968

b) 1991

c) 2002

d) 1986

99. Which is not covered under the Fair Housing Act?

a) an SFR that is corporate owned

b) elderly housing that meets certain Department of Housing and Urban Development guidelines

c) a two-to-four unit dwelling that is not owner-occupied

d) a home owned by an individual who owns more than three properties

100. When real property is held under a trust deed, who uses and occupies the property?

a) the trustee

b) the trustor

c) the beneficiary

d) the mortgagee

324

Real Estate Sales Exam I Answers

1. b. The couple (owner) is granting title to the real property.

2. a. 1 acre = 43,560 square feet.   43,560 x .25 = 10,890 square feet.

3. d. None of the above. The property is the sellers' primary residence which was owned and lived in by then for at least two years during the last five years with a profit less than $500,000.

4. d. The effective gross amount is $4,500 + $150 (the sum of all income generated).

5. a. Not a formal appraisal, so informally, recent sales of similar house are sufficient to render an opinion.

6. c. The children are generally protected under the Fair Housing Act, but owner-occupied dwellings of 3 units or less are exempt.

7. a. The relationship becomes a dual agency with the agent representing both parties. It is necessary to obtain the permission and signatures on the disclosure from both parties.

8. a. A blanket mortgage has more than one property for collateral.

9. c. Both contracts are valid. The contract between neighbors does not fall under the Statute of Frauds and is not required to be in writing.

10. a. The maximum loan to value is 80% in order to eliminate PMI.

11. c. Emblements are generally farming crops that are annually cultivated.

12. b. Each spouse has equal interest in property acquired during marriage.

13. c. Because the father has transferred the property, the lender is allowed to demand full payment.

14. c. In California the agent cannot recommend an inspector.

15. d. Fannie Mae and Freddie Mac purchase conventional loans.

16. b. Processors prepare the loan package for the underwriter.

17. b. Mortgage brokers bring borrowers together with lenders.

18. a. The first step to obtaining home loan financing is to submit the application.

19. c. Agents are strictly prohibited from giving legal advice without a license and must always advise their clients to consult an attorney.

20. b. Shared equity is when the lender offers a low interest rate in exchange for a portion of the equity.

21. c. This contract included a financing contingency in which the purchaser was given the opportunity to withdraw from the contract if they were unable to secure financing.

22. a. The property manager is required to make and keep a copy of collected funds for three years.

23. d. Under the Lead Paint Law, the buyer gets 10 days to test for evidence of lead paint.

24. a. The Commissioner is appointed by the Governor.

25. b. The cost approach is used when the appraiser has difficulty finding comps.

26. a. FNMA purchases conventional loans.

27. a. It is prohibited to ask a borrower if they are planning a family.

28. d. The lender must do an appraisal, ensure the borrower has means to repay the mortgage and meet the lender's credit score.

29. b. Points charged by a lender are to lower the rate for the buyer.

30. d. RESPA prohibits several types of payments to persons who did not perform a service.

31. d. CalBRE is the California Bureau of Real Estate and governs the activities of licensees.

32. c. The Civil Rights Act of 1866 prohibits discrimination on the basis of race in the sale, lease or other transfer of real or personal property.

33. b. A HUD-1 is also known as a Uniform Settlement Statement.

34. a. The title insurance company protects the holder from defects in the title.

35. c. An exclusive-right-to-sell listing allows the broker to receive a commission no matter who sells the property.

36. d. Eminent domain gives the government the right to take private property for public use with payment as compensation.

37. c. In net lease, the tenant pays the maintenance and operating expenses.

38. a. Because he made energy-efficient improvements he has weatherized his home.

39. b. The maximum a California landlord can charge a new tenant is first month's rent + second month's rent + security deposit + cost for new keys and lock change: 3 x $923 + $150 = $2,919.

40. c. Subtract the listing broker's commission from the total commission percentage. Then multiply that number by the home sales price. Then multiply that number by the listing broker's split with his agent. 6 - 3.5 = 2.5%; x $44,900 = $11,225; x 55% = $6,174.

41. b. The lender used different guidelines for homebuyers purchasing in a certain area.

42. d. To be a broker she has to pass the test, complete additional classroom hours of education and be a legal US resident.

43. c. No exam is required to renew a license.

44. a. FHA insured loans protect the lender in the event the borrower defaults.

45. d. All of the above. In 2005 the law added sexual orientation to the list of covered classes.

46. d. Non-freehold estate gives the holder of the estate the right to occupy the property until the end of the lease.

47. c. 3-day Notice to Perform Covenants or Quit. This form is used when the breach does not involve non-payment of rent.

48. a. Short sale is when the bank gives the homeowner the permission to sell the home when he owes more than it is worth.

49. d. The tenant pays rent in exchange for the exclusive right to use and possess the dwelling.

50. c. She would become a dual agent and must get written consent from both parties.

51. d. A broker is not allowed to mix business and personal funds, refuse to pay the client their escrow funds when lawfully instructed, or not pay previously disclosed compensation.

52. c. When no heirs can be found, the state can lay claim to the property.

53. a. Tenants in common can transfer title if all parties agree.

54. a. When the seller holds the note and mortgage, it is a carry-back loan, also known as seller financing.

55. b. Price per square foot is found by dividing the price by the square feet. $328,000/2,980 = $110.

56. d. Multiply the lot dimensions 378 x 296 = 111,888 square feet. Determine how many acres the lot is. An acre is 43,560 square feet; therefore, divide 111,888/43,560 = 2.57 acres. Divide the cost of $198,000 by 2.57 = $77,042.

57. c. New owner leases property back to the person who sold to them.

58. a. Divide the down payment by the sales price. $104,250/$41,700 = .25 or 25%.

59. a. The State of California charges transfer tax whenever real property changes hands and this expense is paid by the seller at closing.

60. c. In a balloon mortgage the remaining lump sum is due at the termination date.

61. c. A broker or sales agent must take 45 hours of continuing education classes within two years to renew his license.

62. c. Market value is the most probable price that an informed buyer will pay.

63. a. Per RESPA, a lender or mortgage broker must give a borrower a copy of a HUD-prepared information booklet within three days of application.

64. c. Any loan-to-value of less than 80% requires PMI. The borrower pays the insurance premium along with the principal and interest payment.

65. d. Under the "unity of time", both owners must acquire the property at the same time.

66. b. The market data approach is also known as the comparison approach.

67. c. DUST is an acronym for the elements that establish value and is associated with appraisals.

Demand for the type of property
Utility (desirable use) the property offers
Scarcity of properties available
Transferability of property to a new owner

68. b. There's a larger inventory of homes than there are buyers

69. a. Value x Cap rate = Net Operating Income $769,000 x .09 = $69,210

70. a. Functional obsolescence highlights features that are no longer considered desirable.

71. b. The Federal Fair Housing Act broadened the prohibitions against discrimination in housing to include sex, race, color, religion, national origin, disability and familial status in connection with the sale or rental of housing or vacant land.

72. d. California allows nonresidents to hold a real estate license if they file a power of attorney appointing the commissioner as their attorney-in-fact for legal issues relating to that individual.

73. c. The fiduciary duties of disclosure and confidentiality, as well as the duties to be honest and fair must be rendered to all parties in a transaction.

74. a. Tenancy in common does not have right of survivorship. Tenancy by entirety is a form of joint tenancy and has right of survivorship.

75. c. Fee simple is a type of freehold estate and is the best form of ownership because the owner has the right to occupy or rent the property, sell or transfer ownership, build on and mine for minerals and restrict or allow the use of the property to others.

76. c. Joint tenancy includes the right of survivorship; the surviving co-owner automatically shares equally in the deceased owner's interest.

77. a. It is an anti-trust violation for brokers to collude with one another to set a universal commission amount.

78. d. A licensed agent who is associated with a brokerage is a salesperson or broker associate depending on the license they hold.

79. c. Personal property taxes are taxes on personal property not real property.

80. b. School ratings can influence whether a person purchases in a certain area.

81. a. A broker may never mix business and personal funds.

82. b. California is one contract. The California Purchase Agreement and Joint Escrow Instructions governs the transaction from offer through closing.

83. b. Because the contract is legal and binding, if the Sellers don't move forward, they will be in breach of contract and the Buyers can sue for specific performance.

84. d. The ads containing "triggering terms" must disclose the loan amount, the down payment, the APR, and the terms of repayment.

85. c. The lender must demonstrate the buyers' ability to repay the loan.

86. b. FHA 203(k) is FHA's Rehabilitation Loan Insurance Program.

87. d. California's minimum age for a real estate license is 18.

88. d. When an agent provides listing information and offers compensation to another agent, this is an offer to cooperate or co-broke.

89. c. The salesperson can work as an independent contractor and/or an employee under the supervision of a licensed broker.

90. c. Fair Employment and Housing Act

91. a. Adverse possession is a method of acquiring title to another person's property through court action after continuous use for more than 20 years.

92. d. The broker must disclose her name and that she is a licensed broker.

93. a. Divide the total commission earned by the sales price. $16,830.62/$67,225 = .025 x 100 = 2.5%.

94. d. All of these are fees and charges typically associated with obtaining financing.

95. b. The Federal Civil Rights Act was passed in 1866 to prohibit discrimination on the basis of race.

96. d. The Uniform Standards of Professional Appraisal Practice (USPAP) sets the minimum requirements for appraisals.

97. c. A section is 640 acres. 640 acres x 43,560 square feet per acre = 27,878,400 square feet.

98. b. The Federal Fair Housing Act of 1968 prohibits discrimination against mentally or physically handicapped individuals. After 1991, it was mandated that all new or rehabbed four-family or larger homes must be designed so the first floor units are accessible for people with disabilities.

99. b. The Federal Fair Housing Act does not cover housing for the elderly that meets certain HUD guidelines.

100. b. In a Trust Deed, the trustor is the borrower and holds equitable title providing for control, use and possession of the property.

Real Estate Sales Exam II

1. Melissa at MY TOWN Realty gets a listing to sell a home representing the Sellers. During one of the open houses, her Buyer client couple comes in and decides to make an offer. They prefer to have a separate buyer client and ask the broker at MY TOWN to assign one of his other sales agents, Keith, to represent them. In this case Keith is acting as a:

a) non-agent

b) designated buyer's agent

c) single agent

d) principal agent

2. A buyer secures a first mortgage for $243,750, puts down 15% and the seller carries back 10%. What was the sales price of the home if she paid full asking?

a) $250,000

b) $300,000

c) $375,000

d) $325,000

3. All are true statements regarding appraisal reports EXCEPT?

a) they can be verbally delivered

b) they must be delivered on the Uniform Residential Appraisal Report

c) they must use guidelines set forth by USPAP

d) they can be delivered in writing

4. Seller competition in the market usually results in:

a) higher home prices

b) lower home prices

c) anticipation

d) progression

5. The disposition, control, right of possession and enjoyment are all:

a) zoning ordinances

b) intangibles

c) corporeal

d) in the bundle of rights of ownership

6. All are real property EXCEPT:

a) air rights

b) refrigerator

c) oak tree

d) pond

7. A local department store property was sold and had an 8% rate of appreciation per year for 12 years. It was originally bought for $713,480. What was the latest sale price?

a. $1,265,439

b. $627,648

c. $515,126

d. $1,398,420

8. A church which has 501(c)(3) status is exempt from paying:

a) a mortgage

b) property taxes

c) hazard insurance

d) licensing fees

9. Felix Munoz decided to pay four points on his mortgage. If the mortgage is $326,000, how much is he paying for points?

a. $10,620

b. $1,043

c. $13,040

d. $107.42

10. Matthew decides to purchase a home, so he gives his landlord of two years a 30-day notice. If his security deposit was $1,345 and the bank interest rate (where the landlord held his deposit) was 1%, how much money should he expect to receive?

a) $1,545.38

b) $1,345

c) $1,358.45

d) $1,372.03

11. Even though Jennifer's lease ended over a month ago, she has not moved out. When she pays her rent this month, what type of tenancy will she now have?

a) tenancy at will

b) tenancy for years

c) tenancy for period to period

d) tenancy at sufferance

12. Realtors are members of the:

a) NAREB

b) NRA

c) NAR

d) REBAC

13. A lender needs to set a listing price on one of his foreclosed homes. He will more than likely order a(n):

a) mortgage payment history

b) appraisal

c) assessed value report

d) BPO

14. Which one is an example of commercial real estate?

a) a 21-unit apartment complex

b) a store for rent

c) a storefront with apartments on the second floor

d) loft apartments

15. Bill and Mara Peterson are in the process of filing their taxes for last year. During that year, they paid $7,500 in mortgage interest. They also paid $976 in property taxes. Since they are in the 10% tax bracket, what will they save in taxes? (Round to the nearest dollar.)

a. $848

b. $1,200

c. $652

d. $1,635

16. *Fructus naturales* refers to:

a) real property

b) emblements

c) natural fruit

d) annually cultivated crops

17. An exploration company purchases the rights to any minerals and oil from an owner. The owner now owns all rights EXCEPT the following:

a) subsurface

b) water

c) air

d) surface

18. In California, a manufactured home is transferred by:

a) mortgage deed

b) mortgage note

c) bill of sale

d) purchase contract

19. Cheri was so happy when she received money from her lender that she could use to pay her contractor. She had taken out a(n) _____ mortgage.

a) equity

b) land sales

c) purchase money

d) primary

20. Bill negotiated the lease for his new apartment on the phone and told the landlord that he could sign the lease and meet in person within three days. However, Bill experienced an emergency and had to fly out of town right away, so he told his twin brother Bob to meet the landlord and sign the lease for him. The lease is:

a) valid

b) void

c) voidable

d) illegal

21. In two days, Jackie was anticipating going to her home loan closing, but instead she received a call from her agent that the home had an old second lien on it that the seller said he paid off. What term best describes the title?

a) the title is free and clear

b) the title is void

c) the title is vested

d) the title is clouded

22. Due to the economy and a loss of jobs in the area, home prices have fallen by 46% and are now valued at about $372,000. Based on the information, what was the average home price?

a) $866,000

b) $689,000

c) $668,000

d) $888,888

23. Janet's landlord locked her out of the building where she lives in Glendale, California. She decides that she wants to file a lawsuit against him but finds that he has filed bankruptcy. She must file her case with which court?

a) Janet cannot file a lawsuit; she must go before the bankruptcy court

b) judicial

c) housing

d) district

24. A couple who had their home listed with Any Town Brokerage, hosted a Christmas party. One of the guests from the party loved the home and came back to ask them several questions about the house and if they could get a formal tour. He ended up purchasing the home and the sellers did not have to pay Any Town Brokerage any commission. What type of listing did they have with Any Town?

a) dual

b) net

c) open

d) exclusive agency

25. An apartment purchaser receives shares and shares in the corporation that owns the property. What type of apartment was purchased?

a) condo

b) cooperative

c) multi unit

d) three-family home

26. Seventeen-year old Arthur, a college student, is told by a landlord that he is too young to rent one of his apartments. Which California state law might the landlord be violating?

a) Fair Employment and Housing Act and Unruh Civil Rights Act

b) ADA

c) Fair Housing Act

d) None of the above

27. Balance contributes to value when:

a) there is homogeneity in a neighborhood

b) there are diverse land uses

c) there is conformity

d) there is regression

28. If an agent is found to have violated California Fair Housing laws, his license can be automatically suspended for _____ days.

a) 60

b) 120

c) 30

d) 90

29. Mrs. Tenant vacated her apartment because her landlord turned off the water. This was a(n):

a) adverse eviction

b) lease back

c) constructive eviction

d) contractual eviction

30. In a 99-year lease, the buyer typically receives all the bundle of rights EXCEPT:

a) enjoyment

b) possession

c) control of use

d) none of the above

31. Missy paid her landlord the first month's rent and a security deposit. What does California state law mandate that he give her?

a) thank you letter

b) keys immediately

c) list of tenant rules

d) receipt

32. Violet and her dog will be leasing a one-bedroom apartment in Sacramento, California. The property manager tells her that she will need to pay first and last month's rent and a security deposit, which are each $1,100. He also tells her she will need to pay a $150 pet fee and a $30 credit report fee. What is the legally acceptable amount she will pay the property manager?

a) $3,300

b) $3,450

c) $3,480

d) $2,380

33. In California, what type of tenancy does a tenant who lives in public housing have if they have additional tenant protections?

a) tenancy at will

b) tenant with written lease

c) tenant by regulation

d) tenant at sufferance

34. Another name for tenancy at will is _____.

a) yearly lease

b) common tenancy

c) sublease

d) month-to-month

35. Which of the following describes the relationship between a property manager and the property owner?

a) non-binding agency

b) partnership

c) fiduciary

d) sub agency

36. The _____ requires that all Purchase and Sale Agreements must be in writing.

a) National Association of Realtors

b) Statute of Frauds

c) US Department of Housing and Urban Development

d) California License Law

37. A seller will pay 3% in closing costs. If the sales price is $378,499 and the buyer is providing a 20% down payment, which is the amount paid by the seller?

a) $2,270

b) $9,084

c) $3,000

d) $11,355

38. California property managers must have a:

a) broker's license

b) two-year degree

c) real estate salesperson's license

d) none of the above

39. Mike and Dana are renting a unit in their 1946 two-family home to a couple with a five-year-old child. What must they (Mike and Dana) do in accordance with the Lead Law?

a) de-lead

b) give the new tenants a Lead Paint Notice

c) have the tenants sign an escalation lease

d) a and b

40. Stan and his business partner decide to sell their four-unit property. They find another investment property in a town closer to where they live which will make it easier to manage. What technique can they use that may ease their current tax burden from the sale?

a) 1031 exchange

b) owner financing

c) hard money loan

d) equity loan

41. If you are a tenant in a property that has been foreclosed, your tenancy will:

a) terminate and you must immediately move out

b) automatically convert to a written lease with the lender

c) automatically turn into a tenancy at will

d) automatically transfer to the new owner

42. Sharon was told that her front and back end numbers were 48/55 and that she did not qualify for a home loan at this time. These are called _____.

a) LTV

b) qualifying ratios

c) cost per unit

d) income to debt ratios

43. Farmer Jedd has _____ rights, in that he is able to allow his horses to drink from the river next to his property.

a) mineral

b) air and surface

c) littoral

d) riparian

44. When two people are co-owners of a property, the three types of ownership are:

a) tenancy in common, tenancy in sufferance, and tenancy as written

b) joint tenancy, tenancy at will, and tenancy in common

c) tenancy by the entirety, tenancy in common, and joint tenancy

d) tenancy in common, tenancy by the entirety, and tenancy in sufferance

45. An agent lost her wallet with her real estate license. In order to replace it, she must_____.

a) follow the instructions on the CalBRE website

b) get a misplaced license form

c) retake the test

d) only send in the applicable fee, no form is needed.

46. Mitzi is a licensed agent but no longer wishes to perform real estate. The only thing she needs to do is:

a) send a resignation letter to her broker

b) send a resignation letter to the Bureau

c) not pay the renewal fee

d) tell the Bureau members in person when they have a meeting

47. A salesperson collects a security deposit for a lease. What is she required to do with the check?

a) immediately deposit into the office's trust account

b) deposit the check in the trust account within 3 days

c) turn the check over to her supervising broker or transaction manager

d) immediately turn the check over to the landlord.

48. The Taxpayer Relief Act was passed in:

a) 1997

b) 1986

c) 1977

d) 2001

49. Flood insurance is:

a) always optional

b) required in certain areas

c) automatically included in the hazard insurance policy

d) only available to homeowners purchasing properties financed by rural housing

50. Patty has gotten a loan pre-approval from Conservative Trust Bank. More than likely, her housing expense ratio does not exceed _____ percent.

a) 38

b) 20

c) 28

d) 33

51. A buyer makes an offer to purchase a home and the seller accepts the offer. But, before the agent can inform the buyer of the seller's acceptance and deliver the signed contract, the buyer delivers a letter to the agent's office withdrawing the offer and requesting the return of the earnest money. Which of the following is true?

a) the agent must return the earnest money immediately before informing the seller of the cancellation

b) the signed contract voided

c) the buyer must proceed with the transaction since the contract was signed by all parties

d) the agent must notify the buyers they are in breach of the contract and forward the earnest money to the seller

52. Under the cost approach, the formula for determining value is:

a) Replacement or reproduction cost – Accrued Depreciation + Land Value = Value

b) Accrued Depreciation – Replacement or reproduction cost + Land Value = Value

c) Replacement or reproduction cost + Accrued Depreciation – Land Value = Value

d) Replacement or reproduction cost + Land Value – Accrued Depreciation = Value

53. Which are examples of a protected class:

a) children

b) veterans

c) elderly

d) all of the above

54. A broker told an elderly couple that for $3,000 she could help them get their loan modified to a more affordable payment, but after the couple gave her the money she disappeared. What California law has the broker violated?

a) The Federal Civil Rights Act

b) ADA

c) California Lead Paint Law

d) California Consumer Protection Law

55. The _____ pledges the property as collateral.

a) mortgage lien

b) mortgage

c) mortgage note

d) collateralization note

56. Land, "bundle of legal rights," and permanent, human-made additions are:

a) personal property

b) emblements

c) real property

d) real estate

57. Lisa and Mike are remodeling their home. The contractor unloads a truckload of drywall and tile in front of their house. The delivered items are:

a) personal property

b) encumbrances

c) real property

d) real estate

58. Which is NOT one of the "bundle of rights?"

a) right to transfer the home to a relative

b) right to live in the home

c) right to refuse entry into the home

d) right to run a neighborhood casino

59. Which economic characteristic of real estate best represents the following example? Two identical homes built by the same developer are located on Milford Street, which separates Old City and New City. House A is in New City and sits on the west side of the street and House B sits on the east side of the street and is in Old City. Because it is a newer area, homeowners believe that the school district in New City is better than Old City.

a) relative scarcity

b) area preference

c) supply and demand

d) improvements

60. A granddaughter inherited a home worth about $225,000 that her grandparents lived in for 50 years. This home had a great deal of sentimental value to her, so she decided to remodel the home to her taste, which cost her well over $380,000 in remodeling costs. While the home's value did increase to $300,000, the appraiser told her that she over-improved the home for that neighborhood. What type of value does this home now have?

a) objective

b) indestructible

c) subjective

d) immobility

61. In California, a brokerage can exist under a temporary broker's license without examination when:

a) the broker travels out of the country

b) the broker decides to appoint one of his agents as a broker

c) the broker is late in completing his continuing education and paying the renewal fee

d) the broker of record passes away

62. The real estate market has slowed. Broker Marcia runs an ad offering a $300 closing cost rebate to anyone buying her listing at 423 East Main St. before the end of the month. Which of the following applies to this ad?

a) the ad must disclose that the rebate is subject to the seller's approval

b) the rebate must be made in cash at the closing

c) the managing broker must pay a portion of the rebate according to the commission split agreement he holds with Marcia

d) Marcia cannot make this offer; rebates are illegal.

63. Who can offer a junior mortgage?

a) Freddie Mac

b) the VA

c) the seller

d) RHS

64. Kelley, Marvin and Andrea are tenants in common. When Andrea and Marvin sell Kelley their shares of the property. As Kelley is now sole owner, she hold title in _____.

a) common

b) severalty

c) entirety

d) life estate

65. Greg has an oceanfront property where he is able to enjoy the ocean at any time. He has _____ rights.

a) bundle of

b) alluvial

c) riparian

d) littoral

66. A(n) _____ is divided into 36 sections.

a) city

b) township

c) commonwealth

d) acre

67. In a deed, *et ux* means:

a) and wife

b) everyone

c) and others

d) and husband

68. Abraham bought a property and later learned that his great-great grandfather may have owned that property. What can he order that will show the property ownership history?

a) deed of trust

b) legal description

c) certificate of title

d) chain of title

69. A chattel mortgage would more than likely be used in a transaction with all of the following EXCEPT:

a) car

b) furniture

c) single family residence

d) mobile home

70. A developer plans to build a new subdivision that is pedestrian friendly. The homes will be on small lots, but the community will have several "green" areas with parks and common areas for the residents. This type of design is known as _____.

a) communal property

b) clustering

c) commingling

d) canvassing

71. Mrs. James' husband passed away about six months ago. Because she is on fixed income she is finding it difficult to meet all of her expenses due to her husband's remaining medical bills. Because she owns her home free and clear and she would like to remain in it, what loan product might work for her?

a) junior mortgage

b) HELOC

c) primary mortgage

d) HECM

72. Which is NOT a method used to satisfy the requirement for legal description in a deed:

a) the Torrens System

b) the metes and bounds system

c) the lot and block system

d) the government survey system

73. Juliet has lived in her apartment for four months and loves it. Because summer is approaching and she does not have air conditioning, she's decided to replace her dining room lighting fixture with a ceiling fan. The ceiling fan will now be:

a) a riparian right

b) an easement

c) real property

d) personal property

74. A hardship associated with acquiring rental property is:

a) the law of increasing returns

b) lack of reserves

c) negative amortization

d) redlining

75. A broker's license is NOT required:

a) when an individual sells his candy store business to another individual

b) when he offers to list real property for sale

c) when he offers to sell his parents' home

d) in exchange for one month's rent, he negotiates the rental of real estate for another individual

76. The ADA is the:

a) American Disabled Vets Act

b) American Disposition of Realty Act

c) American Disposal Act

d) Americans with Disabilities Act

77. Misty works as a sales agent for Real Time Realty as an independent contractor. She should expect all of the following EXCEPT:

a) to assume responsibility for paying her own income tax

b) to be compensated on production

c) to receive employee benefits from the broker

d) that she and the broker will have a written contract

78. Manny and Lisa purchased their home six years ago for $325,000 when they put down 10%. Their interest rate was 6.5% and after making 72 monthly payments, their loan balance was $268,901.96. Assuming the current market value and the sales price are the same, how much equity do the homeowners have?

a) $32,500

b) $56,098.04

c) $29,200

d) none of the above

79. Every homeowner is entitled to the following income tax deductions EXCEPT:

a) loan interest on second homes

b) property taxes

c) discount points

d) penalty-free withdrawals up to $10,000 from an IRA

80. Byron, a first time homebuyer, bought his home for $72,500 with an FHA loan. The contract was executed April 28, 2010. Because he had a 60-day escrow, he finally got his keys on June 30, 2010. How much tax credit money should he expect to receive if he has no other tax liabilities?

a) $7,250

b) $500

c) $8,000

d) $7,500

81. Which physical characteristic of real estate best describes the following: two parcels of land are not identical:

a) homogeneity

b) immobility

c) non-homogeneity

d) a physical characteristic of land

82. Which of these are uses of real property?

a) residential

b) grazing cattle

c) cemetery

d) all of the above

83. The first state real estate license law was passed in _____ in 1917.

a) California

b) New York

c) Colorado

d) Texas

84. A cookie shop owner needs to move to a larger location. When he removed the oven, he repaired the holes from the bolts on the walls and the floors. The oven was a(n):

a) fixture

b) trade fixture

c) real property

d) appurtenance

85. The section on the 1003 form that deals with the race or ethnicity and sex of an applicant is data collected under the:

a) Home Mortgage Disclosure Act

b) Community Redevelopment Act

c) Fair Housing Act

c) Federal Civil Rights Act

86. Broker Connie says the following phrases to her clients, "Better sell the house before too many of them move in the neighborhood," "There goes the neighborhood." These are examples of:

a) redlining

b) steering

c) blockbusting

d) commingling

87. Randy meets with loan officer Jackie so she can prequalify him for a loan. After talking with Randy she learns that he is unmarried and decides to halt the application process. Randy calls her several times only to receive voicemail. Since it appears as though Jackie is discriminating against Randy on the basis of marital status, what law is she violating?

a) The Civil Rights Act of 1964

b) The ADA

c) The Federal Fair Housing Act of 1866

d) ECOA

88. Which is NOT a purpose of the License Law?

a) raise revenue

b) to protect the public from incompetent brokers

c) prescribe minimum standards for licensing brokers

d) protect licensed brokers and salespersons from unfair or improper competition

89. Which is the best acronym to help in remembering the four government powers?

a) DUST

b) OLDCAR

c) PETE

d) PPEDTE

90. Ms. Mary owned the land adjacent to her church and decided to grant it to the church as long as it is used to build a recreation center for the church's youth. This type of estate is known as:

a) fee simple

b) revocable

c) legal fee

d) conventional life estate

91. Sonja gave her $3,500 earnest money deposit to her sales agent. What should her sales agent do next?

a) deposit the check in his (sales agent's) personal checking account

b) give the check to the office's transaction coordinator who deposit it in the company's escrow account

c) cash the check and give Sonja a receipt

d) give the check to the office's transaction coordinator who will place the check in a file folder with Sonja's name on it, along with the contract, and store them safely in the file cabinet

92. Johnny and Donna visit a new home development and fall in love with the model homes. All of the homes in this subdivision will have only one level. After picking a floor plan they like, they ask the sales agent what the cost would be to add a second-story media room and bathroom. The sales agent advises the couple that the developers have created a _____ that does not permit two story homes in the subdivision.

a) planning and zoning law

b) inverse condemnation

c) public control

d) deed restriction

93. Ted received a letter stating that the lender had obtained a deficiency judgment against him. Which scenario below best fits what happened to Ted?

a) One of his creditors from a credit card put his account in collections then filed a judgment against him.

b) The home was sold in an auction for the amount he owed, but because there were no funds to pay the agents, the lenders paid it and are now suing Ted for the deficiency.

c) Ted's loan balance and fees were more than the home sold for at foreclosure; therefore, the lender will claim Ted's other assets in order to satisfy the indebtedness.

d) none of the above

94. When working on behalf of a seller or buyer, an agent must exhibit good business judgment, trust and honesty. These are the mandatory elements of a(n) _____ _____.

a) fiduciary relationship

b) faithful performance

c) implied authority

d) special agent

95. Keith is selling his five-unit complex. He should be prepared to bring all documents below EXCEPT:

a) tax returns

b) lease agreements

c) maintenance contracts

d) estoppel letters from the tenants

96. Baker and Johnson Partnership decides to sell off some of its real estate. If each partner holds title as tenants in common, which signatures will be required to convey the real estate?

a) Only one signature is required since it is a partnership.

b) Since each partner holds title, they will each have to sign.

c) They can sign with a stamp in the name of their partnership.

d) Whenever a partnership sells real estate, only two signatures are required no matter how many partners there are.

97. Theron and Perry are neighbors. Theron builds a fence of which two feet extend into Perry's property. The fence is an example of a(n):

a) eminent domain

b) encumbrance

c) encroachment

d) easement by necessity

98. A couple residing in a community property state have been married for five years. During the marriage, the wife's grandfather decides to give each of his grandchildren their inheritance, which is one of his income-producing properties. The property is:

a) community property

b) sole proprietorship

c) part of a land trust

d) separate property

99. Real estate ownership by a corporation is a(n):

a) tenancy in sufferance

b) tenancy in severalty

c) joint tenancy

d) none of the above as corporations can't own real estate

100. Barbara has been pre-approved for a maximum purchase price of $318,000 based on 90% LTV. What will her down payment be?

a) $10,000

b) $6,400

c) $32,000

d) $23,000

Real Estate Sales Exam II Answers

1. b. Keith was designated by the principal broker in the office and now becomes the designated buyer's agent. Mellisa continues to the be seller's agent, but continues to owe limited fiduciary duties such as confidentiality to the buyers. She may not disclose any information she obtained in confidence as a result of having been the buyers' agent.

2. d. Find the loan-to-value (LTV) which is 100% - 25% = 75% or .75. Since we are given the loan amount and now have the LTV we can solve for the sales price: $243,750/.75 = $325,000.

3. b. The appraisal can be oral or written.

4. b. When sellers are competing it drives home prices down.

5. d. The bundle of rights are the property rights which include the right of possession, control, enjoyment and disposition.

6. b. The refrigerator is not attached to the house. The owner can take this, therefore it is personal property.

7. d. To determine the latest sale price, multiply the original purchase price by the rate of appreciation. Multiply this figure by the number of years. Add this figure to the original purchase price.

8. b. Nonprofits are exempt from paying property taxes.

9. c. To determine how much is being paid for the points, multiply the mortgage amount by the number of points converted to a decimal (0.04).

10. d. 1345 x .01 = 13.45 interest accrued in year one. For year two, add the rent amount, plus the interest in year one for the account total for at the beginning of year 2 and recalculate the interest. 1345 + 13.45 x .01 = $1,358

11. a. Tenancy at will has a termination date

12. c. National Association of Realtors

13. d. BPO or broker price opinion is when the mortgage holder gets a broker's opinion of value based on a competitive market analysis.

14. b. Commercial property is non-residential and must be used to conduct business.

15. a. If they itemize their deductions, taxpayers will save $848. The calculation for tax savings is (the amount paid in interest + the amount paid in property taxes) x the tax rate. ($7,500 + $976) x .10 = $848.

16. a. *Fructus naturales* are considered to be real property. They include citrus fruit, apples, berries and grapes, and remain with the property.

17. a. Subsurface rights are rights below the earth's surface.

18. c. Manufactured homes are considered personal property as most are not permanently affixed.

19. a. Equity mortgage is where the homeowner takes out a portion of the equity on their property.

20. c. The lease is voidable because Bob/Bill lied about their identity.

21. d. Clouded title is when a document, claim or unreleased lien may impair the title to real property or make the title doubtful.

22. b. 100-46 = 54% or .54. $372,000/.54 = $688,889.

23. a. In California if the landlord has filed bankruptcy, the tenant must go before the bankruptcy court.

24. d. An exclusive agency listing means that only one listing broker/agency represents the seller. However, the seller retains the right to sell the property on their own without paying a commission.

25. b. Cooperatives are units owned by a corporation that holds titles to the entire property.

26. d. Minors are not considered competent to sign contracts, including leases.

27. b. Balance is when a neighborhood or town has several different types of land uses.

28. a. An agent's license can be suspended for 60 days if he is found to have violated California Fair Housing laws.

29. c. Constructive eviction is when a landlord has rendered a property uninhabitable.

30. b. In a 99-year lease the buyer does not have full title rights because the leaseholder retains the right of exclusive possession.

31. d. When a tenant pays fees to a landlord, the landlord must give the tenant a receipt.

32. a. In California, landlords can only collect first month and last month's rent and security deposit except in certain circumstances.

33. c. Tenants who live in public housing may have additional protections.

34. d. Tenancy at will has no termination date.

35. c. Property managers have a fiduciary relationship with the owner.

36. b. The Statute of Frauds requires that all Purchase and Sale Agreements must be in writing.

37. d. Closing cost can be found by multiplying the sales price by the closing cost percent. $378,499 x .03 = $11,355.

38. d. California property managers are not required to have any type of license or degree.

39. a. According to the Lead Paint Law, along with giving the new tenants a Lead Paint Notification and Tenant Certification Form, because the new tenants have a child under six, Mike and Dana must de-lead the property.

40. a. By using the 1031 exchange, they can defer the tax on their gain until a future date.

41. c. Tenancies automatically pass with sale.

42. b. Qualifying ratios are calculations to determine whether a borrower can qualify for a mortgage.

43. d. Riparian rights are the rights of a landowner whose property is adjacent to a flowing waterway to use the water.

44. c. There are three types of tenancy for co-owners, tenancy by the entirety, tenancy in common, and joint tenancy.

45. a. The appropriate form is located on the Bureau's website

46. c. The Bureau will make her license inactive if she doesn't pay the renewal fee.

47. c. Salespeople must immediately turn over funds to someone authorized to handle trust funds.

48. a. The Taxpayer Relief Act was enacted August 5, 1997.

49. b. Flood insurance may be required if any part of the property is in a flood zone.

50. c. The housing ratio is the front end or housing expense, and the back end ratio is the total debt ratio. Conservative lenders tend to use more conservative ratios.

51. b. The contract is not in effect until the agent notifies the buyer of the seller's acceptance and receives a signed copy of the contract.

52. a. The formula for determining value: Replacement or reproduction cost – accrued depreciation + land value = value

53. d. A protected class is any group of people designated by law.

54. d. The California Consumer Protection Law (Chapter 93A) prohibits unfair and deceptive trade practices.

55. b. The mortgage deed pledges the property as collateral.

56. c. Real property is real estate plus bundle of legal rights.

57. a. Personal property is not attached and easily moveable.

58. d. Illegal uses are not included in the "bundle of rights."

59. b. The economic characteristics of real estate are relative scarcity, improvements, permanence of investment, and area preference.

60. c. Subjective value is affected by the relative worth an individual places on a specific item.

61. d. The Bureau can, upon application, issue a temporary license without examination to the broker's designated individual or legal representative.

62. a. California allows brokers to offer rebates as long as their client approves.

63. c. The seller can offer to carry back a second mortgage.

64. b. Estate in severalty is sole ownership.

65. d. When a landowner's property borders a large non-flowing body of water such as an ocean, the landowner may have the littoral right to enjoy the water.

66. b. A township is divided into 36 sections.

67. a. Abbreviation for Latin term *et uxor* meaning "and wife."

68. d. A chain of title is a recorded history of conveyances of a particular property.

69. c. A chattel mortgage is used with personal or moveable property.

70. b. Clustering is when a developer groups home sites on smaller lots and leaves the remaining land for use as common areas.

71. d. A Home Equity Conversion Mortgage is another name for a reverse mortgage. This type of mortgage allows an elderly person to remain in their home in which the equity is converted to cash for the homeowner.

72. a. The Torrens System is a system of registering title to land with a public authority.

73. c. The ceiling fan became real property once it was attached to the ceiling.

74. b. Most lenders require three to six months of reserves of the PITI payment when purchasing income property which often creates a barrier to entry.

75. a. A license is not required when an individual sells his business.

76. d. Americans with Disabilities Act.

77. c. A broker cannot offer employee benefits to his/her independent contractors.

78. b. $325,000 - $268,901.96 = $56,098.04

79. d. Only first-time homebuyers can make a penalty-free withdrawal of up to $10,000 from their IRA.

80. a. The tax credit was worth 10% of the purchase price.

81. c. No two pieces of land are ever exactly alike.

82. d. All are uses of real property.

83. a. California

84. b. The oven was a trade fixture and because he returned the walls and the floors to their original condition it can be considered personal property.

85. a. The Home Mortgage Disclosure Act (HMDA) requires mortgage lenders to collect and report data to assist in identifying possible discriminatory lending practices.

86. c. Blockbusting is the illegal act of convincing homeowners to sell their properties by suggesting that a protected class is moving into the neighborhood.

87. d. The Equal Credit Opportunity Act prohibits lenders from discriminating against credit applicants on the basis of race, color, religion, national origin, sex, marital status, age or dependence on public assistance.

88. a. The License Law was not enacted to raise revenue.

89. c. The four government powers are PETE: Police Power, Eminent Domain, Taxation, and Escheat

90. b. This is a revocable estate in which the estate will come to an end immediately if the specified purpose ceases.

91. b. All earnest deposits must be held in the company's escrow account.

92. d. Deed restrictions can control everything from what can be parked in a driveway to what exterior color the homes can be.

93. c. When the proceeds of the foreclosure sale do not cover what is owed, the lender may claim other assets to cure the indebtedness.

94. a. A fiduciary relationship requires that an agent exhibit trust, honesty and good business judgment when working on behalf of the principal.

95. a. He does not have to supply his tax returns.

96. b. Each partner will have to sign since they all hold title.

97. c. The fence is an encroachment because it invades the neighbor's land.

98. d. Inherited property is excluded from community property under "separate" property laws.

99. b. Because a corporation is a legal entity, corporate real estate ownership is held as tenancy in severalty.

100. c. The down payment is 100 - 90 = 10%. 10% of $318,000 = $31,800 or $32,000.

Real Estate Sales Exam III

1. What is the county transfer tax charge the seller will pay if he sells his home for $428,000? Typical tax fees apply.

a) $470.80

b) $12,840.52

c) $1,284.33

d) $1,000

2. The classroom hours were waived for Wendy because she took a real property course in _____ school.

a) business

b) accounting

c) project management

d) law

3. California has reciprocity agreements with _____ states.

a) 9

b) 23

c) 13

d) 0

4. California exempts four groups from paying property tax. They are:

a) disabled, blind, veterans and elderly

b) surviving spouse and children, elderly, blind, veterans

c) surviving spouse and children, disabled, elderly, veterans

d) elderly, disabled, blind, surviving spouse and children

5. Arthur, the owner of three two-family homes, decides to enlist the help of a property management company to aid him in managing the properties. What type of contract will he have with the property manager?

a) a multiple listing agreement

b) a rental agreement

c) a management agreement

d) a multiple use agreement

6. The Federal Reserve Board's Regulation B implements_____.

a) Equal Credit Opportunity Act

b) Truth in Lending

c) RESPA

d) Home Mortgage Disclosure Act

7. The Hemsley family bought a vacation home. Their down payment was 40% and they financed the rest. They became the:

a) mortgagee

b) borrower

c) mortgagor

d) lienor

8. Karen, who purchased new home for $598,000, tells her friend Samantha that her property tax payment is included in her monthly maintenance fee. Samantha suspects that Karen more than likely purchased a:

a) leasehold

b) PUD

c) condo

d) coop

9. The Stemmons family owns 2,000 acres of land with several stands of trees on the property. Every year they sell lumber to a timber company. The cut trees are sold as:

a) real property

b) personal property

c) not considered property since they are not a structure

d) an appurtenance

10. Marla is acquiring an equitable interest in the property located on 926 Elm Street, Any Town, Any State 12345. In this case Marla is the:

a) seller

b) grantor

c) purchaser

d) grantee

11. Your home has a fence that was installed around 15 years ago and you have lived there for four years. You have continuously used your side of the property for three years without any problems. Recently your neighbor had his land surveyed and it appears your fence is on his land. In California, if you continue to use the land and your neighbor doesn't say anything, how many years do you have before you can file for adverse possession?

a) 2

b) 5

c) 8

d) 20

12. Jean Garvey has a contract with a local real estate agency that pays her 65% of 45% of all commissions she generates. If Jean sold three houses for a combined total of $834,000 and all three had 6% commissions to be split between broker and salesperson, how much was her commission check at the end of the month?

a. $1,386.45

b. $14,636.70

c. $2,133.00

d. $47,200

13. A property is worth $214,000 and it has $156,000 in liens tied to it. This difference is known as:

a) the assessed value

b) down payment

c) equity

d) leverage

14. Martha and her daughter made an offer on another home based on their current home selling by a certain date. What type of clause was this?

a) financing

b) contingency

c) recession

d) partial performance

15. An agent meets with a client in their home for the first time and the couple decides to sign the listing agreement authorizing the broker as their listing agent. The agent loves the home and believes it would make a great starter home for Jack, her neighbor's son. The agent holds an open house and receives two offers along with Jack's offer. These offers are all very similar. Then just before she (agent) leaves to present the offers, she gets a new offer which is much better than the current offers. Even though she really wants Jack to get the home, she shows all offers to her client. Which of the six agent responsibilities did the agent demonstrate?

a) loyalty

b) accounting

c) reasonable care

d) confidentiality

16. _____ is when the municipality takes action against a property owner and, through the court land process, attempts to gain ownership of the property.

a) foreclosure

b) eminent domain

c) taking

d) constructive notice

17. Which is true?

a) FHA is hazard insurance

b) FHA guarantees that the borrower will not default on the loan

c) FHA 203(k) loans are for one-to-four-unit investment properties only

d) FHA insures the lender against borrower default

18. Which contract is void?

a) a painter is contracted to paint a home, but two days before he was to begin the job, the home was destroyed by a hurricane

b) an owner who grows marijuana in his backyard agrees to sell it to his next door neighbor

c) an older brother who lives with his younger brother because he is mentally challenged and needs supervised care, contracts a landscaping company to begin cutting the yard

d) a buyer makes an offer to purchase and includes a financing contingency

19. According to California law, borrowers have no _____ rights after a valid non-judiciary foreclosure.

a) littoral

b) air

c) redemption

d) mortgage

20. If a house sold for 175% of its original value of $316,880, what was its selling price?

a. $554,540

b. $712,750

c. $316,182

d. $295,100

21. Another name for the government survey method is _____.

a) the rectangular survey system

b) principal surveys

c) base lines survey method

d) principal meridians

22. The Jackson estate is sold to satisfy a judgment resulting from an $18,000 mechanic's lien for work that began on September 15th, 2012, subject to a first mortgage lien of $310,000 recorded November 17th, 2011, and to this year's outstanding property taxes of $14,000. If the estate is sold at the foreclosure sale for $350,000, in what order will the proceeds of the sale be distributed:

a) $310,000 mortgage lien; $18,000 mechanic's lien; $14,000 property taxes; $8,000 to the foreclosed landowner

b) $18,000 mechanic's lien; $310,000 mortgage lien; $8,000 foreclosed landowner; $14,000 property taxes

c) $14,000 property taxes; $8,000 foreclosed landowner; $310,000 mortgage lien; $18,000 mechanic's lien

d) $14,000 property taxes; $18,000 mechanic's lien; $310,000 mortgage lien; $8,000 foreclosed landowner

23. Which is subject to property taxes?

a) nonprofit hospital

b) one-hundred-unit apartment complex

c) church

d) golf course operated by the city's parks

24. Kiley, a realtor and interior designer, is more than likely a member of these two associations:

a) NRA and AID

b) NAR and ASID

c) NAR and MAR

d) REA and NRA

25. Which of the following actions is a permitted exemption from fair housing laws?

a) the agent, on instruction from her client, advertises the property as for sale to Christian families only

b) a home seller, attempting to sell without an agent, posts a sign in his yard saying, "For Sale - Mature, Single Men Only"

c) the owner of a four unit building advertises an apartment "for rent to married couples, no children, no pets"

d) the owner of a two-family home advertising the apartment below her refuses to rent to a non-Christian

26. Julie owned five acres of land that she wanted to sell to Kelvin for $800,000. But before she could sell the land to Kelvin, she had to first offer it to Angelica - a holder of the right to purchase the land - who decided to exercise her right and follow through with the purchase. What right did Angelica exercise?

a) bundle of rights

b) redemption

c) right of first refusal

d) contingency

27. A developer agrees to purchase 50 acres of land from the owner for $600,000. The owner has agreed to carry back 20%. If the developer takes out a construction loan with a first lien position, the landowner will have to agree to a _____ agreement.

a) subordination

b) percentage lease

c) conformity

d) deferred transfer

28. A listing agreement is a(n):

a) future delivery purchase

b) interest in severalty

c) estimated amount for which a party should exchange hands

d) contract between a broker and seller

29. Deprecation is accounted for in which approach:

a) market value

b) cost

c) comparative market analysis

d) rent history

30. Although Jesse works as an independent contractor under his broker, the broker is still responsible for all of the following EXCEPT:

a) providing a contract which clearly stipulates that Jesse is responsible for paying quarterly federal income tax payments

b) the ethical and legal behavior of Jesse

c) payment of Jesse's licensing and professional fees

d) providing an agreement which defines compensation amounts

31. Windstorm insurance is mandated by:

a) federal government

b) state

c) city

d) county

32. Which of the following calculations does FNMA use to determine the qualifying debt ratios for borrowers:

a) monthly income to monthly debt

b) maximum debt to income

c) monthly housing expenses to monthly debt

d) both a and c

33. A hearing panel found that Mary was in violation of the National Association of Realtors' Code of Ethics. In addition to being assessed a penalty up to $5,000 what course may she be asked to take?

a) ethics

b) principles of real estate

c) accounting

d) consumer information

34. Which is an example of steering?

a) a lender offers only balloon loans to a certain group of buyers

b) a realtor tells his clients to sell his home because one of the neighbors rented his house to a Section 8 tenant

c) an owner decides not to rent his home to a disabled veteran

d) a sales agent begins showing homes to more African Americans in an affluent area because she feels the neighborhood needs to be more integrated

35. Sally's new apartment has a refrigerator that is not included in the lease. Since she doesn't have one of her own, which of the following is true?

a) she must purchase the refrigerator from the landlord

b) the landlord must remove it

c) the landlord is not responsible to maintain or replace it

d) she can void her lease because the apartment is uninhabitable without a refrigerator

36. The following legal description is known as a _____.

Lots 3, 4 and 5 in Block 6 of G. Smith's Subdivision, City of Glendora, Los Angeles County, California.

a) metes and bounds

b) subdivision plat

c) township squares

d) survey system

37. Margaret receives a letter from her homeowners' association that she needs to replace her roof and garage door. She is very upset because she thought these items were covered by the homeowners' association since her unit is attached to other units. What type of unit does Margaret more than likely own?

a) single family residence

b) cooperative

c) townhome

d) condo

38. A house depreciates at 3.56% a year for five years and was worth $154,600 at the beginning of that period. What is it worth today?

a. $145,389

b. $127,082

c. $234,765

d. $109,856

39. A real estate broker refers his client to US Home Warranty Company and in return they send the broker a $125 referral fee. This is a violation of:

a) the Comprehensive Environmental Response, Compensation, and Liability Act

b) the Real Estate Settlement Procedures Act

c) Truth in Lending

d) HUD-1

40. Mrs. Ramirez, the local real estate agent, earned a commission of $19,500 off a house she just sold. The house closed for $325,000. What was Mrs. Ramirez's commission rate for the sale?

a. 11%

b. 8%

c. 6%

d. 15%

41. In a condominium development, which would be considered a "limited" common element?

a) pool

b) elevator

c) parking spots assigned to occupants

d) limited access gates

42. How is a property lien properly terminated?

a) full payment of the debt and recording of a discharge

b) through the Title company on transfer of property

c) recording another lien that is superior to the existing one

d) upon death of either the lienor or lienee

43. One of the most important deadlines in the contract documents is the:

a) home inspection

b) option period

c) loan commitment

d) none of the above

44. An HO-6 policy is an insurance policy for a(n):

a) PUD

b) SFR

c) mobile home

d) condo

45. What monthly income should a building costing $670,000 produce if the annual rate of return is to be 14%?

a. $9,125

b. $7,816

c. $8,150

d. $7,250

46. An appraiser will use the _____ approach to estimate the value of a three-family rental home.

a) reproduction

b) income

c) cost

d) sales comparison

47. Jane bought her home for $279,000 and now it's worth $333,000. It has _____ in value.

a) appreciated

b) regressed

c) vested

d) diverged

48. Sally received a letter that her home loan with ABC lending was being transferred to Community Bank. This is known as a(n):

a) takeover

b) assumption

c) assignment

d) aggression

49. When a borrower signs a security agreement in which he is promising to pay, he is signing:

a) a deed of trust

b) a promissory note

c) a bill of sale

d) an offer contract

50. A disadvantage of a bridge loan is:

a) the buyer does not have to sell their current home before they purchase their next home

b) the lender might not require the buyer to make monthly payments

c) the buyer can immediately put their home on the market

d) buyers may be prequalified based on two mortgages and they might not meet this requirement

51. Henry's title report suggests that the property he's purchasing is free of legal issues and liens, therefore the property has a(n) _____ title.

a) clear

b) cloudy

c) good

d) efficient

52. In a home loan, which is the collateral?

a) the down payment

b) the equity

c) the property

d) the borrower's liquid assets

53. The date an interest rate changes is known as the:

a) payment shock

b) balloon maturity date

c) the adjustment date on an adjustable rate loan

d) none of the above

54. Lisa makes an offer on a home and gives her broker a check to let the seller know she is serious. These funds are known as:

a) security deposit

b) earnest money deposit

c) option period deposit

d) down payment

55. Which best describes an easement?

a) When a tenant who is moving out of the storefront rental takes his cupcake oven

b) A property owner whose land is adjacent to a river, swims and fishes in the river

c) A neighbor who accesses his barn by legally crossing part of his neighbor's land

d) The state legally takes back private land to widen the highway

56. A subdivision is:

a) a neighborhood in a community revitalized area

b) a housing development where tracts of land are turned into individual lots

c) when houses in a neighborhood are the same style and color

d) a neighborhood with a homeowners' association board

57. A home buyer who had limited liquid funds obtained her home through a nonprofit organization, where she helped build her home with her own labor and services. What type of contribution did she make?

a) sweat equity

b) equity deposit

c) money

d) labor

58. Ben, who recently lost his job, is considering transferring ownership of his home to his lender as he is having great difficulty making the payments and has been unable to sell his home. This is known as:

a) foreclosure

b) deed-in-lieu

c) short sale

d) adverse possession

59. Stephanie and Max, first-time homebuyers, are currently living on Stephanie's income as a teacher; but Max will be finished with his medical residency in two years and their income will increase dramatically. In light of this, their loan officer has advised them that they could qualify for a larger house if they took out a loan with payments that increased by no more than 7.5% per year over the next five years. What type of loan are they being offered?

a) four-step mortgage

b) fixed rate

c) 2-1 buy down

d) graduated payment

60. According to their lender, a couple must contribute $71,700 in the form of a cashier's check toward the purchase of the $478,000 home they would like to buy. This amount is known as the:

a) earnest money deposit

b) settlement costs

c) down payment

d) contingency fee

61. For government loans, which statement is true?

a) they are insured by FHA

b) they are guaranteed by RHS

c) they are guaranteed by VA

d) each of the above

62. Heather conveyed her interest in a property to Mr. and Mrs. Olsen, her brother Barry's friend and Mike's parents. Who is the grantee?

a) Mike

b) Mr. and Mrs. Olsen

c) Heather

d) Barry

63. Katy and Mickey's home was completely destroyed by a storm from El Niño. When they returned to check the damages, they found their basement completely flooded and everything destroyed as the water level reached up to the second floor. Which insurance will likely cover the bulk of the damages?

a) hurricane

b) windstorm

c) flood

d) hazard

64. Which is NOT a liquid asset?

a) money in savings account

b) 401(k)

c) parcel of land

d) stocks

65. A homebuyer used a mortgage broker with Finance World to get her home loan. She used the coupon provided to mail her first payment to Finance World. Before her second payment was due, she received a letter stating that the servicing of her loan was being assigned to the Bank of the United States and that the investor Duchess Bank had remained the same. Which is her current lender?

a) Finance World

b) Duchess Bank

c) Bank of the United States

d) Mortgage broker

66. If Justine has power of attorney, what has she been granted?

a) limited or full authority to make decisions on behalf of someone else

b) an opportunity to represent someone in court

c) entrance to law school

d) full power to make medical decisions on behalf of someone else

67. The principal is:

a) that part of the mortgage payment that reduces the unpaid balance

b) the amount borrowed

c) a and b

d) b only

68. Which best describes an encroachment?

a) You legally drive across part of your neighbor's property to access your property.

b) You continuously use your neighbor's driveway for years and he doesn't stop you.

c) You add a second level to your home which completely blocks your neighbor's authorized access to the sea.

d) You allow your horses to drink out of the river which is adjacent to your land.

69. Two sons are tenants in common in a property left to them by their parents. Son A has one child and Son B has four children. In the event Son B passes, who does the property go to?

a) Son B's interest is split equally among the five grandchildren

b) Son B's interest goes to Son A and his child

c) the property goes to Son B's children

d) the property goes to Son A only

70. Ansley wants to see a visual representation of when her mortgage will be paid off as well as how much money she will be paying in interest each year. This is known as a(n):

a) loan payment schedule

b) amortization schedule

c) interest rate table

d) rate sheet

71. A bi-weekly payment is one in which:

a) the homeowner will make her regular monthly mortgage payment every two weeks

b) the homeowner will make her regular mortgage payment every other month

c) the homeowner will make a payment one time every month, but on the last month of the year two payments will be made

d) the homeowner will make half of her monthly mortgage payment every two weeks

72. Kelly is told that her ARM loan has an initial interest rate of 5.5% and that as the rate adjusts it can never go above 9%. Nine percent is the _____ for her loan.

a) buy down

b) APR

c) cap

d) *ad valorem*

73. George and Mary are retiring to their country home on a large lake with a dock where they keep their boat. In this case, what are the retiree's water rights?

a) the high water mark at the shoreline

b) the low water mark at the shoreline

c) the middle of the lake

d) the end of their dock

74. Henry sells his home to his friend Reese; then Henry gets a letter from his lender demanding full payment. The mortgage included a(n) _____.

a) acceleration clause

b) deed restriction

c) due-on-sale clause

d) covenant of seisin

75. Murray had to go to court to get his property back from his nephew because when he granted him the property he told him that he could not sell alcohol on the premises. What type of estate was this?

a) homestead

b) fee simple defeasible with remainder or reversion

c) determinable fee estate

d) fee simple subject to a right of reentry

76. Which provides the best range of property values on a particular property?

a) competitive market analysis

b) broker price opinions

c) appraisal

d) income approach

77. Jenn and Mike finally found the home of their dreams within their budget of $385,000. They had already been pre-approved for a loan based on 75% loan-to-value. If the sales price is $380,000 but the appraisal came in at $365,500, what is the maximum loan the lender will give them for this home?

a) $288,750

b) $380,000

c) $285,000

d) $274,125

78. Many states generate revenue from the sale of real estate through:

a) commissions

b) transfer taxes

c) down payments

d) broker and salesperson license fees

79. Carl is selling his home in a short sale for less than the amount of his current mortgage debt. Which of the following is most critical to Carl avoiding any further court action?

a) obtaining an appraisal value that exceeds his current mortgage amount

b) getting the buyer to agree to make up any deficiencies

c) getting his lender to provide a full discharge of the lien at the settlement

d) reporting the full amount of the debt forgiveness to the IRS

80. Wilford transfers one of his small rental units to his son for $1.00. What will the transfer tax be?

a) $0

b) $1,000

c) $4.45

d) $456

81. Which of the following is the first step in the appraisal process regardless of the method being applied?

a) determining the highest and best use of the property

b) determining the purpose of the appraisal

c) collecting and analyzing the market data

d) determining the value of the land without improvements

82. A very famous couple chooses a city apartment near all of the amenities they enjoy so they don't have to travel too far out and risk being noticed. Their agent notifies them that they did not receive approval because the other owners believe they will disrupt the peace and quiet currently enjoyed by all the residents. Which best describes this scenario?

a) a condo association can vote in or out whoever they feel is a good match (or not) for the condo development

b) the owners are violating the Civil Rights Act of 1866

c) celebrities are a protected class and may not be discriminated against

d) cooperatives can deny or approve the sale of shares of stock if they feel someone may jeopardize the quiet enjoyment the residents currently enjoy

83. The realtor tells a couple that because of regression, they may have to list their home at a different price than anticipated. Which best describes what is happening?

a) the neighboring homes haven't been updated and modernized as much as the subject property

b) the home has an outdated floor plan

c) the home is in disrepair

d) a school was recently built around the corner

84. When Broker Jamie takes his client's earnest money deposit and puts it in his personal account to tide him over until his next commission check comes, which fiduciary duty is he not living up to?

a) dedication

b) accounting

c) obedience

d) confidentiality

85. Bob Carter bought a house for $95,000. Eighteen years later, it is valued at $330,000. What is the amount of appreciation?

a. $235,000

b. $315,787

c. $127,654

d. $301,625

86. The following is which type of description commonly used in legal descriptions: North 34 degrees, East 200 feet to point?

a) reference

b) bounded

c) strip

d) metes

87. Katy has a voluntary lien on her home. Which represents a voluntary lien?

a) mortgage

b) property tax

c) federal IRS

d) mechanic's lien

88. Samantha's condominium unit which recently appraised at $413,000, was recently damaged in a rainstorm. If it was currently assessed at $405,000, what is the minimum amount covered by her HO-6 policy?

a) $81,000

b) $82,600

c) $80,000

d) $84,000

89. A broker is listing a home in California where he knows a homicide was committed. Under California law:

a) the broker has a fiduciary duty to disclose this to potential buyers

b) the broker must disclose the fact that a homicide was committed if it occurred in the past three years

c) the broker cannot hold any open houses

d) the broker has no legal duty to inform buyers

90. Jane has a document which states she has legal rights of ownership for 1324 Elm Street, Any Town, California. This document is known as a(an):

a) affidavit

b) quitclaim deed

c) title

d) trustee deed

91. Gerard has a 30-year loan on which his interest rate is 5% and then changes every 5-7 years for the life of the loan. What type of mortgage does he have?

a) fixed rate mortgage

b) modification

c) adjustable rate mortgage

d) fully amortized

92. The buyers purchasing Geoff's vacation home love his furnishings so much they want to buy all of it. What contract should he use in this type of sale?

a) bill of sale

b) grant deed

c) purchase and sale agreement

d) quitclaim deed

93. Luigi's Pizza Palace was bought eight years ago for $160,000. The property was sold for $145,000. What was the depreciation per year?

a. 0.058

b. 0.078

c. 0.093

d. 0.035

94. Which is the best description of a real estate agent?

a) Anyone, licensed or not, who conducts and/negotiates the sale of real estate

b) The owner and manager of a real estate firm

c) A person who sells both home warranties and property

d) A person who is licensed who conducts and negotiates the sale of real estate

95. Ricky's friend Esther is leaving the country. She has a great loan with a 3.5% interest rate and a remaining term of 20 years. Because Ricky would like to take over this loan, he sends Esther's lender all of his income and asset documents. Ricky is trying to get a(n) _____.

a) primary mortgage

b) assumption

c) refinance

d) equity loan

96. A legal document which conveys title to a property is known as a:

a) deed

b) preliminary title report

c) purchase and sale agreement

d) promissory note

97. Which is the most common type of bankruptcy?

a) Chapter 13

b) Chapter 7

c) Chapter 13 no assets

d) Chapter 11

98. Someone's credit history report is prepared by a _____.

a) mortgage broker

b) underwriter

c) credit bureau

d) notary public

99. Paula made her mortgage payment 30 days past her due date. Her mortgage is now in:

a) arrears

b) default

c) foreclosure

d) bankruptcy

100. What is the age an appraiser uses to describe a property's physical condition?

a) effective age

b) longevity

c) year built

d) average age

Real Estate Sales Exam III Answers

1. a. Typical transfer tax is $0.55 per $500 of the sales price. $428,000/500 = $856; $865 X .0.55 = $470.80

2. d. In California if you take a real property course in law school, the classroom hours are waived.

3. d. California has reciprocity agreements with no states.

4. b. As long as they apply to the correct municipality and get approved, the blind, elderly, veterans, and surviving spouses and children are exempt from property taxes.

5. c. A management agreement is between the owner of income property and the property manager and details the scope of work expected by the property manager.

6. a. The Equal Credit Opportunity Act protects against discrimination in lending.

7. c. They are doing the mortgaging, so they are the mortgagor.

8. d. Coops are transferred as shares of stock in the corporation pays a property tax bill for the development and passes along each member's portion to be paid through their monthly maintenance fee.

9. b. The cut trees are moveable so they are personal property.

10. d. A grantee is also known as the purchaser.

11. a. In order to file for adverse possession, you must prove you have continuously used the property for five years, without any warning from the owner.

12. b. To determine the amount of the commission received at the end of the month, multiply the combined total of houses sold by the commission rate of 6%. Multiply that figure by 45%, converted to a decimal (0.045). Multiply that figure by 65%, converted to a decimal (0.065). $14,636.70

13. c. Equity is the difference between the value and the liens.

14. b. A contingency clause is when a certain act must be accomplished within a given amount of time.

15. a. Of the six agent responsibilities, obedience, loyalty, disclosure, confidentiality, accounting and reasonable care, the agent showed loyalty to her clients by putting their interest above her own.

16. c. "Taking" is when the municipality takes action against a property owner and through the court land process attempts to gain ownership of the property.

17. d. FHA insures the lender against borrower default.

18. c. The contract is void because one of the parties in not competent.

19. c. Redemption

20. a. To determine the selling price, multiply the original value of the house by the percentage of its original value, converted to a decimal (1.75).

21. a. The rectangular survey system.

22. d. In California, order of payment is the municipal lien, federal tax lien, state tax lien, condo fees up to six months, mechanic's lien, and all other liens on order of recording, seller.

23. b. Nonprofits are exempt from paying property taxes.

24. b. Realtors are member of the National Association of Realtors and many interior designers are members of the American Society of Interior Designers.

25. d. is exempt in an owner-occupied dwelling of 3 or less units and no discriminatory advertising was used.

26. c. In a right of first refusal, the owner gives the holder of the right an opportunity to enter into a transaction before the owner can enter into a transaction with a third party.

27. a. Subordination agreements change the priority of a mortgage or lien.

28. d. Listing agreement is a contract between a broker and seller.

29. b. Depreciation is estimated in the cost approach.

30. c. The agent is responsible for paying their own licensing and professional fees.

31. b. Windstorm insurance is governed by the state.

32. b. Rather than using the tradition combination of both front and back end ratios, FNMA considers on a maximum debt to income ratio (DTI).

33. a. She may be asked to take an ethics course through the association.

34. d. Steering is the illegal practice of directing potential homebuyers away from or to particular areas.

35. c. Refrigerators are generally considered personal property. So long as the lease did not specifically include a refrigerator, the landlord has no obligation to provide or maintain one.

36. b. The subdivision plat method uses descriptions of lots and block numbers.

37. c. With a townhome purchase, the buyer purchases the individual unit and the ground below it. As a result, each unit generally has its own roof and home amenities like garages.

38. b. To determine the worth of the house today, multiply the depreciation percentage by five years to get the rate of depreciation. Multiply the original worth of the home by the rate of depreciation. Subtract this figure from the original value of the home.

39. b. RESPA prohibits kickbacks.

40. c. Divide the profit (commission) Mrs. Ramirez made off the sell by the house sale price. $19,500/$325,000 = .06

41. c. Parking spaces assigned to occupants are "limited" to that occupant.

42. a. Liens can only be discharge upon full payment of the debt.

43. c. The loan commitment deadline is one of the most important deadlines.

44. d. An HO-6 policy, much like a hazard insurance policy for a home, is now required for condominiums by FNMA and FHA.

45. b. To determine the monthly income, multiply the cost of the building by the annual rate of return. Divide this figure by 12.

46. b. The income approach is used to estimate the value of income-producing properties.

47. a. When a home appreciates, it increases in value.

48. c. Assignment is when mortgage ownership is transferred from one company to another.

49. b. A note is a promise to pay.

50. d. Oftentimes bridge loan lenders will prequalify buyers for two home loans.

51. a. Clear title is free of liens and legal questions.

52. c. Because the borrower can lose the property due to nonpayment, the property itself is the collateral.

53. c. The adjustment date on an adjustable rate loan is the date an interest rate changes.

54. b. The earnest money deposit lets the seller know the buyer is serious.

55. c. An easement is when someone other than the owner has right-of-way legal access.

56. b. Developers divide up tracts of land to create individual lots.

57. a. When labor or services are provided in lieu of cash, this is known as sweat equity.

58. b. Deed-in-lieu is when the homeowner voluntarily transfers the title of the house to the lender in exchange for release of lien and payment.

59. d. A mortgage in which the payment can increase by 7.5% per year over a period of time, usually five years, and then remains the same for the duration of the loan is a graduated payment mortgage.

60. b. The final settlement costs are generally paid in the form of a certified or cashier's check at the closing.

61. d. Government loans can be guaranteed by the Veterans Administration and Rural Housing, and insured by FHA.

62. b. The individual(s) who receive title to a property is/are the grantee(s).

63. c. Because the home was damaged by the excessive water level and experienced significant flooding, the flood insurance will likely cover the damages.

64. c. A liquid asset is that which can be easily converted to cash.

65. b. The lender is the financial institution that lent the money.

66. a. Power of attorney grants an individual full or limited authority on behalf of someone else.

67. c. The principal is the amount of money borrowed, and the term also refers to that part of each mortgage payment that reduces the unpaid balance.

68. c. An encroachment is an illegal improvement which intrudes upon another's property.

69. c. Tenants in common have no right of survivorship; therefore Son B's interest in the property will pass to his heirs.

70. b. An amortization schedule is a table that shows how much of each mortgage payment will be applied to principal. It also shows the yearly balance of principal as it decreases until it reaches zero.

71. d. With a biweekly mortgage payment, the homeowner pays half of her mortgage payment every two weeks which means she will have made the equivalent of 13 monthly payments by the end of the year.

72. c. The cap is the limit on ARM loans.

73. a. They hold littoral rights to the high water mark of a non-flowing body of water.

74. c. A due-on-sale clause allows the lender to demand full payment if the borrower sells the property that served as security for the loan.

75. b. Fee simple defeasible is subject to a condition that if violated would cause the title to revert to the grantor.

76. a. The competitive market analysis helps the licensed agent/broker to identify a range of values in a given area.

77. d. The lender will lend based on the appraised value which is $365,500. 75% of $365,500 = $274,125.

78. b. States generate revenue from the sale of real estate through transfer taxes.

79. c. Without a full discharge of the debt, the lender could pursue a deficiency judgment.

80. a. When the transfer is less than $100.00, the Registry of Deeds will not charge a transfer tax.

81. b. Determining the purpose of the appraisal may affect the value and dictate which approach is most appropriate.

82. d. While they are bound by fair housing laws and cannot discriminate based on age, gender, ethnicity/race and religion, co-ops have more control than condo associations since they transfer shares of stock as opposed to real property.

83. a. In this case regression describes the fact that improvements have been made to the subject property that are much greater than the neighboring homes.

84. b. The fiduciary duty of accounting states that the agent must give a full accounting of all trust funds.

85. a. The increase in the market value of the house is appreciation.

86. d. Metes description gives both a bearing and a distance.

87. a. A voluntary lien is created by the lienee's action.

88. b. The HO-6 policy must provide for a minimum of 20% of the appraised value.

89. b. California real estate law requires that a homicide be disclosed if it happened within the past three years.

90. c. Title is a legal document evidencing a person's right or ownership to real property.

91. c. An adjustable rate mortgage generally starts out at a set interest rate and then adjusts after five or seven years.

92. a. A bill of sale is used in transferring personal property.

93. b. To determine the monthly income, multiply the cost of the building by the annual rate of return. Divide this figure by 12.

94. d. A real estate agent is a licensed person who conducts and negotiates the sale of real estate.

95. b. An assumption is when a buyer assumes the seller's mortgage.

96. a. A deed is a legal document which conveys title to property.

97. b. A Chapter 7 is the fastest and least expensive, is subject to homestead exemptions and does not liquidate all assets.

98. c. A credit bureau is a third-party company which prepares a summary report of an individual's credit history.

99. b. Generally, payments 30 days behind on mortgages are said to be in default.

100. a. The effective age is a term the appraiser uses to describe a building's physical condition.

Real Estate Sales Exam IV

1. The sum of all of Mr. Slayer's personal property and real property at the time of his death is known as his:

a) probate

b) escheat

c) estate

d) will

2. Melody's dad, a cabinet maker, built her a beautiful entertainment unit that he securely attached to the wall five years ago. Now that she's married and wants to grow the family she and her husband have decided to move. The unit will have to remain in the home because it is a(n):

a) easement

b) trade fixture

c) appurtenance

d) fixture

3. A homeowner's insurance policy:

a) is a warranty service contract that covers repair and replacement of home appliances

b) combines hazard insurance and personal liability insurance

c) is hazard insurance

d) all of the above

4. A servicer:

a) lends money to purchase a home

b) collects mortgage payments from a borrower

c) conducts title searches

d) insures the loan in case of borrower default

5. A three-family home is:

a) a dwelling with one deed and is for three families

b) a commercial property

c) not legal in California

d) a dwelling with three different deeds and is for three families

6. Three homeowners live adjacent to a body of water, but their water use rights are based on the time they first used or applied for use of the water. This is known as:

a) riparian rights

b) littoral rights

c) the doctrine of prior appropriation

d) the doctrine of adverse possession

7. Which of the following would NOT be considered trust funds being handled by a property manager?

a) collected rents

b) operating expenses for the management firm

c) collected security deposits

d) capital expenditure contributions from the owner

8. All are "improvements" except:

a) sidewalk

b) street light

c) pizza oven

d) paved road

9. Which is NOT a physical characteristic of land?

a) scarcity

b) non-homogeneity

c) immobility

d) indestructibility

10. Over several years, the Parsons' land ownership has increased by means of:

a) regression

b) accretion

c) diversion

d) avulsion

11. David allows Mike to store his pickup truck in his driveway for several weeks free of charge. David gave Mike a (n) _____.

a) acknowledgment

b) tenancy right

c) license

d) easement by prescription

12. Marty receives a notice for specific performance of a real estate sale contract, which is asking for:

a) an earnest money deposit

b) conveyance of the property

c) a new contract

d) a deficiency judgment

13. Which is NOT an acceptable means by which a contract can be terminated?

a) sellers decide to get a divorce during transaction

b) destruction of premises

c) mutual agreement of the parties to cancel

d) impossibility of performance

14. Timothy is out of town when his broker tries to inform him that she has a buyer for his home who has made a full price bid and given her (the broker) the $3,000 earnest money deposit. What does the broker have at this point?

a) implied contract

b) executed purchase and sale agreement

c) voidable contract

d) offer

15. Patricia, who fell behind on her mortgage payments, requested assistance from her lender. Her lender helped her by replacing her old mortgage with a newer one in which they lowered her interest rate and extended her term. What term best describes what happened?

a) refinancing

b) novation

c) accelerating

d) none of the above

16. Which of the following statements is TRUE of a listing contract?

a) It obligates the broker to convince the seller to convey the property to the first person to make an offer.

b) It maintains that the broker act as a non-agent with a seller.

c) It is a contract between the broker and the principal.

d) It is an agreement that lasts indefinitely.

17. Which statement represents what an exclusive agency listing and an exclusive-right-to-sell listing have in common?

a) Both provide for only one broker to represent the seller.

b) Both are net listings.

c) With both, the seller allows only one salesperson to show their property.

d) With both, the seller can sell the property without paying a commission.

18. Margaret's broker listed and advertised her property, to find Nathan, a ready, willing and able buyer. After reviewing the offer and sleeping on it, Margaret decided to reject the offer, telling her agent she had remorse and no longer wished to sell her home. In this case Margaret:

a) will have to pay the buyers for any damages

b) must sell the property

c) owes her broker the commission

d) is within her rights to change her mind

19. Highest and best use is:

a) the effective age of a property

b) what results in its "highest value"

c) the most marketable value

d) the book value

20. All are significant factors in comparing property with the sales comparison approach EXCEPT:

a) original purchase price

b) financing terms

c) physical appearance and condition

d) sale date

21. PITI stands for:

a) payment, insurance, taxes and investment

b) principal, insurance, tariff, interest

c) payment, interest, taxes, insurance

d) principal, interest, taxes and insurance

22. Samantha has a 15-year loan at 4.5% interest rate. This is a:

a) conventional fixed rate loan

b) fixed rate loan

c) variable loan

d) pay option arm loan

23. You will use which formula to calculate the gross income multiplier (GIM)?

a) GIM = annual gross income/sales price

b) GIM = rate x value

c) GIM = sales price/annual gross income

d) GIM = value/rate

24. When a property is pledged for a loan without giving up possession, this is known as:

a) substitution

b) acceleration

c) hypothecation

d) alienation

25. Greg is someone who has received training and education, and is experienced in estimating real property value. His job title is a(n):

a) loan processor

b) mortgage banker

c) underwriter

d) appraiser

26. Another name for Homeowners' Association dues is:

a) community property fees

b) common area assessments

c) common law dues

d) apportionments

27. A(n) _____ is when a tenant is lawfully expelled from the property.

a) aversion

b) eviction

c) conviction

d) avulsion

28. Which of these does NOT describe a recorder?

a) a public official who maintains public real estate records

b) county clerk

c) transcribes real estate transactions

d) collects fees for documents filed

29. Hank and Cheri use a 1003 to:

a) apply for a mortgage loan

b) write out a land contract

c) list a property for sale

d) make an offer on a home

30. Once the appraisal was completed, Jet's lender received a CRV or Certificate of Reasonable Value. What type of loan is he getting?

a) Fannie Mae

b) FHA

c) RHS

d) VA

31. _____ and _____ are government-sponsored entities.

a) FHA and VA

b) Ginnie Mae and Freddie Mac

c) Fannie Mae and Freddie Mac

d) RHS and Agricultural loans

32. According to Regulation Z, Jasmine has _____ to rescind the transaction.

a) 5 days

b) 3 days

c) 4 days

d) 1 day

33. An employer-sponsored tax-deferred retirement plan that homebuyers can borrow against is a:

a) 401(k)

b) 203(k)

c) 403(b)

d) a and c

34. Jumbo loans refer to loans greater than _____.

a) 80% LTV

b) $650,000

c) current conforming loan limits

d) $471,000

35. The Fair and Accurate Credit Transactions Act of 2003 (FACTA) deals with:

a) mortgage fraud

b) commingling of funds

c) prepayment penalties

d) identity theft

36. Which statement about mortgage insurance is NOT true?

a) is also known as private mortgage insurance

b) covers the lender when a homeowner defaults

c) is required when the borrower's down payment is 20% or more

d) is included in the mortgage payment

37. The Barksdale family just learned that the city is planning to build a small commuter airport near their family farm in which the home will sit below the flight path. They were hoping to sell the farm in a year but now fear that their values may be decreased due to:

a) functional obsolescence

b) functional regression

c) economic obsolescence

d) economic regression

38. Two years ago, 17-year-old Jonathan inherited five two-family homes from his late father. Now two years later, Jonathan has decided to sell one of them. If he conveys his interest in the property to a purchaser by signing a deed, the contract will be:

a) valid

b) void

c) voidable

d) invalid

39. Valid exclusive listings must include:

a) an expiration date

b) a forfeiture clause

c) an automatic renewal clause

d) an allowance for the listing broker to appoint subagents

40. Meredith wanted Haley to know that her signature was genuine as she was signing a deed transferring ownership of her property to Haley. The declaration that Meredith made before a notary was a(n):

a) sheriff's deed

b) acknowledgment

c) promissory note

d) affidavit

41. Title to real estate can be transferred by involuntary alienation by all of the following except:

a) escheat

b) erosion

c) seisin

d) eminent domain

42. During her closing, Hillary reviewed a legal document which requires that she repay her mortgage loan during a given period of time based on a stated interest rate. This document is known as a:

a) mortgage

b) deed of trust

c) lien

d) note

43. Zachary, whose home is set to close in two weeks, gets a call from his builder saying that his new home won't be ready for another three weeks. Zachary's realtor works out a deal where he can remain in his old home one week after closing. This is known as a:

a) leasehold

b) leaseback

c) lease at will

d) lease purchase

44. A trustee is:

a) a fiduciary that acts for the benefit of another person

b) always the executor of the estate

c) a trustworthy individual

d) an attorney

45. The best type of estate to inherit is:

a) a leasehold estate

b) a life estate

c) a fee simple estate

d) a general estate

46. The time and date a document was recorded establishes:

a) chain of title

b) subrogation

c) escrow

d) priority

47. Rich sells a parcel of land to Tom. Tom quickly records the deed. If Rich tries to sell the same parcel to Kevin, which of the following statements is TRUE?

a) Tom will have to bring a quitclaim deed to court, since Rich is trying to sell the same property.

b) Kevin has been given constructive notice of the prior sale because Tom quickly recorded the deed.

c) Kevin was mailed the notice of the prior sale since Tom recorded the deed.

d) none of the above

48. The acquisition of real estate through the payment of money is:

a) a sales transaction

b) a truth in lending transaction

c) a purchase money transaction

d) a deed-in-lieu

49. A property sales price on a HUD-1 is a:

a) debit to the buyer and a credit to the seller

b) credit to the buyer only

c) debit to the seller and credit to the buyer

d) credit to the seller only

50. Wilma collected a security deposit from each of her tenants when they signed their lease agreements. Now that she is selling her property, who should get the security deposits?

a) Wilma

b) buyer

c) tenants

d) lender

51. Because Jimmy has the right to control his property, he has a right to do all of the following except:

a) refuse to host a neighborhood block meeting at his home

b) turn away the meter reader from the local utility company

c) put a sign in his front yard that says "no soliciting"

d) host a family barbeque

52. Two properties A and B are separated by a private road. Landowner A owns the road but Landowner B has unrestricted access, as he needs to use the road to reach the main highway. What type of access does Landowner B have?

a) an easement by necessity

b) an encroachment

c) an easement

d) an assessment

53. Mena was so excited as she was purchasing her first home and everything, so far, had gone smoothly. The home inspection came back with minimal issues and her loan was fully approved. But two days before her closing date, the home caught on fire and was totally destroyed. Who will more than likely bear the loss?

a) Mena

b) the seller's lender

c) the seller

d) the buyer's lender

54. A building with 30 apartments renting at $1,400 each has just been sold. If the buyers have been told to expect a 12% rate of return, what was the selling price?

a. $4,200,000

b. $3,915,000

c. $4,150,000

d. $2,636,000

55. The Martins enter into a sales contract with the Haggardy family in which they will pay $1,500 per month for their family farm. The Martins will pay all insurance premiums, property taxes, and any maintenance and repair costs, but the Haggardys will maintain title to the property for 20 years. What type of contract do the two families have?

a) lease with option to buy

b) contract for deed

c) contract at will

d) mortgage contract

56. Harry lists his home with Broker Bill. He tells Broker Bill that as long he gets a profit of $203,000 from the sale of his home, Broker Bill can keep the difference as commission. This type of listing is known as:

a) an exclusive-agency listing

b) an open listing

c) an exclusive-right-to-sell listing

d) a net listing

57. The original capital outlay for labor, materials, land and profit is known as:

a) the market value

b) the market price

c) mortgage value

d) cost

58. Kenny, a single man, died and left all of his real estate to his niece, 23-year-old Ashley, in his will. Title passes to Ashley at what point?

a) when she executes a new deed to all of the properties

b) after she pays all of the property taxes

c) immediately upon Kenny's death

d) once she receives a title report that the properties are free and clear

59. The major organizations operating in the secondary mortgage market are:

a) FNMA, Freddie Mac and MGIC

b) Fannie Mae, Freddie Mac and Ginnie Mae

c) FNMA, HUD and FHA

d) all of above

60. A rate and term refinance:

a) is also known as a no cash-out refinance

b) generally covers the previous balance plus the costs associated with obtaining the new mortgage

c) puts cash in the borrower's hands

d) both a and b

61. Existing mortgages are usually bought as a "pool" on the _____.

a) primary market

b) secondary market

c) government market

d) black market

62. Liens and encumbrances shown on the title commitment, other than those listed in the contract, must be removed so that the title can be conveyed free and clear. It is the _____ responsibility to remove these.

a) seller's

b) buyer's

c) lender's

d) title company's

63. The principal amount of the buyer's new mortgage is a:

a) debit to the real estate company

b) credit to the real estate company

c) credit to the buyer

d) debit to the seller

64. Jay's lender would like to ensure that he is paying a fair price for the home he is purchasing. In order to determine this, the lender will order a(n):

a) appraisal

b) broker price opinion

c) comparative market analysis

d) chain of title

65. For property tax purposes, a(n) _____ establishes the value of a property.

a) broker

b) recorder

c) appraiser

d) assessor

66. Which tenancy automatically renews itself at each expiration?

a) tenancy at sufferance

b) tenancy for years

c) tenancy from month-to-month

d) tenancy at will

67. A valid lease has all of the requirements EXCEPT:

a) valuable consideration

b) offer and acceptance

c) capacity to contract

d) county clerk recording

68. Money set aside for the replacement of common property in a condominium or cooperative project is called:

a) replacement reserve fund

b) savings fund

c) capital improvements fund

d) contingency fund

69. Judith had to replace her boiler. This type of repair is classified as which type of maintenance?

a) construction

b) corrective

c) preventive

d) routine

70. Which does NOT affect zoning?

a) The principle of conformity enhancing value.

b) The city requests that a new building conform to specific types of architecture.

c) Values have remained the same because owners have the freedom to develop land as they please.

d) A new city ordinance mandates that the street floors of office building be used for delis and cafes.

71. Happy Family Realty received a *lis pendens* for their recent listing located at 7892 Oak Street. They now have:

a) a notice of special assessment

b) a notice that legal action has been filed which could affect the property

c) a loan commitment letter

d) a home inspection report

72. New agent Barbara was so excited to close her first sale that she gave her friend Nicholas $200 for referring the client to her. What Barbara did was:

a) give Nicholas what is considered a kickback and is illegal under RESPA

b) legal as it is the cost of doing business

c) as long as Barbara had her attorney draw up an agreement between her and Nicholas, this was legal

d) illegal because she should have given the money to her broker

73. Which is an example of a unilateral contract?

a) a real estate sales contract

b) an agreement which states that you will provide sweat equity as your contribution in having your home built

c) a contract between a broker and his agent

d) The sales manager says he will offer a 20% bonus if you sell $3.5 million in real estate.

74. The Gramm-Leach-Bliley Act (GLBA) requires that companies give consumers privacy notices. Which jurisdiction does this fall under?

a) The Equal Credit Opportunity Act

b) Community Reinvestment Act

c) The Federal Trade Commission

d) The Sherman Antitrust Law

75. All are loan payment plans EXCEPT:

a) 30-year-fixed loan at 5.5% interest rate

b) executory mortgage

c) reverse mortgage

d) graduated payment mortgage

76. A primary mortgage loan is funded by:

a) a mortgage banker

b) a mortgage broker

c) both a and b

d) neither a nor b

77. What should the owner of an apartment complex do if he has determined that his vacancy rate is less than 4%?

a) Nothing

b) He should lower his advertising budget.

c) He should make property improvements.

d) He should survey the rental market to determine whether he can raise his rents.

78. Jacob and Leslie have a beautiful 2,700 square foot home just outside the city, but most of the other homes are about 1,800 square foot. Their home value has decreased because of what appraisal principle?

a) regression

b) assemblage

c) diminishing and increasing returns

d) contribution and conformity

79. Under FIRREA, appraisers need to be licensed by the _____ in order to appraise real property valued at over $1,000,000 in federally-related transactions.

a) state

b) federal government

c) county

d) bank

80. The house on Elm Drive is for sale because last year someone committed suicide in the home. In California, if it occurred within the last three years, a listing agent:

a) must tell the buyer

b) must tell their managing broker

c) must tell the lender

d) brokers do not have to disclose this information according to California general laws.

81. A buyer's agent should NOT disclose which of the following to the seller?

a) the relationship between the buyer and the agent

b) agent compensation that will be paid from the broker's commission

c) that the agent may benefit from referring the parties to a subsidiary of the broker's firm

d) that the buyer is anxious to find a place to live

82. The art of weighing the findings and analyzing from three approaches to value is known as:

a) substitution

b) reconciliation

c) assumption

d) capitalization

83. A prospective buyer is attracted to a property that has a negative cash flow. The following is very likely to be TRUE:

a) the depreciable base is large

b) there is no deferred maintenance

c) there is a substantial increase in property value

d) the new buyer will have to make a huge down payment

84. What provision can stop Cary from losing her home to foreclosure if she files for Chapter 13 bankruptcy?

a) automatic stay provision

b) automatic stop provision

c) repayment provision

d) payment restructure provision

85. Lisa is frustrated with her homeowners' association as they have neglected to fix the walkway where her mother fell. She should:

a) stop paying her HOA dues

b) continue to pay her HOA dues because HOA dues take precedence over all other liens

c) place the money she would normally pay for her dues in an escrow account until the repairs are made

d) fix the walkway with the money she would normally pay her HOA dues and send the HOA a bill

86. Dean Metzger has a seven-acre property he wants to subdivide into as many 1,000 square foot lots as possible. How many lots can he make?

a. 175

b. 256

c. 304

d. 108

87. Raymond's commitment letter, which has not expired, states that his interest rate will be 4.75%. But now his lender tells him that he forgot to lock that rate in and his new rate will be 5.25%. Being that Raymond has met all of the lender requirements, which is true?

a) he will have to pay the new rate of 5.25%

b) the lender will be reprimanded

c) under the law the commitment letter may be a binding agreement

d) Raymond will have to pay the discount points to get the 4.75% rate

88. In some states the sellers must sign a seller's disclosure. Which of the following is true?

a) sellers should never sign the disclosure

b) sellers must disclose all known defects

c) sellers are always required to sign the disclosure

d) sellers do not have to disclose a defect unless they are asked

89. Melissa Ross has purchased a property that is one half of an acre. How big is the lot?

a. 32,670

b. 21,780

c. 58,080

d. 5,808

90. Janice purchases a home from Joe along with a one-year option to buy the adjoining lot for $10,000. A few months later, Joe gets an offer for $12,000 for the lot. Which of the following is true?

a) If Janice wants to buy the lot, Joe must sell it to her for $10,000

b) If Janice wants to buy the lot, she must now pay $12,000

c) If Janice doesn't want to pay $12,000, Joe can sell to the new person

d) If Joe tells Janice, whichever party signs the contract first can buy the lot

91. Which type of ownership is created between a husband and wife when a single instrument transfers property to both of them, but isn't specific about how the title will be held?

a) joint tenancy

b) tenancy in common

c) tenancy of sufferance

d) tenancy by the entirety

92. All are public records that may not be found through a title search EXCEPT:

a) mistakes in recording legal documents

b) unpaid liens

c) forged deed

d) fraud

93. The Banks have made their last mortgage payment. What document do they need?

a) discharge

b) lien

c) acknowledgment

d) promissory note

94. Which is NOT a condition that makes a purchase offer conditional?

a) home inspection

b) financing contingency

c) earnest money deposit

d) an appraisal contingency

95. Ownership of a property by one person is known as:

a) remainder interest

b) entirety

c) severalty

d) reversionary interest

96. The words of conveyance in a deed are in the:

a) purchase clause

b) selling clause

c) granting clause

d) heading

97. Which of the following properties will have the highest capitalization rate?

a) a modernized school

b) an SFR

c) a convenience store

d) a small shopping center with limited traffic access

98. Open listings are also known as:

a) multiple listings

b) non-exclusive agreements

c) exclusive rights to sell

d) net listings

99. Gilbert's defaulted on his loan that the lender foreclosed. Which clause requires the lender to look only to the property for satisfaction of the debt?

a) power of sale clause

b) deficiency judgment

c) acceleration clause

d) defeasance clause

100. Grantees are protected by express covenants found in:

a) bill of sale deed

b) quitclaim deed

c) general warranty deed

d) sheriff's deed

Real Estate Sales Exam IV Answers

1. c. The sum total of an individual's personal and real property at the time of death.

2. d. A fixture is personal property that is attached to the real property.

3. b. A homeowner's insurance policy combines hazard insurance and personal liability insurance.

4. b. A servicer collects mortgage payments from borrowers.

5. a. A three-family home is a dwelling for three families and ownership is evidenced by one deed.

6. c. The doctrine of prior appropriation is generally in areas of water scarcity. Water rights are assigned by priority, based on when the right was either first used or applied for.

7. b. Trust funds cannot be commingled with the management company's operating expenses.

8. c. A trade fixture is an installed item that the tenant can take with them when they end their lease.

9. a. Scarcity is an economic characteristic of land.

10. b. Accretion is the addition of land when sand or soil is naturally deposited from rivers, streams or lakes.

11. c. Permission was granted for a specified period of time.

12. b. A suit for specific performance seeks to force the defaulting party to perform under the terms of the contract.

13. a. Reasons to discharge a contract include: operation of law, impossibility of performance, mutual agreement of the parties to cancel, substantial performance, partial performance.

14. d. At this point, the broker has a signed offer to present to the seller.

15. b. Novation is where the lender substitutes a new obligation for an old one.

16. c. A listing is a contract in which the broker provides professional services to the client.

17. a. Both the exclusive-agency and the exclusive-right-to-sell listings have only one broker.

18. c. Since the broker performed his duties she owes him his commission.

19. b. Highest and best use is the use for which a property is used or suited resulting in its "highest value."

20. a. Original purchase price is not compared when using the sales comparison approach.

21. d. PITI stands for principal, interest, taxes and insurance.

22. b. In a fixed-rate loan the interest rate stays the same for the duration of the loan.

23. c. Gross Income Multiplier = sales price/annual gross income.

24. c. When a property is pledged for a loan without giving up possession, this is known as hypothecation.

25. d. An appraiser is an individual who is qualified by training, education and experience to estimate value.

26. b. Common area assessments are also known as homeowners' association dues.

27. b. Eviction is when a tenant is legally expelled from the property.

28. c. A recorder is a county clerk who collects fees for documents filed as well as maintains public real property records.

29. a. A 1003 is the loan application form used by most lenders.

30. d. In a VA loan transaction, once the appraisal is done, the VA issues a Certificate of Reasonable Value.

31. c. Fannie Mae and Freddie Mac are government-sponsored entities that were chartered by Congress.

32. b. Regulation Z gives most borrowers three days to rescind a transaction.

33. d. 403(b) and 401(k) are employer-sponsored investment plans.

34. a. Conforming loan limits are set annually by FHFA.

35. d. FACTA was designed to enhance the accuracy of borrower financial information, fight identity theft, and expand consumer access to credit.

36. c. Mortgage insurance is required when the LTV is greater than 80%.

37. c. Economic obsolescence is when a property loses value due to surrounding factors such as environmental and social forces.

38. a. The contract will be valid as his age at the time of conveyance will be 19.

39. a. Listing agreements must have a "from and to" date.

40. b. An acknowledgment is a formal declaration before a public official such as a notary public.

41. c. Involuntary alienation transfers are generally carried out by operation of law.

42. d. A note is a legal document requiring a borrower to repay a mortgage loan during a specified period of time at a stated interest rate.

43. b. A leaseback is where a seller conveys the property to a buyer and the seller then leases the property back from the buyer.

44. a. A trustee is a fiduciary who acts for the benefit of another person.

45. c. A fee simple estate is unconditional unlimited ownership interest.

46. d. Time and date of recording establish priority.

47. b. Constructive notice is based on the legal presumption that an individual may obtain information by diligent inquiry.

48. c. A purchase money transaction is the acquisition of real estate.

49. a. Property sales price results in a credit to the seller and a debit to the buyer.

50. b. The buyer should receive the security deposit credit when the deed is transferred to him.

51. b. Utility companies, i.e. those companies that own the equipment, are generally granted an easement because they have a right to enter and work on the property.

52. a. An easement by necessity is an easement granted by law and a court action that is necessary for full enjoyment of the land.

53. c. Most sale agreements state that the seller must maintain insurance on the home. The purchasers can terminate the contract or they can accept the damaged property and an assignment of the proceeds from the insurance company.

54. a. To determine the selling price, multiply the number of apartments by the rental rate to get the total monthly income. Multiply this figure by 12 to get the total annual income. Divide the total annual income by the rate of return to get the price the buyers paid.

55. b. Contract for deed, also known as a land contract, is where the buyer pays installments to the seller for a specified period of time, but the seller maintains title to the property.

56. d. A net listing designates the commission as being all of the money above the net price the seller will receive if the property is sold.

57. d. Cost is the original capital outlay for labor, land, profit and materials.

58. c. A will takes effect upon the death of the testator.

59. b.

60. a. A cash-out refinance puts funds into the hands of the borrower. A rate and term refinance does not.

61. b. The secondary market is where "pools" of existing mortgages are bought and sold.

62. a. The seller must pay off and/or remove any liens before the title can be delivered free and clear.

63. c. The principal amount is the buyer's credit; this is what will be used to purchase the property.

64. a. The lender will order an appraisal which will be done by an appraiser, someone who has been trained and educated and is experienced in estimating value.

65. d. A public official who establishes the value for property tax purposes is an assessor.

66. c. Month-to-month tenancy renews itself at each expiration.

67. d. A lease does not need to be recorded.

68. a. Money set aside for the replacement of common property in a condominium or cooperative project is called a replacement reserve fund.

69. b. Corrective maintenance involves the repair of the building's equipment.

70. c. Zoning is a tool for implementing a local plan to prevent incompatible land uses.

71. b. A *lis pendens* is a legal notice that a suit has been filed which could affect the property.

72. a. Per RESPA, kickbacks are illegal.

73. d. A unilateral contract requires only one party to act in order to initiate the contract.

74. c. The GLBA falls under the jurisdiction of the Federal Trade Commission.

75. b. a, c & d are all mortgage options.

76. a. A mortgage banker is a firm that can originate, sell and service mortgage loans.

77. d. A vacancy rate lower than 5% generally indicates that rents are too low.

78. a. The principal of regression states that value is diminished by proximity to lesser valued properties.

79. a. Under FIRREA, appraisers need to be licensed by the state in order to appraise real property valued over $1,000,000 in federally-related transactions.

80. a. Under California general law, brokers must disclose that a suicide or homicide occurred in a home within the past three years.

81. d. Confidentiality is an agent responsibility.

82. b. Reconciliation is the art of weighing the findings and analyzing from three approaches to value.

83. c. Negative cash flow can be offset by an increase in property value.

84. a. Chapter 13 bankruptcy has an automatic stay provision.

85. b. HOA dues in California take precedence over other liens and the association can take the homeowner to court and even force a sale.

86. c. To determine how many lots can be made, multiply the square feet in one acre by seven. Divide this figure by 1,000.

87. c. As long as the borrower has met lender's requirements and the commitment letter has correct wording, it is a binding agreement.

88. b. Seller are always required to disclose any know information affecting the condition, value or desirability of their property.

89. b. To determine the number of square feet in the lot, multiply the number of square feet in an acre by 0.50.

90. a. The terms and conditions of an Option are binding on the Optionor through the full term of the contract.

91. d. Tenancy by the entirety is a form of ownership between a spouses.

92. b. Unpaid liens are generally found in a title search.

93. a. A discharge is generally the document recorded.

94. c. The earnest money deposit is not a condition of an offer to purchase a home. It the consideration that creates a valid and binding contract.

95. c. Severalty means that all others have been severed or cut off.

96. c. The words of conveyance can be found in the granting clause.

97. d. Because traffic is limited, the shopping center will have the greatest risk and therefore the highest cap rate.

98. b. Open listings are also known as nonexclusive agreements.

99. a. The "power of sale" clause allows the lender to pursue a non-judicial foreclosure and precludes them from seeking a deficiency judgment.

100. c. General warranty deeds contain covenants that warrant the new owner's clear and undisturbed title.

Made in the USA
San Bernardino, CA
01 August 2017